AF838414

Human and Technological Progress Towards the Socio-Economic Paradigm of the Future

Interdisciplinary Thought of the 21st Century

Management, Economics and Law

Series Editors
Elena G. Popkova and Artem Krivtsov

Volume 1

Human and Technological Progress Towards the Socio-Economic Paradigm of the Future

Part I

Edited by
Elena G. Popkova and Marina L. Alpidovskaya

DE GRUYTER

ISBN 978-3-11-063221-7
e-ISBN (PDF) 978-3-11-063614-7
e-ISBN (EPUB) 978-3-11-063239-2
ISSN 2626-7063

Library of Congress Control Number: 2020935237

Bibliographic information published by the Deutsche Nationalbibliothek
The Deutsche Nationalbibliothek lists this publication in the Deutsche Nationalbibliografie; detailed bibliographic data are available on the Internet at http://dnb.dnb.de.

© 2020 Walter de Gruyter GmbH, Berlin/Boston
Cover image: janeb13 / pixabay.com
Typesetting: Integra Software Services Pvt. Ltd.
Printing and Bindung: CPI books GmbH, Leck

www.degruyter.com

MIX
Papier aus verantwortungsvollen Quellen
FSC
www.fsc.org
FSC® C083411

Introduction

The combined problem of the digitization of the economy, the digitization of humanity as a whole and human existence in time and space as a subject has been actualized in recent times. Indeed, the projects of the future world economy are inextricably connected with the achievements of scientific and technological progress linked with global social and economic transformations at the system and intersystem levels.

Nevertheless, the question of urgency and the imminent necessity of these events arises. Is this process so necessary for modern Russia and other countries of the globalized world and what is its impact on the economic and social life of socio-historical organisms? Back in the early 2000s, Robert Solow, winner of the Nobel Prize in Economics, wondered how the introduction of information technologies had an effect on the growth of labor productivity in various industries. The USA gave the answer – the staff of their Bureau of Statistical Analysis found out that the bi-factor productivity did not increase in any of the branches of the American economy, except for one – computer production. At the same time, there is a steady trend towards a decline in labor productivity and capital in the economy as a whole. In addition, the problem of universal access to information due to global Internet networks plays a less positive role in creating a favorable background of social comfort in the population of the countries of the global world. The standard of living of the notorious "golden billion", formed in the late 1950s and early 1960s due to the introduction of innovative technologies in all possible industries and a sharp jump in bi-factor productivity, is still not achievable for the remaining almost 5 billion people using all sorts of "Gadgets". This leads to the inevitable growth of social tension . . . Against the background of the "failures" of the modern socio-economic system, some projects are offered to get out of this situation. Not all of these projects and proposals are unequivocal. Consequently, the outcome of their implementation is the same.

In modern society, it is very difficult for a person to manifest his or her creative purpose. The consumer function of administration has become the embodiment of life ideals, aspirations, ambitions, social significance and status weight. The problem of human creative and generative self-realization and realistic realization of ideas in the economy of the future has faced the present society.

Today, the variants of the future society are mostly drawn archaically harshly. However, we should not forget that, in accordance with the already established views, the acceleration of economic growth over the past 200–250 years of human existence was caused by three successive scientific and technical revolutions (STDs). The world is on the verge of the fourth. The West has always independently carried out technological "breakthroughs", relying on all sorts of incentives: trade and production incentives, financial advantages, better conditions for the functioning of capital, as well as global integration. Moreover, Russia has always been able

https://doi.org/10.1515/9783110636147-202

to choose the path of forward-pragmatic-rational-emotional movement, which is able to bring out not only her and her satellites, but the rest of the world from the dimension of non-existence . . . In addition, if the future takes place, it will go along the development trajectory emotionally – an intuitive relationship space, remembering, of course, the ratio . . .

This volume is about these major trends in the development of humanity, society and economy.

This first part is devoted to the social consequences of digitization. The authors determine the problems, substantiate the perspectives, and offer applied recommendations for determining the role of human in the modern digital society and its adaptation to the conditions of Industry 4.0. The scientific concept "homo digital" is developed, and the essence of its formation in the process of evolution of "homo economicus" is studied. In addition, the transition from the post-industrial to information society is considered. A socio-technical environment in which modern human functions are modelled, and the challenges in this environment are determined.

The authors show that in the context of the digital economy the problem of economization (commercialization) of non-economic (non-profit) spheres and types of economic activity becomes more urgent; they are analyzed through the prism of the Theory of time in economics. Based on this, the increase of the influence of the consumer society on the modern social environment is shown. The key role of human capital in formation of a new quality of economic growth in the digital economic environment is substantiated, and transformation processes in the structure and practice of application of human capital are analyzed. The idea of social justice is reconsidered through the prism of digital society as a social environment with equal opportunities but different competences and motives.

Attention is paid to the modern Russian practice of the influence of the digital economy on society on the whole and on each human being. Scientific and methodological recommendations for indicative evaluation of the quality of economic growth in the conditions of digitization of Russia's economic system are offered, and the specifics of the problem of socio-economic differentiation of the Russian population in the conditions of technological progress are shown. Based on this, it is proved that the digital economy has a contradictory influence on society, increasing the accessibility of goods and services, in particular hi-tech ones, but also causing an urgent need for adapting to the new economic conditions. This adaptation is largely determined by the capabilities of people, the flexibility of their thinking, and their ability for learning and development. Thus, instead of the expected provision of balance of society, its disproportions could grow in practice. Also, specific features of regional migration in modern Russia in the context of digitization are determined.

The role of emotional intellect in the formation of the critical thinking of a company's employees is indicated. Because of this, it is shown that the so-called "human factor", which is traditionally treated as a source of economic risks and costs, acquires a new role in the conditions of the digital economy – a source of value creation and reduction of risks of technological progress, due to justified opposition to unfavorable changes. Informal labor relations based on digital communications, as the highest form of evolution of these relations that is achieved in the conditions of Industry 4.0, is considered. The central role of higher education in the process of social adaptation to the conditions of Industry 4.0 is outlined. The economic and legal issues of the digital economy are considered – in particular, the issue of democracy in the digital society in the conditions of e-government.

For a better understanding all Russian sources have been translated into English. The responsibility lies with each author.

Marina L. Alpidovskaya and Elena G. Popkova

Contents

Elena E. Nikolaeva, Alla B. Berendeeva

1 Man as an Element of the Economic Mechanism of the Information Society in Modern Social and Economic Theories and Concepts

Introduction

Modern society is characterized as the information society, as the digital economy. When writing about the digital economy, the authors mean the system of network relations between economic entities on the production, distribution, exchange and consumption of goods, based on the use of information technology and the possibilities of the Internet. In such an economy, information is a part of productive forces, which also changes other elements: the means of labor, the technologies used, the forms of organization of labor and production, the person him or herself. Informatization of modern society and the digital transformation of the economy requires rethinking many established theories, economic categories (including economic mechanism, along with a variety of flexible forms and methods of management), their compliance with the changing conditions of economic development and the nature of tasks (Thought, 1986, p. 3).

The economic mechanism does not exist outside the technological and economic activities of people within the framework of social reproduction, which has a multi-level nature of the structure. Therefore, a person acts as an active element of a complex multi-level economic mechanism of society through economic relations, in which people enter into the process of social reproduction, interacting with other elements of productive forces (technical and economic, organizational and economic, social and economic relations). As noted by L. I. Abalkin, "human activity, including in the management process, is socially determined, it is always determined by objective factors. But it does not imply unambiguity and stereotyped behavior. A person as a subject of social development (and a subject of management) is always faced with the situation of choosing one or another line of behavior, making a certain decision" (Abalkin, 1986, p. 219–220).

Any decision made by people at different levels of the socio-economic system is based on the analysis of available information. At the same time, the economic mechanism of the company itself appears like a carrier and processor of a huge amount of information. It is necessary to solve problems with uncertain conditions

Elena E. Nikolaeva, Alla B. Berendeeva, Ivanovo State University, Ivanovo, Russia

https://doi.org/10.1515/9783110636147-001

in which actions in accordance with a template will not promote the progressive development of the society. Therefore, human economic behavior can be used to reveal the essence of the economic development of the society.

Methodology

Before we talk about the person in the system of economic mechanism it should be explained what we mean by this mechanism. In a broad sense, we can say that it is a system of dialectical interactions, spontaneous and consciously regulated economic relations between people which act as a set of tools and projects that ensure the movement of subjects and objects. This movement occurs partly in the order of self-development, partly under the influence of external regulatory influence.

We proceed from the fact that the general goal of economic development is the person whose level and quality of life is considered as the starting point. One of the tasks of the modern economic mechanism is to activate human activity, the direction of its efforts to develop and implement innovations, the technological base of which is information technology. To implement the proposed task, it is necessary to rely on socio-economic theories and concepts that reveal various factors that affect the economic activity of people, their behavior and the adoption of certain decisions.

In the second half of the 20th century, scientists from different countries actively developed the concepts, reflecting the increasing role of the person in social reproduction, that are *a theory of human capital, the concept of social resource, social capital, human factor, human resources, human potential, social capital, theories of "an economic ethical person", "an information man", "an innovative person", etc.* These theories and concepts interact and complement each other, express different structural and functional aspects of the person at all levels of management. The development of these theories is associated with social changes in society, the causes of which were the progress in the development of science, engineering and technology, the development of production and the growth of the productive forces of society, the complexity of the structure of the society, ever-growing needs of people, contradictions and conflicts over the distribution of various resources between social groups and layers of society, increasing the importance of the environmental component of life, etc.

These theories and concepts reflect current trends in the development of science. They are interdisciplinary knowledge, combining economics, sociology, psychology, management. This is reflected in the fact that various authors speak a lot of socio-economics as an interdisciplinary science, an academic discipline in the scientific literature (Shabanova, 2006, 2010; Shulus, 2008; Surin, 2009 etc.). We are methodologically based on the system-reproductive approach, the symbiosis of political economy and institutionalism, interdisciplinary interaction of economics, sociology, ecology, psychology, the unity of economic, social and spiritual spheres of social life. These methodological approaches have been effectively used in our other studies (Berendeeva, 2006, p. 152–182; Babaev and Nikolaeva, 2017; Babaev and Berendeeva, 2018; Nikolaeva, 2012).

Results

Theories and concepts of human understanding and research that have developed in modern Russian and foreign literature can be considered in the context of the goals and objectives of the economic mechanism of the society, management at various levels of the socio-economic system, including the municipal level. Significant investments are required in modern conditions for infrastructure development of territories, including the construction of social facilities, to improve the quality of life of the population in small settlements. But if there are not always enough material and financial resources, then there are huge social resources, which, unlike material ones, are inexhaustible. They tend to multiply with the development of the society, forms of self-government, the creation of innovative products, services, change of the person in the process of communication with other people, self-education, self-realization of the creative abilities, the formation of civic consciousness.

In this regard, attention should be paid to the *concept of social resources and social potential* (Makasheva and Kalinikova, 2002; Maltsev, 2006; Semchenko, 2012 etc.). Social resource refers not only to labor resources, but also to the totality of the relationship between man and business, not only within the production enterprise, but also outside it (KnoRus et al., 2006, p. 3, 30, 33); reserves of creative energy of the individual (social, cognitive, activity ones), social organization and society as a whole (community of people, organizations, institutions, social groups) (Makasheva and Kalinikova, 2002). An urgent task today is a problem of disclosure of all the possibilities of this huge potential of both an individual and social organizations, the use of powerful energy of social resources in the creative direction. Such concepts as *"social activity", "social well-being"* are close to the category of *"social resources" in their content and logic.* The following directions can be identified in the issue of the development of social potential: preservation of human health, the functioning of educational and cultural institutions, social protection of certain groups of the population, educational and patriotic work with young people. For the implementation of the above tasks, coordinated interaction of both local self-government bodies and public authorities and public organizations is necessary. The volunteer movement, the activities of various public organizations, charitable foundations can be given as an example of the successful implementation of social resources. Such structures operate on the basis of self-development, internal motivation, besides, they are supported by government agencies at various levels.

In the early 2000s academician D. S. Lvov put forward the idea of moral economy, which suggests that economic and other decisions are made taking into account the humanistic component, "an ecological man", "a moral personality", a man with developed moral qualities, open to interethnic communication is formed in the society (Lvov, 2004). Thus, there is an acute problem of environmental pollution by plastic debris of the earth's surface and the oceans in Russia. It is widely described in the literature. Various solutions to this problem are offered – collection and recycling of plastic waste, replacement of plastic materials difficult to decompose with ones, which are similar in their properties, but subject to rapid decomposition, the transition to the use of paper bags instead of plastic packaging, and so on. But one thing is clear: these problems cannot be solved by market mechanisms, since all these methods require additional costs for the construction of new production complexes, lead to a rise in the cost of consumer goods (paper packaging is more expensive than plastic), etc. There is a need for serious state support for science in the development of new materials, entrepreneurship in the field of waste collection and processing, other measures of industrial and environmental policy, but the main thing is to educate an environmentally responsible, moral person who cares about the preservation of nature. The designated problems cannot be solved without taking into account this side of the case and without the formation of the appropriate environmental behavior of people.

Many modern researchers focus on the development of spirituality, education, the socio-cultural dominant. In this regard, the models of the "psychological", "social" and "sociological man" are offered as an alternative to the model of the economic man in the literature. Thus, the *concept of "the ethical economic man"* justifies the ethics of the economic choice and the motivation of the behavior of a business entity (Rodionova, 2006). The proposed model is intended for practical application in the structures of management systems and macroeconomic regulation of socio-economic processes.

The increasing importance of the human factor of development in modern conditions is linked to the fact that the opportunities for choice are expanding in the information society and, consequently, the responsibility for the quality of decisions is also increasing. This leads to the emergence of the *concept of "an information person* who is distinguished by the presence of an increasing information need and a certain dependence on information" (Orlova, 2010, p. 214) from various gadgets. The modern man is *a network man* who is included in many networks which are independent entities that form the inherent thinking and behavior of its participants.

There is a change in human qualities (it is necessary to have competencies in the field of new technologies, to be an expert in their field, to quickly learn and implement new solutions), the transformation of the labor market (the growth of the need for highly qualified personnel, employment opportunities for persons limited socially or geographically, a change in the structure of employment in the direction of new competencies, etc.). NTP leads to a change in the position of the employee in the system of social reproduction due to the fact that intellectual work is put forward at the forefront as a combination of education and science ("intelligence of the nation"). Thus, the driving force is not just labor, but innovative labor (the literature refers to the *"the innovative man")* (Islamutdinov and Shangaraev, 2011). Factors of activation of innovation at the enterprise level are: "creative freedom delegation of the part of the administrative powers to personnel, the increase of liability, professional and psychological readiness to change (the subjective quality of the person: adaptability, susceptibility to innovation), the collective nature of work (competition and mutual assistance, mentoring), proactive leadership (feedback between management and staff), the humanization of working conditions and relationships" (Shangaraev, 2013: p. 16–17).

The theory of human capital is still relevant (Verenikin, 2005; Dobrynin, Dyatlov, and Kurgansky, 1999; Dyatlov, 1994; Ivanov, 2004; Mayburov, 2004, 2006; Shchetin, 2001). This theory implies the need for significant public and private investment in human development. This approach is implemented in practice. In particular, *the index of human capital per capita* (calculated by the Bureau of labor statistics, USA) expresses the level of costs of the state, companies and citizens on education, health and other branches of social sphere counting per person (Dovbenko and Osik, 2011).

The development of the theory of human capital is related to the concept of "*human potential*", taking into account all the peculiar features of an employee (from values to health), affecting the efficiency of his work (Sen, 1996, 2016; Coleman, 2001). *The concept of human potential* is directly related to the topic of improving the economic mechanism. The theoretical foundations of the study of human potential were laid by W. James, J. Moreno and A. Maslow (James, 1902; Maslow, 2008; Moreno, 2001). As noted by O. I. Ivanov, W. James made a program of research on human potential, which provided the development of methods designed to stimulate effective activity. A. Maslow is the founder of the modern psychological approach to human potential, the creator of the concept of "peak experiences", that is a state of man in which his capabilities are activated (Ivanov, 2014).

There are different opinions about the structure of human potential in the literature: "the stock of physical and moral health, general cultural and professional competence, creative, entrepreneurial and civic activity accumulated by the population, realized in various spheres of activity, as well as in the level and structure of needs", "health (physical and spiritual), ensuring the general viability of a person; readiness for family life and upbringing of children; knowledge and skills"; "adaptability to social infrastructure; cultural and value orientations and psychological competence"; "health, abilities of people, values and spirituality of citizens, their activity" (see Ivanov, 2016). T. Zaslavskaya believes that human potential is "the readiness and ability of the national community to active self-development, timely and adequate response to multiple challenges of the external environment and successful competition with other societies". The main components of human potential are socio-demographic, socio-economic, socio-cultural, activity ones (Zaslavskaya, 2005).

The theory of human capital is complemented by the original *concept of the individual, society and the state*. This social theory was developed by I. Larionov. The essence of it is that the measure of all social processes is a creative and creative potential, and "the criterion of positive social dynamics and social activities is the extent to which society creates conditions for the disclosure of the creative process in individuals and to what extent society provides an opportunity for each individual to find his place, adequate disclosure of its creative potential" (Larionov, 2001, p. 11, 13–14). This theory is the result of a systematic study of social processes in Russia, and the methodology is consistent and systematic accounting of the trinity of economic, social and spiritual spheres.

The theory of social capital is *being further developed*. This theory allows "overcoming the main contradictions between "labor" and "capital", increasing labor productivity and revenue of companies" by facilitating to the redistribution of the part of the company's income in favor of hired personnel (financing of the company's social policy, participation of employees in profits) (Sysoev, 2015). The concept of social capital was introduced into science by French sociologist *P. Bourdieu* in the early 1980s. The 20th century for the quantitative and qualitative characteristics of social relations of society (Bourdieu, 2002). The term capital here reflects changes in the society that have the properties to persist and accumulate for a long time. Social capital, like other types of capital, acts as a resource, but unlike, for example, financial capital, it is accumulated, maintained, multiplied and expands, deepening social interaction between people. In the future, this concept has become a measure of humanity of society, as a kind of value. The researchers note that this type of capital promotes the spread of knowledge and innovation, forms the norms of trust and determines the behavior of people in the society. Countries that have a high degree of public trust are characterized by political stability, stable economy, low risks of social conflicts.

This theory is close to the institutional direction in economic theory, as the presence of public institutions, social networks, associations, laws, generally recognized norms, rules, which subordinated life in civil society; trust between different social structures, which is closely related to ethics, morality are identified as indicators that allow assessing the state, trends in the development of certain aspects of the social capital. All this echoes the above-mentioned concept of ethical economic man and the theme of moral economics.

The success of a country's development depends on the nature of its national social capital. *The concept of national collective capital* was formulated by the German economist F. List in the middle of the 19th century. It is closely related to the theory of social capital. F. Fukuyama's *idea that any* society needs social capital at the national level is widely known (Fukuyama, 1999). The motivation of the individual, business and government representatives is necessary for the socio-economic development to actually take place. Russian society on the part of national well-being does not have very good characteristics, but it still preserves features of passionarity. (Passionarity is the activity manifested in the individual's aspiration to the goal (often an illusory one) and in the ability to overstrain and sacrifice in order to achieve this goal.) Passionarity of the nation is determined not only by the motivation of material interests but also by spiritual values, patriotic ideas, high goals that can really move people. There must be an idea of pride for the country. A strong social state, which activities are aimed at ensuring well-being for all, improving the level and quality of life of the population, the development of science, education, sports, health, culture, etc. can become such a great idea.

Conclusions/Recommendations

Summing up, we will present the concepts and theories considered in Table 1.1 and outline the main directions of their practical application to increase motivation for human economic activity as an element of the economic mechanism.

Table 1.1: Modern theories and concepts devoted to man as an element of the economic mechanism.

The name of a theory or a concept	Main areas of application
1. The concept of social resources, social potential	The main directions of development of social potential: preservation of human health, the functioning of educational and cultural institutions, social protection of certain groups of the population, educational and patriotic work with young people.
2. The concept of the moral economics	Economic and other decisions are made taking into account the humanistic component, there is a formation of the "ecological man", "moral personality", a man with developed moral qualities, open to interethnic communication in the society
3. The concept of "the ethical economic man"	With the introduction of the model of the ethical "economic man" in the structure of management systems of organizations, the latter will acquire the status of institutions of ethical and legal cooperation of all persons interested in the economic activity
4. The concept of the "information man"	There is a change in human qualities, competencies, the formation of a network person

Table 1.1 (continued)

The name of a theory or a concept	Main areas of application
5. The concept of "the innovative man"	Innovative labor becomes a driving force; there is a change in the position of an employee in the system of social reproduction due to the fact that intellectual work is put forward at the forefront as a combination of education and science
6. Human capital theory	Knowledge of employees is considered as a form of investment, they become one of the key assets of the employee, and for the economy as a whole it is one of the most important factors of production
7. The concept of "human potential"	It is aimed at improving the economic mechanism. It allows implementing annual cross-country comparisons through the human development index – HDI
8. The concept of the individual, society and state	It is aimed at revealing the creative potential of the individual
9. The theory of social capital	It promotes trust and behavior in society, knowledge and innovation, provides a basis for cooperation, reduces the risks of social conflict and violence
10. The concept of national collective capital	The national idea can increase the passion of the nation, motivate people to solve important national problems

Human decision-making, socio-economic behavior can be seen as a subjective basis within the economic system as an objective basis. This leads us to understand the variability of economic systems that change under the influence of the type of management (administrative, centralized or liberal, spontaneous ones), the conditions of functioning and national characteristics. In addition to economic factors, the economic system and its mechanism are significantly affected by non-economic factors (social, spiritual, environmental, moral, etc.). The subjective (human) factor becomes a necessary condition for the implementation of the objective requirements of production, economic laws. The considered concepts pay attention to the person and the problem of his self-realization. Therefore, in the context of the development of the digital economy, the focus of society on the comprehensive development of the person, the training of competent personnel to solve the problems facing the country is a necessary condition for the development of the national socio-economic system.

Acknowledgments: The article was prepared with the financial support of RFBR in the framework of the scientific project No. 19-010-00329 "Theoretical and methodological foundations of an extended understanding of the economic mechanism in the modern economy".

References

Babaev, B. D., Berendeeva, A. B. (2018), Sotsial'nyye svoystva ekonomiki: pokazateli i faktory narastaniya, tormozheniya [Social properties of the economy: indicators and factors of growth, braking]. Theoretical Economics, no. 2, pp. 29–43 (in Russian).

Babaev, B. D., Nikolaeva, E. E. (2017), Obshchestvennoye vosproizvodstvo kak sistemnoye yedinstvo prirodnykh, ekonomicheskikh, institucional'nykh i social'nykh protsessov [Social reproduction as a system unity of natural, economic, institutional and social processes]. Vestnik of Tver State University. Series "Economics and management", no. 2, pp. 22–27 (in Russian).

Berendeeva, A. B. (2006), Sotsial'nyye svoystva ekonomiki: nauch. izdanie [Social properties of the economy: science edition]. Ivanovo: Ivanovo State University., 300 p. (pp. 152–182) (in Russian).

Bourdieu, P. (2002), Formy kapitala [Forms of capital]. Economic sociology, vol. 3, no. 5, pp. 60–74. URL: https://ecsoc.hse.ru/data/2011/12/08/1208205039/ecsoc_t3_n5.pdf (Accessed 15.12.2018) (in Russian).

Verenikin, A. O. (2005), Chelovecheskiy kapital: kontseptual'nye osnovaniya i osobennosti proyavleniya [Human capital: conceptual foundations and specific features of manifestation]. The US. Canada: Economy-Politics-Culture, no. 3, pp. 85–100 (in Russian).

James, W. (1902), Nauchnyye osnovy psikhologii [Scientific foundations of psychology]. Saint-Petersburg: St. Petersburg Elektropechatnya, 375 p (in Russian).

Dobrynin, A., Dyatlov, S., Kurganskiy, S. (1999), Chelovecheskiy kapital (metodologicheskiye aspekty analiza) [Human capital (methodological aspects of the analysis)]. Saint-Petersburg: Publishing house of SPSUEF, 209 p (in Russian).

Dovbenko, M. V., Osik, Yu. I. (2011), Sovremennyye ekonomicheskiye teorii v trudakh nobeliantov: ucheb. posobiye [Modern economic theory in the writings of Nobel laureates: work book]. Moscow: Academy of natural sciences, URL: https://monographies.ru/en/book/section?id=4232 (Accessed 01. 02.2019)(in Russian).

Dyatlov, S. A. (1994), Teoriya chelovecheskogo kapitala [Human capital theory]. Saint-Petersburg: Publishing house of SPSUEF, 141 p (in Russian).

Zaslavskaya, T. I. (2005), Chelovecheskiy potentsial v sovremennom transformatsionnom protsesse [Human potential in the modern transformation process]. Social sciences and modernity, no. 3, pp. 5–16 (in Russian).

Ivanov, N. (2004), Chelovecheskiy kapital i globalizatsiya [Human capital and globalization]. World economy and international relations, no. 9, pp. 29–43 (in Russian).

Ivanov, O. I. (2016), Novyye konfiguratsii neravenstva i potokovyye struktury glem-kapitalizma [New configurations of inequality and stream structures of glam capitalism]. SOCIS, no. 6, pp. 13–23 (in Russian).

Ivanov, O. I. (2014), Chelovecheskiy potentsial: voprosy teorii i metodologii issledovaniya [Human development: issues of theory and methodology of research]. SOCIS, no. 6, pp. 89–95 (in Russian).

Islamutdinov, V. F., Shangaraev, R. G. (2011), K voprosu o kontseptsii innovatsionnogo cheloveka [To the question of the concept of innovative human]. Issues of innovation economics, no. 4 (4), pp. 3–12, URL: http://bgscience.ru/lib/8934/ (Accessed 18. 11.2017) (in Russian).

Coleman, J. (2001), Kapital sotsial'nyy i chelovecheskiy [Social and human capital]. Social Sciences and modernity, no. 3, pp. 121–139 (in Russian).

Larionov, I. K. (2001), Sotsial'naya teoriya: Obshchie osnovy i osobennosti Rossii: ucheb. posobie [Social theory: General principles and features of Russia: work book]. Moscow: Dashkov and K °, 242 p (in Russian).

Lvov, D. S. (2004), Nravstvennaya ekonomika [The Moral economy]. Moscow: Institute of economic strategies, 45 p (in Russian).
Mayburov, I. (2006), Ekonomicheskoye obosnovaniye nakopleniya chelovecheskogo kapitala [Economic justification of human capital accumulation]. Society and economy, no. 7/8, pp. 245–263 (in Russian).
Mayburov, I. (2004), Effektivnost' investirovaniya i chelovecheskiy kapital v SSHa i Rossii [Investment efficiency and human capital in the USA and Russia]. World economy and international relations, no. 4, pp. 3–13 (in Russian).
Makasheva, Z. M., Kalinnikova, I. O. (2002), Sotsial'nyy menedzhment: ucheb. dlya vuzov [Social management: work book for universities]. Moscow: YUNITI-DANA, 207 p (in Russian).
Maltsev, V. A. (2006), Tekhnologii optimal'nogo ispol'zovaniya sotsial'nykh resursov regiona [Technologies of optimal use of social resources of the region]. Scientific and research institute of synergetics: collection of research papers. Issue 9. Belgorod, pp. 54–60 (in Russian).
Maslow, A. (2008), Motivatsiya i lichnost' [Motivation and personality], 3rd edition, translated from English. Saint-Petersburg: Peter, 352 p (in Russian).
Moreno, I. L. (2001), Psikhodrama [Psychodrama] / Translated from English by G. Pimochkina, E. Rachkova. Moscow: April Press, Eksmo-Press, 521 p (in Russian).
Nikolaeva, E. E. (2012), Vzaimodeystviye politekonomicheskogo i institutsional'nogo podkhodov v ekonomicheskikh issledovaniyakh kak trebovaniye sovremennoy ekonomicheskoy teorii [Interaction of political and institutional approaches in economic research as a requirement of modern economic theory]. Theoretical Economics: scientific electronic economic journal, no. 4, pp. 14–21, URL: http://www.theoretical-economy.info (Accessed 8. 10.2018) (in Russian).
Orlova T. V. (2010), Informatsionnyy chelovek v sovremennom obshchestve [Information man in modern society]. Social reproduction as a multi-level process: theory and practice issues: collection of research papers / ed. by B. D. Babayev. Ivanovo: Ivanovo State University, pp. 212–215 (in Russian).
Rodionova, N. (2006), Model' etichnogo ekonomicheskogo cheloveka [Model of ethical economic man]. Man and labor, no. 1, pp. 67–70; no. 2, pp. 76–79; no. 3, pp. 77–79 (in Russian).
Semchenko, I. V. (2012), Obmen sotsial'nymi resursami v sovremennom obshchestve [Exchange of social resources in modern society]. Generation of the future: View of young scientists–2012: collection of papers of the International Youth Scientific Conference: in 3 volumes; edited by A. A. Gorokhov; The South-West State University, pp. 41–42 (in Russian).
Sen, A. (1996), Ob etike i ekonomike [On Ethics and Economics] (translated from English). Moscow: Science, 160 p (in Russian).
Sen, A. (2016), Ideya spravedlivosti [The Idea of Justice]. Moscow: Publishing house of the Gaidar Institute; the Liberal Mission Foundation, 520 p (in Russian).
KnoRus. (2006), Sotsial'noe razvitiye predpriyatiy: ucheb. posobie [Social development of enterprises: work book] (2006) / A. N. Averin and others; under the general editorship of N. A. Volgin, A. N. Averin. Moscow: KnoRus, 543 p (in Russian).
Surin, A. V. (2009), Sotsioekonomika: ot teorii k paradigme [Socio-Economics: from theory to paradigm]. Vestnik of Moscow University. Series 21: Management (state and society), no. 1, pp. 3–24 (in Russian).
Sysoev, S. A. (2015), Spetsifichnost' aktivov i social'nyy kapital [Specificity of assets and social capital]. Theoretical Economics: scientific electronic economic journal, no. 3 (27), pp. 37–41, URL: http://www.ystu.ru/download/TheorEconom/3_(27)_2015.pdf (Accessed 26. 01.2019) (in Russian).

Thought. Hozyaystvennyy mekhanizm obshchestvennykh formatsiy [The economic mechanism of social formations] (1986) / under the general editorship of L. I. Abalkin. Moscow: Thought, 269 p (in Russian).

Shabanova, M. A. (2006), Sotsioekonomika kak nauka i uchebnaya distsiplina [Socio-Economics as a science and academic discipline]. World of Russia: Sociology, Ethnology, vol. 15, no. 4, pp. 94–115 (in Russian).

Shabanova, M. A. (2010), Sotsioekonomika i sovremennost' (o pol'ze i riskakh ekspansii ekonomicheskogo podkhoda) [Socio-Economics and modernity (on the benefits and risks of economic approach expansion)]. Social sciences and modernity, no. 4, pp. 100–115 (in Russian).

Shangaraev, R. G. (2013), Sovremennyye vyzovy i formirovanie cheloveka innovatsionnogo tipa [Modern challenges and formation of an innovative type of the person]: the author's abstract . . . PhD in economics: 08. 00.01/ Shangaraev Renat Gabdullaevich. Ivanovo, 23 p (in Russian).

Shulus, A. A. (2008), Sotsioekonomika kak mezhotraslevaya nauka: predmet, metody, formy institutsionalizatsii [Socio-Economics as an interdisciplinary science: subject, methods, forms of institutionalization]. Labor and social relations, no. 1, pp. 4–11 (in Russian).

Shchetinin, V. (2001), Chelovecheskiy kapital i neodnoznachnost' yego traktovki [Human capital and ambiguity of its interpretation]. World economy and international relations, no. 12, pp. 42–49 (in Russian).

Fukuyama, F. (1999), The Great Disruption: Human Nature and the Reconstitution of Social Order. New York: Free Press, 354 p.

Anatoly V. Denikin, Zoya D. Denikina

2 Digitalized Reality as a Concept of Modern Economic Knowledge

Introduction

Digital economy as a studied subject is an aspect of a broader ontological formation. Comprehension of digitalized reality serves as a prologue for solution of one of the most complex problems of economic theory and economic philosophy – conceptual distribution of indicators of mega-economy and transformation economy.

The notion of mega-economy is currently used in two different meanings according to regulatory and positive economic science. In the first case, it means nomologic understanding of mega-economy, complimenting the notional microeconomic range. It indicates various details of openness of national economies existing in interrelated, slightly nonequilibrium global world. The nomologic definition is relevant to ideal essential features, fully realizing the advantages of international division of labor (Zhuravlyova et al., 2019).

In the second case, "event-based" definition of mega-economy is applied, defining it as a contradictive, ambiguous functioning of open national economies. The notion of "economy of transformation" is aimed at updating the problem of mechanism and forms of economic changes amidst super-complex, strongly nonequilibrium conditions of the global world.

Methodology

Introduction of digital economy broadens the methodological base of system study of modern open economy. The term "system", deeply rooted in the economic science, has not yet received the status of a basic ontological and gnoseological notion. Its insufficient explication leads to mostly political-economic interpretation of system as a total of productive relations (Zhuravlyova et al., 2019) and prevalence of structural-organizational perceptions in various management concepts (Krivosheyeva, 2015).

The main hypothesis of the article is that comprehension of digital economy requires aligning two classes of problems: categorial-notional update of economic theory and broadening of its subject area with the help of the achievements of scientific philosophy. One of methodological tools for such conjunction is differentiated

Anatoly V. Denikin, Zoya D. Denikina, Financial University under the Government of the Russian Federation, Moscow, Russia

https://doi.org/10.1515/9783110636147-002

system analysis of digital economy with respect to differences between classic, neoclassic and post-neoclassic types of scientific rationality (Stepin, 2015). Such angle of research allows tracing back the logic of evolution of digital economy and revealing ontological and gnoseological substantiations of the said process.

Results

The notion of information plays an important part in step-by-step study of the phenomenon of digitalized reality. Let us compare the notions of "information" and "digitalization". In our opinion, within the framework of classic scientific rationality, information is understood as the process of production, storage and transfer of knowledge in order to move closer towards the absolute-relative truth.

Another understanding of information relates to neoclassic rationality type, the thrive towards consensus between heterogenous discourses. Information is a process of production, storage and broadcast of subject-object senses. Unlike the phenomenon of knowledge, sense features a subject content and expresses the value-appraising character of information technologies. Information becomes a learning and practical resource of a subject if the performed communication results in formation of a sense having value from the sender and the receiver. In other words, information becomes symbolic communication.

In post-nonclassical science, information interpretation is updated as intrasystem communication affecting the level of self-organization of the system amidst falling or rising chaos. Through interior monitoring, the system learns the level of its disorder and the influence of external environment, and with the help of system information resources, it stabilizes its condition or reestablishes the communications it requires (Luhmann, 1989). In this sense, information technologies are beneficial for the achievement of efficient functioning of economic and social existence. At the same time, the scientific literature is becoming increasingly assured that public life is already saturated with information instruments and information products, that informatization of social space has already happened. This idea allows speculating about the completion of informatization stage (Nikoulina and Starchenko, 2018).

Let us adapt the notion of digitalization to the conceptual and categorical framework of social philosophy and philosophy of science. The fact that digitalization is a means of data transfer speaks of the practice-oriented nature of this technology, and the fact that digitalization serves as a means to bind this data signalizes the intellectual character of the technology. The term "data", dominating digitalization definitions, is interesting in the context of the family of ontological and gnoseological notions.

Firstly, data are neutral in relation to subject-object nature of the cognitive process, they reflect both subjective and objective reality in equal measure. Secondly, data are ontologically indifferent towards objective and virtual reality. Both realities act as sources of cognition and action space (online games, social networks, etc.). Now digitalization already includes information resources and communicatory data bulks, “limiting” the infinity of information (photo, audio, etc.).

Digitalization is not merely bound with technical availability by analytic analysis procedure, it itself acts as a subtype of analytic activity. Digitalization acts as a mechanism of a certain kind designed for input of information about reality phenomena into the conscience of subjects, ensuring its treatment and certain processing. Digitalization can also be reviewed as a type of system methodology. It seems that comprehension of digitalization phenomenon reveals the epistemic potential of such types of system methodology as modelling and projecting. In relation of informatization, digitalization serves as a metatheoretical level of learning, as infoworld is an observable reality for digital technology. Digital world is the observing reality, modelling the objective world and the world of communicatory data.

Undoubtedly digitalization has a target-oriented, practical focus. The efficiency of the procedure much depends on the final result of the operation of choice and comprehension of data flow. In this regard, the notions of “technology” and “method” interrelate just as methodic and method. It seems that in case of digitalization, one can witness a post-nonclassical epistemic effect of “turnover” of theory and method of ontologization of methodology. The way of data connection turns out to be a projecting activity and reality which is further operated by communication subjects. Thus, digitalization is often defined as both an instrumental method and an existential environment (Nikoulina and Starchenko, 2018).

Digitalization presumes logically substantiated information offer, as in digitalization, the object of learning is constituted and cloned, knowledge of this object is organized and its practical, system value is determined. In our view, in terms of digitalization, information equals knowledge in its post-nonclassical meaning. Knowledge is any form of intrasystem or intersystem monitoring, beneficial to system self-organization.

Thanks to digitalization, the process of learning is incorporated into reality itself. Uniformity of extraction, processing, treatment and use of information, achieved by digitalization, is fixed contensively and functionally, forming intersubjective semantic field. The subject of learning is inside the slightly nonequilibrium reality, selection and processing of communicatory data points out the rational character of constructive actions of the subject.

Let us discuss the term “digital economy”, which gives us two different meanings when translated from English: a real economy sector and scientific field. There is no mixing between meanings here, we are talking about post-nonclassical interpretation of system reality, according to which, scientific knowledge is involved in the process of system self-organization. The most widely known study of digital economy is a book by the Canadian economist Don Tapscott (Tapscott, 1999). Among Tapscott achievements, one must note his research on consequences of digitalization within the framework of the theory of Ronald Cows company. They include a reduction of expenses for information search when executing contracts, arrival of new business forms, exclusion of mediators. In other words, digitalized reality is studied within the scope of microeconomics with the aim of finding stable, equilibrium forms of business activities. The reference to the company theory was made due to the subject-subject communicative content of digital technologies.

In the Russian Federation, the topic of digital economy was first raised by the President at the Eastern economic forum in 2016. The Presidential Decree of May, 9 2017 provides a definition of digital economy: "Digital economy is business activity key production factor of which is data in digital form, treatment of large volumes and the use of analysis of which in comparison with traditional business forms allows for a significant increase of the efficiency of various types of production, technologies, equipment, storage, sales and delivery of goods and services" (Decree of the President of Russia, 2017).

Let us divide this definition into fragments and provide it with a philosophical and economical interpretation.

Production of data is a traditional interpretation of economy through the notion of production. The nonclassical moment lies with the fact that data are attributed to factors (conditions) rather than production instruments.

Treatment of large volumes of data is a technological aspect of digitalization and a reference to its systematic character. A large volume of data inevitably leads to a functioning disbalance and deficit of knowledge about system components and its interrelations.

The use of analysis results. Economic systems always perform analytic activities, which result in circulation of system-related sense as knowledge. The definitions "economy of knowledge" and "knowledge management" are currently in active use. The topic of knowledge is discussed in intellectual capital theory, and knowledge management lies within the scope of management studies. The author of the term "economy of knowledge", Fritz Mahlup did not make any difference between information and knowledge yet. In the 90s, knowledge became an example of public benefit. At the same time, the system-related definition of benefit defines it as a product, for which the use of a unit of this benefit by one agent does not impede its use by other agents (Mahlup, 1962). Such understanding is important from macroeconomic point of view, takin into account the equilibrium between market factors in an economic system.

Increasing the efficiency of various types of production. In our view, this is a representation of aspects of self-regulation and self-organization of economy as a system in micro-, macro- and mega-economic sense. Digitalization is understood as precise data transfer, reduction of super-complexity, an instrument to lower uncertainty. Economic system becomes standardized, and in this sense, digital economy remains a subject of study in neo-institutionalism.

Studying digitalized reality in post-nonclassical science is productive within the scope of macro-economy and mega-economy, understood as open systems, interacting with the environment in positive and negative senses.

This is the exact reason why digital economy is real economy and a scientific field at the same time. For economic theory, the object of studies is economic reality itself, while for economic metatheory it is the analysis of economic reality and its presentation in economic cognition. In other words, digital economy is the kind of system that monitors itself in order to maintain steady development. Digitalization promotes "switching" between economy transformation modes: a) from regressive changes and zero growth towards development; b) transition from crisis-prone strongly nonequilibrium states to stabilization and steady development.

The second type of changes has not been studied and is currently not studied in classic social-economic science. It has not been studied because the initial statement of classic science presumes manifestations of essential market properties in any scenario, and it is believed that temporary anomalies do not cancel the effect of objective laws. The essential aspect of economic phenomena is closed, and there is no place for external influence of aggressive environment in such ontological picture. The said abstract thought does not exist in pre-Marxist and Marxist political economy.

In modern classic views, such economy transformation mode is not studied because some researchers identify transformation with development, mistakenly presuming that dialectic laws of development are relevant to all kinds of strongly nonequilibrium states (Lousse, 1999). One of the reasons of such misconception lies with the absolutization of regulatory aspects of economic theory. The following principle is set at the top of the mind: "How should it be? How does economy look under ideal parameters?" Such assumption is true in the sense that without ideal parameters, it is hard to determine the essential properties of economic phenomena. Accordingly, differentiating macro- and mega-economic processes is hardly productive for modern classic views. Regulatory-systematic views ideally fit macroeconomic explanations which do not require venturing into nonequilibrium external global environment.

At the same time, post-nonclassical economic science requires differentiating the essential type of economic development and scenario-specific form of structural transformations. In the first case, it is logical to speak about changes in national economies resisting unfair competition and converted (in Hegelian sense) international division of labor. Studying the second type of changes presumes studies of macroeconomic problems of national economies in unstable mega-economic conditions (Kolontai, 1999).

For the first time, the notion of information as economic category was used by Oliver Hart. Let us compare the notions "information economy" and "digital economy" within the framework of economic philosophy and social philosophy. In the case of information economy, technological aspect of postindustrial society will prevail (Antipina, 2009). From the standpoint of digital economy, one can witness the symbolic aspect of the society of knowledge, which means transfer of senses significant for the whole system and stabilizing it (Behman, 2010).

The topic of virtual economy has been discussed a lot lately. Let us compare the notions "virtual economy" and "digital economy". Virtual economy is a characteristic of digital economy, accentuating various forms of economic existence. Accordingly, one can outline the following shades of understanding of virtual reality from the perspective of the philosophy of science.

In classic understanding (according to Hegelian categories) virtuality is a transition from possibility to reality. The ability itself is present in reality in form of capability for further development of its major essential properties. On one hand, in classic interpretation of virtual economy, virtuality is viewed as the condition of target setting of an economic subject, which is later realized in rational existence. On the other hand, virtuality means ability of effective existence, reality to develop predictably and consistently within essentially set variative borders.

In nonclassical science, due to the assumptions of quantum mechanics, the topic of virtuality is discussed in the context of instrumental reality. The question is how technical equipment affects objective reality and whether it creates new additional parameters. From this standpoint, virtual economy is regarded as electronic economy and artificial environment. In other words, the neoclassic sense of virtual economy lies with recognition of conventional character of economic reality. Different groups of conditions result in essentially different variations of functioning of economic existence. The conditions may be created artificially or form naturally, being an inseparable interior component of economic existence of this type. In economic literature one can sometimes see the opinion that electronic economy reflects the material carriers of economy. It becomes clear that the term is being narrowed down.

In post-nonclassical science, all of these senses are preserved, and system-related meanings begin to stand out. What was earlier defined as an economic function (e.g. money) or economic conditions (e.g. investments) are now becoming the way of existence for the whole economic system. This is why virtual economy is often defined as movement of financial capital.

Noncompliance of the terms virtual economy and digital economy features yet another aspect. Virtual economy may become a type of system-nonrelated reality, functioning alongside and destroying the rational condition of economy. In this case virtual economy looks, for example, like movement of fictious financial capital, threatening to create critical system-related situations.

Conclusions/Recommendations

Thus, in post-nonclassical science digitalized reality is a variety of system reality, combining actual and potential, complex and ultra-complex, material and spiritual, valuable and evaluating, true and false, necessary and accidental. Oppositions are eliminated, as all these manifestations exist simultaneously, and no entity is dominating ontologically. Digitalized reality looks like a system solution, system evaluation, system communication.

In the first case, system logic is determined and the mechanism of system actions is launched, and in the second, their targets are defined. In the third case, the system is self-organized, its stable condition is supported and its aims and targets are realized.

System entropy cannot be infinite, from time to time systems turn to stability and development. Slightly nonequilibrium conditions require stable communications, valid intrasystem information, productive intrasystem and external monitoring followed by expert evaluation. Epistemic productivity of the digital economy concept is explained by the key idea of retaining the integrity of running processes amidst crisis and amidst slightly nonequilibrium conditions. Economic or financial crisis interrupts system existence, and digital reality ensures its continuity.

Digitalized reality problems are relevant from both practical and theoretic standpoints. Turn to digital economy is caused by the need to react accordingly to cardinal changes in international and national economies. Constitution of the modern economic theory is impossible without respect of the results of interdisciplinary knowledge and methodological resources of economic philosophy. The categorial and notional analysis conducted on the interfaces between economic theory and scientific philosophy is aimed at lowering the "temperature" of conceptually methodological tension in economic mainstream. The task of adapting the notion of digitalization for economic theory and economic philosophy complicates further research in this direction.

References

Antipina, O.N. Informatsionnaya ekonomika: sovremennyye tekhnologii I tsenoobrazovaniye. [Information Economics: modern technology of price formation]. M.: TEIS. – 2009 (in Russian).

Bekhmann, G. Sovremennoye obshchestvo: obshchestvo riska. informatsionnoye obshchestvo, obshchestvo znaniy. [Modern society: society of risk, information society, knowledge society]. M.: Science. Logos. – 2010 (in Russian).

Zhuravleva, G. P. Ekonomicheskaya teoriya. Makroekonomika1, 2. Megaekonomika. Ekonomika transformatsiy. [Of the Economic theory. Macroeconomics 1, 2. Megaeconomics. Economics of transformation]. M.: 2019. – p. 704. Phoenix (in Russian).

Kollontay, V. O neoliberal'noy modeli globalizatsii [On the neoliberal model of globalization] // M·E i MO, 1999. No. 10. p. 3 (in Russian).

Krivosheyeva, T.D. Instrumental'nyy potentsial proektnogo podkhoda k razvitiyu elektronnogo pravitel'stva kak faktor sovershenstvovaniya sistemy publichnogo upravleniya [Instrumental potential of the project approach to e-government development as a factor of public administration system improvement]: dissertatsiya . . . kand. ekonom. nauk. Ros.akad.nar. khoz-vai gos. sluzhby pri Prezidente RF. Rostov-on-Don., 2015 (in Russian).

Luhmann, N. Sotsial'nyye sistemy: Ocherk obshchey teorii [Social systems: Sketch of the General theory] // Zapadnaya teoreticheskaya sotsiologiya 80-kh godov. Referativnyy sbornik. M., 1989. pp. 41–64 (in Russian).

Lusse, A. Makroekonomika. [Macroeconomics]. SPb.: Piter, 1999 (in Russian).

Machlup, F. The production and distribution of knowledge in the United States, 1962. PRINCETON UNIVERSITY PRESS. - 462 p. (pp. 3–4). (in England).

Nikulina, T.V., Starchenko E.B. Informatizatsiya i tsifrovizatsiya obrazo-vaniya: ponyatiya, tekhnologii, upravleniye [Informatization and digitalization of education: concepts, technologies, management] // Pedagogicheskoye obrazovaniye v Rossii. No. 8. – 2018. p. 109 (in Russian).

Stepin, V.S. Istoricheskiye tipy nauchnoy ratsional'nosti: problemy demarkatsii i preyemstvennosti [Historical types of scientific rationality: problems of de-marking and continuity] // Filosofiya, metodologiya i istoriya nauki. 2015. No. 1. pp. 6–27 (in Russian).

Tapskott, D. Elektronno-tsifrovoye obshchestvo [Electron-digital society]. – K.: "INT-press". – M.: "Relf-buk", 1999 (in Russian).

Ukaz Prezidenta RF ot 9 maya 2017 g. No. 203 "O Strategii razvitiya in-formatsionnogo obshchestva v Rossiyskoy Federatsii na 2017–2030 gody" [Decree of the President of the Russian Federation "On the Strategy of information society development in Russian Federation to 2017–2030"] (in Russian).

Elena M. Skvortsova

3 Spiritual Bare of Digital Calving of Anthroposphere

Every STR changes the world.
(Simon Kuznets)

Introduction: Rubicon

When humanity left the world of nature, it embarked on the path of instrumental completion of its own habitat. About one and a half million years have passed from the manual chop of a Homo habilis to modern life support technologies of Homo sapiens. Mankind overcame many technological rubicons, but made only one spiritual transition – a person awared himself, gained personal reference points of creative activity in the axis era. The gods punished Prometheus and similar anthropophiles for violating the ban on the dissemination of completely confidential information. The biblical God has cast out Adam and Eve for disobedience from Eden to the world of suffering and labor. What is so jealously guarded by higher powers from evolving humanity? Fire, secrets of the letter, secrets of skill? The Bible provides the most comprehensive answer. Gods defended people from premature cognition, with the negative consequences of which slowly developed in spiritual terms, humanity will not be able to cope. And while the speed and depth of such knowledge somehow remotely corresponded to the spiritual evolution of our species, everything was more or less safe for him. But nothing remains unchanged, at a certain stage of self-development the process inevitably qualitatively transforms.

On the threshold of the third millennium, humanity stood before the line that the gods of antiquity had foreseen. We live in an era of demographic transition. Fertility and mortality are rapidly declining, with the result that the reproduction of the world's population trends in the limit to a simple replacement of generations. The law of hyperbolic population growth on Earth, described by Heinz von Förster, A.V. Korotaev and S.P. Kapitsa, on the basis of the theory of self-organization of processes developing with aggravation, ceases to reflect the current demographic situation, although it was correctly described from the moment of the Neolithic coup until today (Kapitsa, 2010). The hyperbolic law of the economic development of mankind was the trigger of all the improvements of our kind and the engine of progress of the last three scientific and technological revolutions. Now the demographic curve

Elena M. Skvortsova, Financial University under the Government of the Russian Federation, Moscow, Russia

https://doi.org/10.1515/9783110636147-003

acquires a logistic form. Scientists predict that from the mid-2020s, when the upward movement of the curve ceases, the logistic law will adequately reflect the nature of the demographic dynamics of the Earth until the next anthropological turn.

If in the previous anthropological epoch, the growth of the population of the Earth was determined by the accelerated extensive accumulation of life-supporting technologies and the improvement of the means of transmitting them in time and space, then in the new conditions this interaction will have paradoxical feedback – there will be more and more information that will influence on the creation of life enduring technologies less and less. The immense flow of information and the means of navigation available to the masses threaten to bring down the tsunami on humanity who is carried away by gadgets. Modern means of communication in our world are primarily social, and secondly – economic functions. Computers are turning not only into the killers of people's free time, especially in the zone of gaming that has swept humankind, but also weaken the colorful interpersonal communication of individuals. A person, especially a young one, ceases to understand the other without words, the language of facial expressions and gestures is less and less accessible to him, the areas of the brain responsible for the regulation of communicative connections are degrading.

Methodology

Anthropological Phenomenology of Virtualization of Reality

Virtual reality today seeks to dominate human relationships. It tactlessly bursts into our lives, threatening to substitute a person, promises him digital immortality and salvation, as, for example, in the novel "The Digitized Man" by Baal Malrad. Today, technologies are being seriously developed for preparing the human brain for digitizing its existence, digitizing the brain after a person's death, and connecting the brain to the Internet. According to the leading specialist of the Internet Brain project group (Brainternet) Adam Pantanovich, the maximum danger awaits a person at the stage when people learn to download information directly from the network to the brain. It is then that a hypothetically possible deep penetration into human consciousness will become possible, and the irreversible tragedy of total control and manipulation of people will acquire its insidious reality.

The Pantanovich group's proposed method of protecting a digitized brain is based on the idea of a quantum network reflecting the quantum nature of the very nature of consciousness. Breaking the network can immediately change the entire subjective configuration. The user, therefore, will be instantly warned about the dangers of the intervention. Religion has a special opinion on this. In its language, consciousness is beyond the control of anyone except God, who created man in such a way that he could not be spiritually unprepared to create an ideal copy of some arbitrary unknown state. Still, NetCom, funded by the US National Institute of Mental Health and the Y Combinator Venture Fund, is making no attempt to trick the old God. And these attempts are only the beginning of a tsunami in the depths of the ocean of human curiosity, instigated by the search for a way out of its organic nature.

Problem Areas of Anthroposphere Virtualization

At the modern, relatively safe stage of exploitation by a person of information technologies and networks, big problems await us. And the very first of them, according to Dawkins, is the "egoistic gene", or "meme", a semantic unit capable of fast spontaneous duplication and translation through people, creators and carriers of information (Dawkins, 1989). A paradoxical idea is expressed that it is not so much the biological species of a person that is twice rational that evolves, but the product of its conscious activity, which turns its source of origin into a simple nutrient medium. The information itself chooses its carrier and creates favorable or unfavorable conditions for the reproduction of this or that person. The imperative behavior of the information environment is becoming more assertive, and people lose control of their own child.

Serious is the danger of information networks being clogged by cognitive, verbal, spiritual memes-viruses on the one hand, and uncontrolled reproduction of information patterns harmful to humans on the other. The most contaminated source of the network is the site "VKontakte" – a sample of information oncology of modern Russia. It is reasoned that the leading scientists of the country sounded the alarm, created the Sretensky, in the manner of Rome, a club within which they discuss, among other things, the problems of noomonitoring and cognitive programming of subjective reality: Ageev, E.L. Loginov, V.G. Budanov, V.S. Kurdyumov, A.V. Oleksin (Budanov, 2009; Budanov, Kurdyumov and Oleksin, 2016; Ageev and Loginov, 2017; Oleksin, Kurdyumov and Kolesova, 2017).

Their idea of pushing the spontaneous self-organization of the virtual network space by launching "social chaperones" seems interesting. The idea is taken from biology. Chaperones are molecules that regulate the assembly of molecular networks. *"It is intended to develop a personality-adapted configuration of basic characteristics (including political bias and intellectual preferences) of individuals and their aggregated groups as the basic reference point for managing groups of interconnected people, machines, technical, including information, systems and natural objects."* (Ageev and Loginov, 2017)

There is another development of the problem of virtualization of reality. In the near future, it will inevitably have to push "extra people" out of life. According to the Me Kinsey Global Institute estimates, by 2020, high-tech companies in the world will suffer from a deficit of 40 million top specialists in the fields of programming, analytics, engineering and mathematics. The staff with secondary special education, on the contrary, will be a surplus of 100 million people. Automatics will replace medium-level jobs, with the middle class of society facing the inevitable extinction. By 2050, robots will be able to leave more than 1 billion people out of work around the world, depriving them of their wages of 16 trillion dollars.

Results

Development Trends of the Anthroposphere Within the New Technological Era

Polarization of the workforce, the growing demand for highly qualified and highly paid specialists will inevitably have to lead, on the one hand, to widening the gap between people's incomes, and, on the other hand, to reducing the consumer demand of the population. Under the conditions of the new demography, the economy will radically change its priorities. As the automation of the production processes of the third STR period inevitably came the time of digitalization, with its almost absolute transparency of the total clue for everything that happens in the world leaving the digital trace of activity, so the digital economy will inevitably have its modest place and means highlight the task conscious optimal organization of man-made habitat. Members of the Sretensky Club named after S.P. Kurdyumov proclaimed: man has lost a reserve of time for an experienced comprehension of the world, it is time to transform reality with the help of science. Such a manifesto makes us seriously think about the questions: what do people expect from their activities, what are the ideals of their fathers-designers, what generally happens to people in the era of the new technological revolution?

Maybe we are afraid that once again the machines will replace people, but only replace them so that the return path of human development closes for us forever? But, in fact, let us not reject in the old manner the fruits of scientific and technological progress, fighting with the windmills of its ghosts. New Luddism today is absolutely inappropriate. The logic of the instrumental development of mankind cannot be canceled, and it is not necessary. The human genius makes our living environment comfortable and releases a lot of free time, which people can use for personal self-improvement, being realized in creative activity, each in their own unique manner. Philosophers have always dreamed of this paradise for people. Now he is close to us, and we are able to finally see with our own eyes its real charms and threats.

In the postindustrial economy of developed countries, out of 100 people only a quarter work, feeding themselves and all the rest. What remains for people who are free from life-supporting activities? Rich countries are ready to maintain an army of unoccupied people at a fairly high level of living. In Switzerland, a referendum was held to assess consumer preferences of the country's residents and to find ways to maintain the potential demand of the population in terms of minimizing productive activity on the new demographic wave. People were asked to answer the question of whether they agree to receive a monthly basic income of $ 2,800 per person as compensation for a hypothetical loss or decrease in employment. To the surprise of sociologists, the answer was negative. Citizens are rightly afraid of the devaluation of labor incentives and the ability to positive goal setting, especially among the younger generation.

Noosphere or kakosphere? Socio-Humanitarian Flaws of Civilization and the Goals of Society

What follows from the above? It seems that our main duty to future generations is to achieve a twofold goal – to preserve the control of humanity over the world around it and over ourselves. It can be done only with the concomitant resolution of the problem of a radical restructuring of people's attitudes toward their environment as an object of irresponsible manipulation. In order to carry out this task it is necessary to save man for humanity, to save the life of the anthroposphere, which more and more becomes kakosphere. The term was introduced by G.A. Zavarzin in 2003 to refer to the antipode of the noosphere concept, developed in the works of V.I. Vernadsky and P. Teilhard de Char din at the beginning of the 20th century (Pierre Teilhard de Chardin, 1987; Vernadsky, 1988; Zavarzin, 2003; 2011).

The transformation of the Earth's biosphere into a garbage dump, into a septic tank of human activity, has its own social flaw. Human relations can get out and already partly go out of people's control. War as a form of aggression regulated by society today gives way to terrorism, preventing the spread of which will inevitably strengthen the punitive functions of power against the whole society and lead to a narrowing of the zone of political freedom and public will of the people.

In the cage with this negative are the humanitarian disadvantages of civilization, changing the face of the person. He leads a sedentary lifestyle, uses genetically modified foods that lead to obesity, cancer and genetic diseases. The culture of fitness clubs, aimed at combating a sedentary lifestyle and unhealthy diet, is becoming a kind of physical culture business with all the costs associated with this. But an even more dangerous symptom of the destruction of the anthroposphere is the weakening of the spirituality of the new generation of people who grow up on the products of show business, artificial stimulants and virtual communication.

The emergence of the international youth subculture of self-isolated people in the developed countries of the world has become an extreme manifestation of the harmful state of a person. Their share in the respective age categories today almost reaches the mark of 10%. Psychologically, they are tied to gadgets, which are literally in symbiotic relationship, and are addicted to gaming. They do not go out into the white light and do not tolerate fresh air. They work in networks, communicating with their own kind in chat rooms in a language incomprehensible to the uninitiated, they receive food through the delivery system. Without exception, all of them suffer from diseases of civilization, they are closed, unsociable, psychologically unstable, intellectually developed.

Panacea from the Dehumanization of Society

Is it necessary to resist? Not everyone will answer this question positively. For some, this is the logical outcome of the evolution of the human race. But it is unlikely that a modern healthy person will want to become a home-worker, give up a full-blooded life in favor of a ghostly wander through the maze of virtual spaces. To prevent this from happening, thus the person will have not changed himself, he needs to help as soon as possible to recall the answer to the question of what sets the trajectory of his integrity, that is, humanity. This answer has long been known: it is its ability to reasonably restrain itself on the basis of benevolence towards others, expedient comprehension and use of knowledge about the world, and opposition to phenomena that destroy the natural habitat, that is, what people call morality, moral values, high intelligence.

All these meanings fit into a single concept of *spirituality*. It reflects the highest level of development and self-realization of a mature personality, the purpose of which is the highest human values: good, honor, generosity, selflessness, justice and independence. A person acquires these qualities in the course of his socialization, carried out through family relations, educational and labor activities. They are based on interpersonal communication. Values, ethics, morality are transmitted only and exclusively from person to person. A person cannot be raised by an immature person with an impaired ability to judge and make decisions independently. Immanuel Kant called the ability to assess the highest measure of man. Alexander Sergeevich Pushkin expressed a thought in his own way: *"The self-state of man is the guarantee of his greatness."*

Epicrisis of the Modern State of the Anthroposphere

What do we observe in today's human habitat? The sharp decline in the value of interpersonal relations, the crowding out of the culture of the word by the cult of teaching manipulations in the humanities, the separation of online learning from the traditional, the display of barriers that divide not only different subject areas, but also the branches of the same disciplines. The modern smart generation of

Google demonstrates the wonders of ingenuity in the exploitation of the pocket memory of the "flat brain", however, in the search for high meanings, its ability to navigate immediately disappears as if by magic. Symptoms are too obvious, indicating the defeat of the human principle in modern society. It is significant that even humanitarians, scientists, teachers manage to write textbooks on human development, putting it in the context of scientific and technological progress, including any components there, but not the spiritual vector of the evolution of our species (Human development: a new dimension of socio-economic progress, 2008).

The contemporaries of the 21st century need to think about overcoming the catastrophic shortage of humanity in people, diminished by the circumstances of their life. Alber Schweitzer spoke about this shortage in the previous century: "We must fight the circumstances for our humanity" (Schweizer, 1992). Today, these circumstances set the vector of personal modernization, which is based on success at any cost. It is shaped by social expectations that support the family, school and university. Education and career are two of its fundamental interests. Here we are not talking about a person, his soul and morality. The inevitable consequence of such a scenario is the growth of aggression, the coarsening of interpersonal relations, the deterioration of the mental health of the population and, especially, the youth.

The accelerating growth in the number of divine adolescents indicates a violation of social ties and a deep crisis of pedagogy. The stubborn facts of the report on the state of health care in the world, and, in particular, on the mental state of modern humanity, clearly demonstrate the deep spiritual disease of society at the turn of the II–III thousand: *"Today, approximately 450 million people suffer from mental and neurological disorders. Acute depression is currently the leading cause of disability in the world. In the whole world, 70 million people suffer from alcoholism, 50 million – with epilepsy, 24 million – with schizophrenia. Every year 1 million people commit suicide, from 10 to 20 million people commit suicide attempts. One out of every four people will be afflicted with a mental disorder at some time in their life."* (World Health Report, 2001)

Conclusion: "Ab ovo"

We once again stand up to the eternal question – what shall we do? What the people of the modern post-industrial era should start their recovery with, while they managed to find a lot of comfortable, but bad habits? The Romans replied that the first step was taken "ab ovo" (from the egg). A child begins with a family, spiritually grows and develops in school, and acquires activity independence in a higher educational institution.

The main problem of modern family relations is the pernicious and ever-increasing trend of replacing the live communication of people of different generations, who always acted as the starting navigator for the child's life, immersed in virtual reality and eternal employment. Both adults and children are drowning in these evils, and the older generation, as a rule, is doomed to silence and oblivion. When a person himself takes away the past by losing respect and interest in antiquity and elders, he loses his destiny, condemns himself to the role of tumbleweed, and is easily pushed out of people's inherent habitat. The anthroposphere shrinks just as it does during apoptosis of cells in the human body. Adults who create families now need to be taught not only how to properly swaddle and care for a child, but also how to maintain a warm spiritual climate in the family, how to pay attention to the elderly and children, showing a keen interest in them, how to prevent a pernicious addiction to hang networks. Western sociologists have presented a bleak picture. Modern men give the family 45 minutes a day, and 4.5 hours – to their gadgets. *Emotional harmony is the basis of family relationships.*

School is the next step in the *humanization and spiritualization* of children. Smart learning technologies should be used here only as a convenient means of educating the child's personality, raising his abilities for independent and sound judgment. Weekly lessons in the history of logic, ethics, aesthetics, rhetoric, psychology, linguistics, literature and etiquette are necessary. Schoolchildren should talk more, learn to express their soul. The culture of the word is the basis of spiritual perfection. Natural sciences are called upon to open to students an amazing connection of everything with everything in the universe. In their teaching, it is high time to abandon the tradition of formal logical training, which does not give room for imagination to either the mind or the soul of a child. *The creativity of adolescents should become a spiritual imperative of school education*, but at the same time not likened to the protrusion of their own point of view "for peanuts".

The university completes the preparation of a person for independent living, figuratively speaking, it boils a hard-boiled egg. High temperatures are the main sign of the final stage of training. Here the personality is driven around, learning to make weighted responsible independent decisions and put them into practice. The activity competence approach to higher education is justified only if it contains the vector of spiritual activity. Any form of cognitive and performative activity of a student should be developed in the direction of developing an understanding of the consequences of the anthroposphere response to human intervention in the holy saints of the whole world. *Fostering the student's responsible attitude towards their own transformational activities is the spiritual imperative of higher education.*

The younger generation is different today, it can accommodate much more than its predecessors. This must be taken into account. But teachers themselves must be brought up in the ideals of high intelligence and spirituality. This path is not fast, rather thorny, but only it will lead humanity to the cherished goal, the motto of which will be the words of the Hippocratic oath "Do no harm!", applicable now not to an individual, but to the anthroposphere as part of a living integral world. Humanity must stand before a new phase of its spiritual development, which will come, according to P. Teilhard de Chardin, when it is generally aware of itself, as once an individual did (Teilhard de Chardin P., 1987).

References

Ageev A.I., Loginov E.L. The battle for the future: who will be the first in the world to master noomonitoring and cognitive programming of subjective reality. // Economic strategies. 2017. No. 2. pp. 124–139.

Budanov V.G. How is the quantum-synergistic anthropology possible (synthetic myths of physicality) // Body as an epistemological phenomenon / resp. ed. I.A. Beskova. – Moscow: Institute of Physics, RAS, 2009. pp. 55–70.

Budanov V.G., Kurdyumov V.S., Oleksin A.V. Social chaperones. // Economic strategies. 2016. No. 7. S. 92–100.

Dawkins R. Egoistic gene. - M.: Corpus, 1989.

Human development: a new dimension of socio-economic progress. The manual edited by prof. V.P. Kolesova (Faculty of Economics, Moscow State University), second edition, supplemented and revised. – M.: Human Rights, 2008.

Kapitsa S.P. Paradoxes of growth. The laws of human development. - M.: Alpina non-fiction, 2010.

Oleksin A.V., Kurdyumov V.S., Kolesova L.A. Network structures, matrix and chaperones. Practical opportunities and organizational steps. // Economic strategies. 2017. No. 5. pp. 94–105.

Schweizer A. A reverence for life. – M.: Progress, 1992.

Teilhard de Chardin P. The Phenomenon of Man / Preface. and comm. B.A. Starostin; trans. from Fr. by N. Sadovskiy. – M.: Science, 1987.

The world health report. Mental Health: New Understanding, New Hope. – M., 2001.

Vernadsky V.I. Philosophical thoughts of a naturalist / resp. ed. A.A. Yashin – M.: Science, 1988.

Zavarzin G.A. Like the sphere. Philosophy and journalism / G.A. Zavarzin. – M.: Ruthenika, 2011.

Zavarzin G.A. The antipode of the noosphere // Bulletin of the Russian Academy of Sciences, 2003. Vol. 73. No. 7. pp. 627–636.

Bronislav D. Babaev, Elena E. Nikolaeva, Dmitriy B. Babaev

4 STP as a Human Society Development Factor: Resource Support of STP

Introduction

The overall objective of the proposed material is to give a detailed modern understanding of scientific and technological progress, taking into account its resource support and then show the role of STP in the life of a person. The authors are guided by the materials on the economy of the Russian Federation, referring to the world experience when necessary. The relevance of the topic is related to the major economic advances expected in the economy of the Russian Federation. There is a turn of economic policy in the infrastructure-regional direction, when the theme of the infrastructure arrangement of the economic territory is put at the forefront with the emphasis on establishing the optimal relationship between centralized tasks and problems of various regions in the country. The attention of the authorities and business is clearly increasing in order to more fully realize the most important competitive advantage of the national economy, which consists not only in a huge economic territory, but also in innumerable natural resources, which implies an intensification of efforts in the field of material production. People will always have a need for food, clothing, housing and other material benefits. An important role in the future will be taken by the program of transit of goods and people between Europe and Asia using our resources; if managed effectively, it will give a tremendous gain in its various forms – the development of territories, currency, etc. The main discussed topic is in-depth development of raw materials and materials received on the territory of our country in order to get a higher benefit. At the same time, the tasks of import substitution as a factor of national security are being solved, and the emphasis is placed on the high role of the Russian regions. Since the world is dominated by aggressive competition, it is necessary to achieve success in the organization of scientific and technical progress as a leading factor in economic activity.

Note: The material was prepared with the financial support of the Russian Foundation for Basic Research in the framework of the scientific project No. 19-010-00329 "Theoretical and methodological foundations of an expanded understanding of the economic mechanism in the modern economy".

Bronislav D. Babaev, Elena E. Nikolaeva, Ivanovo State University, Ivanovo, Russia
Dmitriy B. Babaev, Ivanovo branch of the Russian Presidential Academy of national economy and public administration, Ivanovo, Russia

https://doi.org/10.1515/9783110636147-004

The authors pay tribute to the cohort of domestic and foreign scientists who have studied the problems of scientific and technical progress. An example of the classical work on the theory of productive forces, in the framework of which the STP is considered, is the work of A. I. Anchishkin (Anchishkin, 1986). The books by J. K. Galbraith (Galbraith, 1973) and J. Schumpeter (Schumpeter, 1989), which at one time became bestsellers, are useful within the framework of the theoretical analysis of the productive forces and the STP.

Methodology

The basis of the methodological principles is systemness, integrativity, reproducibility, and also contradictions as a driving force.

Usually, researchers seek to present their material in some kind of systemic form, which is characterized by integrity, interpreted as a structure, as an organization of direct and inverse relations. In this case, an overview of the whole complex of the problems being raised is provided, while development points are extracted.

Integrity, in turn, means the coherence and complementarity of those scientific propositions, which together form a system, in our case – a system of research character.

The moment of reproducibility should be understood traditionally, as phenomena or processes that are constantly renewed (if there are appropriate prerequisites) and occur constantly. Processes of a pivotal plan and phenomena of a basic nature are being advanced, but at the same time, phenomena are also singled out in the system of relations, the task of which is to maintain and provide the movement of basic phenomena. Both in theory and in practice, the ratio of the core and supporting types of economic activity is easy to show on the example of clusters (complexes of a national or regional level).

As for the contradictions, with the usual look, quite often they are interpreted as certain flaws of the economy, as something that does not move as much as it slows down the process. But within the framework of the dialectic of the movement (development) of a contradiction there is a necessary signal to action, and the resolution of contradictions is a movement forward. For example, in the economy and finance of our country there is always some kind of dissonance in relations between the center and the regions, it concerns primarily the distribution of funds of the consolidated budget. At the same time, the steps taken to optimize this ratio are undoubtedly a positive move, when the conditions for financing certain responsible projects are improved. In general, contradictions are an extremely important scientific motive substance. If we split up one process or another, then mental interaction between the two sides arises. The topic of their correspondence is actualized, but partly internal and mainly external factors generate a discrepancy. In the end, the current tendency to conformity acts as a driving force. For example, in well-known processes of stimulating any activity, for example, at the enterprise level, one can divide the two sides in the order of analytics – the economic interest of the collective and its social responsibility. The tendency to establish balance is the driving force.

Results

Now, let us review the consideration of the main scientific results.

We start with the fact that the STP is the highest form of human economic activity, which is characterized by at least four fundamental points. First, there is an intensive type of economic growth where integration takes place: science and technology (one version); science, technology and education, where science and education form the intelligence of the nation (another version); science, technology, economics, education (third, expansion version, possibly controversial). Secondly, this process fits into the framework of the expanded social reproduction of the innovation type, which involves periodic technological breakthroughs with the provision of fundamental shifts in the growth of labor productivity, resource saving and expansion of the range of goods created, works performed, services rendered. Thirdly, the STP as a process has an anthropogenic nature. It is inextricably linked to a person, a creative one (an innovative person), which results in the fact, that this economic phenomenon occurs only at a sufficiently high level of human society development. Fourthly, the interrelation of the process self-development (it's autonomization) and existence as a controlled process (projects, programs, etc., implemented by people in an organized manner) is distinctive.

In a structurally informative and functional-evolutionary form, the STP is disclosed in the works of B. N. Kuzyk and Yu. V. Yakovets (Kuzyk and Yakovets, 2005).

Scientific and technical progress as a techno-economic phenomenon originated at a sufficiently high level of human development. Artificially man-made means of labor evolved and pre-emerged as a system of machine production. The various movements of the objects of labor were also related, for example, as a result of the success of chemistry and other sciences, a "second nature" arose, the fruit of human hands and mind labor.

Along with transformable means of labor, technologies and methods of organizing the case play a prominent role. For interest, you can recall the revolutionary role of the conveyor, as well as assembly methods from finished parts of industrial and non-industrial buildings and structures at their deployment sites. In general, many industrial and other upheavals have shifts in technology as a starting point, and only then their technical arrangement arises.

In the literature there are holistic theories devoted to the influence of STP on the economy of society. As an example, let us refer to the works of S. Yu. Glaz'yev, where the subject of technical-economic structures and long-term systems is proclaimed (Glaz'yev, 1993, 2018). V. V Ivanter and his institute are actively involved in predictions in the field of STP, generally believing that the importance of STP as a factor of development increases as science penetrates the macro- and microworld and improves the mechanisms for introducing science into practice (Ivanter, 2017). In some areas, the concept of STP is structured and applied to the Russian conditions. The development topic is deployed for the future – a large group of scientists is working on this under the direction of A. R. Belousov (Belousov, 2006). The role of technological upheavals in certain industries, which entail changes in technology, organization and economy, is emphasized.

The third point that we treat as a prerequisite for STP is the formation of a cohort of creative people. Apparently, there are special methods created by nature and society itself to select people constituting the economic, political and other elite. Even in ancient times, priests, for example, in ancient Egypt, were carriers of special knowledge that amazed people. Another prerequisite for STP is the formation of new ideas, which from the organizational side can be represented as schools (for example, in Ancient Greece there were philosophical schools in favor, and philosophy itself was viewed as a science of science, which included both theoretical knowledge and applied knowledge.

Among the factors that determined the need for STP is the public demand for this type of economic activity, which is innovative in nature. So, mankind has always had a need for means of transportation. Especially sharply this kind of need manifested itself in the 19th century, when the railways began to grow as mushrooms and river and navy received powerful pushes. After some time, there was a new breakthrough associated with the air fleet, and later with the space. In general, the request forms for STP are extremely diverse and represent a certain mixture of centralized and decentralized moments. So, the central government takes care of the army, the regions are concerned with strengthening the rule of law, there is also a request for weapons, uniforms, etc., but this is not a request of an army type.

There are new concepts in relation to changing conditions – as an example we can cite the concept of V. Mayevsky, dedicated to macroproportions (Mayevskiy, 1997). Economic and mathematical methods and models that "look into" the future have been described by V. Leontief and his school (Leontief and Duchin, 1986).

Speaking about the origins of STP, let us point out the different organizational forms of its existence – projects, comprehensive target programs, departments responsible for innovation, etc.

The topic of STP from the plane of technology and organization is often transferred to the management plane and is included in the general scheme of the national economy called "management economics" – a similar concept was professed, for example, by K. Seo (Seo, 1991). STP was interpreted not only within the national and global economy, but also within the enterprise. For example, this idea was promoted by A. Thompson and J. Formby (Thompson and Formby, 1993). There are, however, concepts that suggest “replacing” the topic of STP as a driving force for the influence of finance on the economy – M. Friedman with his monetary approaches can be cited as an example (Friedman, 1953). We note, however, that there are primary factors of development, among which are the STP, but there are also derivatives, for example, the role of money circulation and the company’s finances.

Based on our understanding of the STP as a phenomenon that has a content-structural fullness and a certain functional purpose, we highlight the following points.

The starting point is the formation of ideas. On this account there is a whole science, and not even one. Scientists are consolidating, forming schools, associations and other formations, which allow combining individual and group views and forming such points of view that are widely spread and even widely accepted. In the sector of scientific knowledge, fundamental and applied directions are distinguished. Currently, there is increasing attention in the RAS to basic research, because, firstly, it is the scientific basis of applied knowledge, and secondly, it is a reserve for the future. We often hear that these or other developments are based on the Soviet legacy, and from this side the research of a fundamental nature is similar to a long-playing disc. Technological breakthroughs are only possible on the basis of such studies, and we really need them to strengthen our position in the world market. In the field of scientific research there are a lot of problems, but we will not particularly consider them.

The second step is the materialization of ideas, the creation of prototypes, the carrying out of necessary experiments, etc. This kind of work should apparently be carried out to a significant extent on the basis of guaranteed budget financing, especially when it comes to large-scale development. At the same time, large economic structures have their own scientific divisions, financed at the expense of enterprises. It is regrettable that we have not only damaged fundamental research, but also sectoral and departmental science. Media says that it is necessary to establish by law the rate of deductions from gross domestic product to science support. Sometimes these figures are called – 2%, 3%.

The third step is the replication of new developments, the release of new products, services provided. At this point, traditionally (this is also characteristic of the Soviet period) were failures. The reasons for the fact that at this stage the scientific and technical progress was significantly inhibited were diverse. We point out some of the most important points.

Low wages, low labor costs are the number one topic. Such a paradoxical moment is interesting: our natural resources, their accessibility also do not have a very positive effect on social progress, in particular, they do not stimulate a rational use of available resources (this can be shown on the example of water, electricity, etc.). The economy is arranged in such a way that, in the part in which it is aimed at the domestic market, it does not compel producers and consumers to take due care to increase the efficiency of economic activity. For example, in oil production there are a lot of abandoned wells, where there is still oil, but it is difficult to extract. If it is possible to create new wells, then why take care of old, abandoned? Torches are burning, which means losses for the national economy. Accident rate of oil transportation is high. In this case, this industry is heavily indebted to the country; natural resources are not used efficiently enough.

There are other circumstances that slow down the STP. The literature gives an example from the practice of relations between trade unions and business in the United States. Since very long time, positions have been fixed in contracts: for each percentage increase in labor productivity, wages increased by 0.7% (a common standard). It is customary to emphasize the importance of this innovation in explaining the reasons for success in the US economy. This practice has not spread in our country. It is necessary to ascertain the undesirable moment that our long-term work of managers is not sufficiently stimulated. As a result of market reforms, the salaries of enterprise managers have increased dramatically, but this is not always properly tied to performance. There is a world practice of awarding shares, using bonuses, etc., in order, firstly, to raise the responsibility of managers for the activities of teams, secondly, to authorize them for lack of success in activities, and thirdly, to interest them in the implementation of long-term projects.

In a market economy, it is important not only to produce a new product, but also to be able to offer it to the consumer. The task is facilitated in the conditions when the contractual system is in place; it is very widespread in the world. But some of the new goods are bought in the order of free trade. This is where problems that are well known in the literature arise. In any case, marketing as an intermediary has a very serious impact on the scope and course of the STP.

Typically, the problems of STP are over if the product is sold. But in real life the movement continues. Various issues arise related to the achievement by the enterprise-consumer of the design capacity of the equipment used, the regulatory use of raw materials, etc. Moreover, in relation to machines and equipment, periodically there are issues of spare parts, maintenance, repair, etc. Because of this, the practice of after-sales service of equipment, machinery, appliances and other things concerning household is widespread. Finally, let us notice a series of plots on the disposal of worn out tools. Apparently, all these issues should be included in the problems of STP. We believe that in analytical and practical work it is necessary to use an expanded view of scientific and technological progress as an innovative form of economic activity.

It is necessary to pay attention to what acts as a product of scientific and technological progress. We can say: new ideas, new goods, works, services, this is correct, but this is not enough. Without renouncing this, more convincing language should be used.

First, the STP allows humanity to maintain economic activity at the competitive level that has developed (or is taking shape) in the economy. For example, at present, the speed of movement on the railways (Japan, France and other countries) has sharply increased, on this side Russia needs to pull itself up. The movement of goods and people between Europe and Asia has noticeably increased, our country needs to dramatically expand this transit, which allows it to obtain greater benefits. By the way, now the work on the development of the Northern Sea Route has become more active.

There is an increase in the number of types of economic activity. Thus, in the United States, the number of manufactured products, semi-products, work performed, services rendered exceeded 30 million items. The figure is impressive. Such processes are associated with what has received the name of roundaboutness. In some cases, it increases, in other cases it decreases. If you fish with bare hands, then the roundaboutness is zero, but if fishing is carried out by modern vessels with extensive use of divided labor and resources, then the quantitative value of roundaboutness is high.

Any kind of economic activity has its own life cycle; here it is important to maintain optimization decisions that fall within the competence of the STP.

Due to internal laws and external circumstances, humanity is moving forward, making new and new requests for products and services. A new product is not just a new circle of consumers, it is some kind of movement in the production, circulation, consumption of the product, it is a natural movement that cannot be stopped. If you "close" the STP, then it can be likened to stopping the Earth, when the atmosphere will demolish everything that is on this Earth. G. Wells in one of his stories used a similar plot. Modern civilization is characterized by a close bunch of "new needs – STP".

We have already entered the plot topic of resource provision of STP. All wisdom lies in the fact that this process is ensured by the whole economy, one of which tasks is to form and maintain social progress as a continuously ongoing process. It is possible with a certain convention to isolate those parts of the national economy that, in aggregate, "support" STP.

1) Personnel is undoubtedly the first to be discussed. Especially important are those who form schools and directions, being able not only to create research teams, but also to provide a targeted result. In fact, the topic of results has always been the subject of great discussions in science, but without clearly set guidelines one will have to work on the well-known proverb "Go there, I don't know where, bring it, I don't know what".
2) The overall focus of the economy on the allocation of a group (complex) of industries that set the tone for economic growth. For example, in the 1930s, it was a heavy industry with its core – mechanical engineering. With a bit of conventionality, it one can say that the military-industrial complex now dominates, if it only steadily supplies civilian spheres with the necessary technologies.
3) Supply of machinery and equipment. In this case, especially when it comes to basic research, there is a big specificity, which implies a broad global cooperation in the design and creation of scientific equipment. Our dependence on external supplies in this situation is obvious. There is no big trouble in this, if we, in turn, supply the scientific equipment produced by us to the same world market.
4) Formation of a public request for new products, works, services, that is, the support of STP. From this side the state order is very important. As an example, the construction of space centers, Kerch Bridge, high-speed highways.

5) Financial support of STP. We have already spoke on this topic. This question, despite all its triviality, is theoretically and practically not simple. What about the STP in general? What innovative activities do the state, business, households, foreign participants take on themselves? Usually they tend to think that the infrastructure should, if possible, be handed over to the state. At the same time, the topic of the need to increase the investment burden on households is being raised, although there are 19 million poor people in the country. It is primarily about the construction of people of their own housing. As for the purchase of cars, the level of motorization in the country is high. Even in such a depressed region as the Ivanovo region, on average, every second family has a car.
6) Organizational and managerial forms of organization and regulation of the STP. Here we must be careful, because there is an interconnection between self-development (autonomy) and managed development (projects, etc.). Sometimes it is said that in the country, due to the high socialization of production (in production and technology), spatial scope, and the special role of infrastructure, a kind of governmental plan is needed. We also support the creation of a system of regulatory centers. For example, these centers could coordinate the interaction of large enterprises with their long technological chains and small towns with their enterprises that need orders.
7) Development of strategies for the socio-economic development of the country and its constituent regions and types of economic activity. The presence of such a document makes it possible to define more clearly the tasks of the STP as the highest form of economic development. Currently, there is not enough complete clarity on this issue. One of the aspects of this topic is finding out how the regions should position themselves within the national and world markets. So, the country's position on world markets is not entirely clear, but it is still difficult to determine from here what it is to develop on a wide scale within the national economy itself. There is a general consideration – more electricity, more coal, oil and gas, more grain, etc. However, there is no clearly thought out sequence with balance linkages. However, society is waiting for it to appear. Ones argue: there are strategies. Nevertheless, these strategies are often revised and refined, it is possible that this cannot be avoided, but, nevertheless, it is necessary to determine it: first, on a large scale, then on a smaller scale. The use of the economic space of the country as a bridge between Europe and Asia is tremendous in terms of its objectives and an extremely difficult project to implement, on which it is necessary to work for years. But as such, it is necessary to fix it in law, highlighting the appropriate resources for project and other work.

Households that form large-scale requests for innovations and provide important resources for the formation of these innovations need to be introduced into the topic of ensuring the STP. Let us note some points. The household itself is extremely saturated with household appliances, which forms the appropriate national economic and regional services. The domestic situation of households and their relationship with the external environment develops an interesting direction – house science, when homemaker takes on so much knowledge, the totality of which requires us to be aware that the modern woman as the head of the family represents a certain profession (knowledge of home appliances, the ability to understand the variety of goods, etc.)

An automobile, that became a necessary accessory for people, produced a genuine coup in the household. The form of rest and leisure changed. Much has changed. The STP has made a huge contribution, but the household, in turn, supports scientific and technical progress, creating the prerequisites for it and offering appropriate guidelines.

Conclusion

STP is a phenomenon that requires its development an innovative economy as a providing and stimulating start. This is the general conclusion.

We formulate a number of proposals.

1) To discuss via media the question of creating a kind of governmental plan in the country as a whole and in the regions with recommendatory functions and combining analytical and managerial activities.
2) Expand a movement for the active use of the project form of economic and other activities, firstly, in scientific circles, then among managers, as this allows revealing the development opportunities.
3) To study within the framework of the country the experience of training executives with entrepreneurial skills at different levels, thinking out how to use this experience in the specific conditions of the country's regions.
4) To increase attention to large-scale projects as engines of the economy, supporting scientific and technical progress. A country like Russia cannot hold onto small and medium-sized businesses.

References

Anchishkin, A. I. *Nauka. Tekhnika. Ekonomika.* [The science. Equipment. Economy]. Moscow, Publishing house Economika, 1986, 383 p (in Russian).

Belousov, A. R. *Evolyutsiya sistemy vosproizvodstva rossiyskoy ekono-miki: ot krizisa k razvitiyu* [The evolution of the reproduction system of the Russian economy: from crisis to development]. Moscow, MAKS Press, 2006, 393 p (in Russian).

Friedman, M. (1953). Essays in Positive Economics, Chicago, University of Chicago Press, 329 p.

Galbraith, J. K. (1973), Economics and the Public Purpose, Houghton Mifflin, Boston, 334 p.

Glaz'yev, S. YU. *Ryvok v budushcheye: Rossiya v novykh tekhnologicheskom i mirokhozyaystvennom ukladakh* [Breakthrough into the future: Russia in the new technological and world economic structure]. Moscow, Publishing house Knizhnyy mir, 2018, 765 p (in Russian).

Glaz'yev, S. YU. *Teoriya dolgosrochnogo tekhniko-ekonomicheskogo razvitiya* [Theory of long-term technical and economic development]. Moscow, Publishing house VlaDar, 1993, 310 p (in Russian).

Institute of Economic Forecasting of the Russian Academy of Sciences. *Strukturno-investitsionnaya politika v tselyakh obespecheniya ekonomiche-skogo rosta v Rossii: monografiya* [Structural and investment policy in order to ensure economic growth in Russia: a monograph]. Edit. akad. V. V. Ivanter. Moscow, Publishing house Nauchnyy konsul'tant, 2017, 196 p (in Russian).

Kuzyk, B. N., Yakovets YU. V. *Rossiya-2050: strategiya innovatsionnogo proryva* [Russia-2050: Innovative Breakthrough Strategy]. Moscow, Publishing house Economika, 2005, 618 p (in Russian).

Leontief, V., Duchin, F. (1986), The Future Impact of Automation on Workers, Oxford University Press, New York, Oxford, 169 p.

Mayevskiy, V. *Vvedeniye v evolyutsionnuyu makroekonomiku* [Introduction to Evolutionary Macroeconomics]. Moscow, Publishing house YAponiya segodnya, 1997, 106 p (in Russian).

Schumpeter, J. A. (1989), Essays: on entrepreneurs, innovations, business cycles, and the evolution of capitalism, Transactions Publishers, Paris. 341 p.

Seo, K. K. (1991), Managerial Economics. Text, problems and Short Cases, Irwin, Homewood, Boston. 643 p.

Thompson, A. A., Jr., Formby, J. P. (1993), Economics of the Firm. Theory and Practice. Prentice-Hall, Upper Saddle River, New Jersey. 591 p.

Elena V. Ivanova, Galina A. Rodina, Irina A. Smirnova

5 The Role of Human in the Process of Technological Transformation of the Modern Economic System

Introduction

The study of human nature, its potential, creative qualities and diverse abilities has always occupied and continues to occupy a central place in scientific research. At the same time, in the field of economic theory (meaning the traditional theory of neoclassical synthesis), a person continues to be regarded as either a production factor or a rational consumer. As a result, the issue of the development of the human personality largely remains outside the sphere of interests of economic disciplines.

In fairness it should be recalled that the theory, being a reflection of practice, only explains the objective processes occurring in the real economy. These processes, until recently, were associated with the accelerated development of the material and technical base of industry in the course of national industrialization. As a result, for many years among all the abilities of a person his productive abilities stood out, which, along with physical capital, had the status of one of the main factors of production. The main thing was the successful combination of these factors (capital and labor) in the production process. At the same time, there was a stable understanding of the superiority of the technical component over the human.

Today, humanity is entering a new, post-industrial era. Its basis is fundamentally new, different from the previous, technologies, the value of which increases so much that it makes it possible to speak of deep transformations of the entire resource base of the modern economy, including humans.

Methodology

The issues of both technological and human development are beyond the interests of economic paradigm of the contemporary market. The neoclassical synthesis methodology, based on break-even analysis, is unable to assess fundamental, qualitative, increasingly fast and active changes in the resource base of the modern economic system.

Elena V. Ivanova, Irina A. Smirnova, Financial University under the Government of the Russian Federation, Moscow, Russia
Galina A. Rodina, The Yaroslavl State Technical University, Yaroslavl, Russia

https://doi.org/10.1515/9783110636147-005

These phenomena are considered outside the framework of official economics, on the basis of a methodology different from break-even methodology, for example, on the basis of developmental approach methodology. Still, for the modern "main stream", principles that date back to the stage of laissez-faire capitalism with its inherent ideology of marginalism according to which the market feature of any economic element, including capital and human resources, is an outstanding feature, continue to be relevant.

The place and the role of technological transformation in the formation and development of the modern economic system are assessed in the works of such foreign scholars as D. Bell, D. Hamilton, H. Kumamoto, F. Machlup, S. Sato, G. Stigler, E. Toffler, L. White, T. Umesao. In Russian economic science, papers by S.K. Abachiev, A.I. Anchishkin, I.E. Artemyev, L.S. Blyakhman, A.O. Verenikin, D.I. Voloshin, B.C. Inozemtsev, S.M. Klimov, B.N. Kuzyk, D.S. Lvov, V.I. Mayevsky, O.Y. Mamedov, D.Y. Miropolsky, R.M. Nizhegorodtsev, O.S. Sukharev, V.M. Tslaf, Y.V. Yakovets, Y.V. Yaremenko and other economists deal with these issues. In most of these works, the understanding of technology is expanded to the general boundaries of socio-economic processes in which a man comes first.

A natural question arises: what is the relationship between technological changes, on the one hand, and "human" changes, on the other hand. We can find this out by identifying the patterns of technological transformation of the modern economic system.

Results

Regularities of Technological Development of the Modern Economic System

The laws governing the development of a modern economic system are determined primarily by its inherent technological changes, among which one of the main ones is the transformation of technology into a *basic resource of a modern economy.*

This does not mean that technology as an economic resource was absent at the previous stages of human development. However, it played a "supporting" role.

In the era of the appropriating economy, the issue of production was solved through the direct interaction of man and nature, and the technologies that used the muscular power of animals and man were primitive.

With the transition from the economy of the person appropriating to the economy, the interaction between man and nature became more and more mediated by artificial tools of labor – machines. The first industrial revolution finally determined the replacement of machine-less technologies by machine technologies embodied in the means of labor. It is the principles of machine self-development that determined the logic of the formation of an industrial society. The man, servicing the car, began to adapt to it, as a result of which the car acquired dominance over it. It was the logic of "machine self-development" that determined the patterns of the formation of industrial technologies.

The modern economic system has entered the post-industrial era, remaining largely technical and mechanical. It turned out that building up industrial potential has its limits. Firstly, the economic limits associated with a decrease in production efficiency; secondly, the ecological limits, manifested in the growing contradictions between man and nature; thirdly, the humanitarian limits, due to the increasing loss of human creativity; fourthly, the social limits consisting in the growth of disunity of society. The list could be continued by considering the limitations of a political, moral, cultural nature, which, one way or another, relate to any aspect of human life.

Among all the listed, there are separated technological limitations that determine the life of the next technological mode and are fundamental to the formation of a new economic order.

The position and role of man in this case changes fundamentally: the industrial era "appreciated" the working man, and the post-industrial "values" the human creator. In post-industrial technologies, human abilities, information and intelligence come to the fore, and material and technical factors become secondary.

Today, an intellectual firm may not have any business assets in their traditional sense at all, intellectual replaces tangible assets, and information assets replace current assets. According to experts, at the beginning of the 21st century in the United States about 45 million people used only their intellect, supported by a personal computer, as means of production (Moskovsky, 2009, p. 54). The calculations of American economists M. Boskin and L. Lau showed that in developed industrialized countries, on average, 40% of economic growth comes from the introduction of new information technologies, while the other 60% is provided by labor and capital (Boskin and Lau, 1996, p. 93). Further scientific studies showed that in the average parameters of the modern production function, the technological component takes 50%, capital (including natural resources) 35%, labor 15% (Klochkov, 2005, p. 12).

In general, the process of "replacing" technical parameters with technological ones can be characterized as a process of qualitative dynamics, as a result of which a fundamental change occurs in the resource base of a modern economic system. It is these changes that determine the fundamental differences between the post-industrial (new) economy and the traditional and market economies (Table 5.1).

From the foregoing, it follows that at any stage in the development of an economic system, technology played an important role. However, it was at the turn of the century *that it became an all-penetrating phenomenon, forming the basic essential*

Table 5.1: Characteristics of the main stages of the technological transformation of the economic system.

No.	Main characteristics	Technological methods of manufacture (stages of civilization development)		
		Pre-industrial	**Industrial**	**Post-industrial**
11.	Type of economic system	Traditional economy	Market economy	New economy
2.	Base resource	Labor (personal factor)	Capital (real factor)	Technology (integrated factor)
33.	The share of material factors in technology	Low	High	Low
44.	Share of personal factor in technology	High	Low	High
55.	The nature of the base resource	Physical work: agricultural, handicraft	Technique: machines, equipment	Information and communication and other new technologies
66.	Nature of technology	Labor intensive	Capital intensive	Scientific intensive
77.	Driving force	Natural resources	Open source of energy	Creative activity of the person himself

Source: Compiled by the authors on the basis of: Abachiev, 2004; Sato and Kumamoto, 2002.

quality of all types of human activity. The world basically becomes tech. And the role of the main driving force in it is performed by human activity.

The Evolution of the Human Factor in the Context of Technological Changes

Scientific and technological development, causing a change in the status of a person, is accompanied by the evolution of its main feature – the ability to work. Labor is a purposeful, conscious, productive activity and takes most of a person's life. It is subject to the most dynamic transformation, depending on the corresponding technological transformations. In this case, a modification of the dependence of production volume expressed on a production function on the quantity of resources invested in it occurs. This relationship has always had a clear structural organization and an asymmetrical appearance, illustrating the predominant influence of one of the factors: labor or capital.

The pre-industrial stage of the socio-economic development of society was characterized by the superiority of the personal factor over the material one. During the medieval period, man, using primitive equipment and manual labor, creating and trading handicrafts, dominated the means of production. At the same time, the skills and abilities of the worker were valued (Ivanova, 2017).

In the period of transition to the industrial era, the equipment still continued to play a supporting role, but the main asset was the employee's life fund. Accordingly, the economic theory of the industrial revolution era was precisely labor that considered the source of value, and the growth of its productivity as a source of economic growth.

Gradually, in the process of industrialization as a capital asset, machines became a full-fledged material embodiment, ensuring the priority of engineering and machine technology. That is, capital in the full sense of the word has become the technical means of production, on the basis of which socio-economic relations have been formed, known as "capitalism".

The further progress of technology and the development of large-scale machine production led to the fact that capital and labor were separated, which "gave rise to" the problems of their optimal combination. But in any case, the machine received priority over the person, and the real factor – over the personal one. This circumstance is fixed in Marx's famous thesis about the real subordination of labor to capital (Buevich and Karamova, 2018).

In a postindustrial society, a person again "rises" above the means of production. However, in this case, the efficiency of social production is provided not by manual labor, but by the creative potential of the worker and his personal abilities. In other words, the means of production in their interaction require the "intellectual" and not the "physical" human participation. At the same time, socio-economic development is considered as a process of expanding human capabilities, which ultimately determine the quality of life of the population (Rodina, 2017, p. 4–8).

Increasing the role of the human factor and reducing the role of traditional technical means does not mean the replacement of capital by labor. Labor and capital do not oppose each other, but complementing each other, they create a new technological resource. Modern technologies are not based on the allocation of any separate factor of production, but on their combination, not on the analysis of structural elements, but on their synthetic perception.

Intellectual work becomes the main form of work and requires new social foundations, economic forms and ideological orientations of social production, incompatible with the principles of "classical" capitalism (Izmailova, 2018). The increasing importance of the human factor leads to the humanization of all aspects of social production. At the same time, one of the main signs of humanization is the ability of a person to produce and use new information – a unique resource that has a high beneficial effect, resulting in disproportionately made costs. This ability, providing the opportunity to generate income, turns a person into the owner of a new information (intellectual) capital. It, acquiring an ever more applied character and practical significance, contained in new technologies, forms a new social and institutional environment.

Technological Aspects of Modification of Social-Institutional Environment

Each technical and economic paradigm should be considered from the standpoint of characterizing not only the content of the technological structure, but also the socio-institutional form of its implementation. This may be the financial and credit system, the ratio of public and private sectors, income distribution, forms of organization of interest groups, the education system, conditions for the development and protection of inventions, the distribution of labor, the balance of forces of different social groups (Beck, 1994), etc.

In turn, institutions, folding objectively in accordance with certain technological changes, act as factors determining the behavior of an individual human being. At the same time, they are an object of creative activity of people, subject to change due to their collective social actions. The social nature of technological change is expressed in the need to preserve and transfer some members of the community experience in implementing activities aimed at achieving sufficient satisfaction of various needs.

As is well known, human nature contains both rationality and sociality, which, on the one hand, are the result of its evolution, and, on the other hand, a way to adapt a person to the external environment. The rational motives of human behavior are determined by calculations of their own benefit. However, as a rule, people behave irrationally, being under the influence of emotions, fears, memories, stereotypes and prejudices. At the same time, it is impossible to separate some motives from others. It is impossible to "dismember" a person into separate elements, highlighting his economic, social, moral, and spiritual or any other component. He simultaneously contains all possible coexisting aspects, each of which carries its own purpose. If for the economic person the main thing is to get his own benefit, then it is important for the moral person to know what price was paid to receive it. For a person of spiritual benefit, benefit is conditional. For a social person, the most important is public recognition, for which one can sacrifice personal gain. As a result, there are many shades of human behavior, which, in the end, determine the order of making any decision, including those related to technological changes.

National motives of technological change are determined by the technological activity of individual economic entities. "Theoretically speaking, there are certain actors who act as agents of collective action. They organize a collective transition, during which they force the most numerous group of followers to expect this collective transition, and the expectation comes true by itself if the critical mass is really reached" (Witt, 2004, p. 15). This thesis is quite applicable to the characteristic of technological transformation. And this means not only the creation, but also the use of new technologies.

Modern society not only creates, but increasingly consumes ready-made technologies (healthy lifestyle, fashion, appropriate behavior). Many see the problem precisely in the fact that technologies invade art, politics, culture and religion, that is, those areas of human life where manufacturability is not an essential attribute. Currently, technological nature has acquired a significant part of the culture. Books, songs and films are not created, but are produced by analogy with commercial products based on the use of special technologies, and their sale is organized by analogy with the sale of laundry detergent. "The process of artistic creativity is divided into separate components – in order to get the product that is in demand" (Werther and Berman, and Vasconcelos, 1997, p. 98).

The well-known methodologist and philosopher P. Shchedrovitsky concluded that technologies of consumption processes are replacing technologies in the field of production activities, which, in turn, are replaced by technologies for the distribution of resources, including finance, the biosphere, human capital, etc. (Schedrovitsky, 2003). As a result, just as industrialization at one time "formed" a corresponding social and institutional environment: lifestyle, customs, traditions, morality, spirituality, social relations, norms and rules of behavior, the whole variety of parameters of human activity is being formed in relation to the requirements of modern technological changes. At the same time, if, for example, culture comes into conflict with the requirements of technological progress, then the needs of ensuring the viability of humanity will determine its restructuring (Antonyuk, 2003, p. 8).

In other words, each stage of technological development forms the corresponding moral and ethical aspect. The industrial mode of production is based on rigid technologies of machine production. This kind of technology involves unambiguous actions, not allowing the intervention of ideological goals, moral and social attitudes, and, moreover, emotional impulses. As a result, industrial technologies acquired the same, characteristic for any country using technology, design and appropriate (industrial-technological) processing of all public life (Smirnova, 2017).

The newest post-industrial technologies, on the contrary, "humanize" the production process, ensuring its specificity in each country, including Russia.

Russian Specification of the Process of Technological Transformation

The modern Russian economy is currently characterized by the interaction of two main sectors: the traditional and the innovation. The traditional sector is characterized by the influence of the industrial mode of production, and the innovation sector by the development of post-industrial technologies.

Unfortunately, the existing method of statistical evaluation does not allow distinguishing the participation of these sectors in the creation of GDP. In this regard, the calculation of the share of expenditures spent on research and development in the growth of the country's GDP (Table 5.2) Can be considered as the most indicative.

Table 5.2: The share of research and development costs in the growth of GDP of the Russian Federation (statistical yearbooks, 2001, 2006, 2011, 2016, 2017, 2018).

No.	Indicators	2000	2005	2010	2015	2016	2017
1.	GDP growth (billion rubles)	2482.4	4577.3	5832.5	2859.2	5344.3	5888.6
2.	Research and development costs (billion rubles)	76.7	230.8	523.4	914.7	943.8	1019.2
3.	Share of research and development expenses in GDP growth (%)	3.1	5.0	9.0	32.0	17.7	17.3

Source: compiled by the authors on the basis of Russian statistical yearbooks: 2001, 2006, 2011, 2016, 2017, 2018.

Corresponding calculations show that over the past 17 years, the share of expenditures on research and development in Russia's GDP growth has increased more than 5 times[1] (from 3.1% in 2000 to 17.3% in 2017). However, in general, the calculated data confirm the conclusion that a large part of the national product is currently being created in the traditional rather than in the innovative sector of the Russian economy. At the same time, the share of innovation factors that ensured the growth of GDP in developed countries at the beginning of the new century was 34.6% in the USA, 42.3% in Japan, 50% in Europe (Kirdina, 2003) and continues to grow (Pulyaeva, 2018).

One of the reasons for this is that past investments in previously emerging technologies, while demanding proper returns, may hinder the rapid spread of the latest technologies. At the same time, the availability of opportunities for real improvement of old technologies for a certain time will support their competitiveness and reduce the attractiveness of a relatively "raw", insufficiently "run-in" alternative (Dementiev, 2009, p. 35). Therefore, where the less inertial influence of previous technologies is less significant, new technologies may spread more dynamically. At the same time, the reinvestment of income derived from the use of new technologies can give the development of these technologies such an acceleration that will provide technological advantages to those countries that have dared to take this step.

1 At the same time, a sharp increase in this indicator to 32% in 2015 is obviously due not so much to the rising costs of research and development, but to the fall in GDP growth rates.

Thus, the policy of creating and replicating new technologies must comply with the objective laws of technological evolution, including its two main components (Ivanova, 2018):

Firstly, the policy of deindustrialization, i.e. liberation of economic space from objects of an obsolete industrial structure;

Secondly, the innovation policy for the creation and replication of new technologies.

The implementation in Russia of the first component is largely “facilitated” by the current depressed state of the economy, creating, according to S. Glazyev, the opportunity to reduce its burden “with . . . excess capacity in technological aggregates of an obsolete way” (Glazyev, 2008, p. 7). The implementation of the second is “hampered” by the influence of the factors of the socio-institutional environment of the industrial economy.

This refers, in particular, to the style of thinking of the national industrial elite. Its interests are associated with a high appreciation of the role of industrial tradition, mass production, commodity exchange, and the predominant value of tangible assets in comparison with intangibles. Therefore, the industrial worldview of the industrial elite does not allow initiating an innovative process of technological transformations (Rodina, 2018, p. 48–50). As international experience shows, business connects to innovations, at best, only after the state allocates money for the development of priority areas of technological development.

The state is the main bearer of the demand for high technology and the only institution capable of accelerating the development of the country’s scientific and technological sphere. It plays a special role in solving the problem of modernization and the effective integration of the Russian complex of research and developmental works into the current socio-economic reality. However, since any state apparatus consists of people, the human factor is also present in state administration. In the case of the conservatism of the state apparatus, its lack of interest in innovations and, moreover, direct opposition to them, the country is doomed to a technological lag (Smirnova, 2018).

The dominant bureaucratic environment in the current political space is unable to ensure the emergence of a modern post-industrial reality. As a result, the scientific and technological sphere in fact has not yet become a priority for the development of Russia, and the attention of the state is still aimed at solving the problems of quantitative growth. Modern socio-economic programs of the Government, reproducing the logic of industrialism, do not give answers to the challenges of post-industrial development.

Conclusions/Recommendations

The technological transformation of the modern economic system is an objective phenomenon. It is connected with the transition of the world economy to a new post-industrial phase of development. In the process of this transition, a change in the resource base of the economic system takes place, when the main source of development is technology, in which the "greater proportion" is occupied by human, personal, intellectual, not machine, material, physical factors. At the same time, the labor activity of a person acquires a creative character, and the role of the human person in the formation of the corresponding socio-institutional environment increases substantially.

It is clear that in practice, the transition of the economy to a new technological state proceeds with difficulties. However, many of them can be overcome by carrying out a consistent, based on the knowledge of objective laws, technological policy of the state.

References

Abachiev, T.K. *Evolutsionnaya teoriya poznaniya. Opyt sistematicheckogo postroeniya* [Evolutionary theory of knowledge. The experience of systematic development.] – M.: URSS, 2004 (in Russian).

Antonyk, G.A. *Obyektivnaya tsel' chelovechestva i ego standartizatsiya* // [The objective goal of mankind and its standardization] // East Slavic countries in the era of globalization: the choice of development paths. Proceedings of the International Research-to-Practice Conference held on November 26–27, 2003 - Grodno, 2003. – pp. 194–199 (in Russian).

Bek U. *Ot industrialnogo obshchestva k obshchestvu riska* [From the industrial society to the risk society] // THESIS. – 1994. – Vol. 5 – pp. 5–55 (in Russian).

Boskin, M.J. *Contributions of R & Development to Economic Growth* / M.J. Boskin, L.J. Lau // Technology, R & D, and the Economy. – Washington, D.C .: The Brookings Institution and American Enterprise Institute, 1996 – pp. 90–98.

Buevich, A.P. and Karamova O.V. *Ot "Kapitala" K. Marksa k intellektualnomu kapitalu v kontekste innovatsionnoy economiki budushchego*. [From "Capital" by K. Marx to knowledge-based capital in the context of the innovative economy of the future] // Bulletin of Tver State University (Tver State University); Series: Economics and Management. – 2018. – No. 1. – pp. 258–265 (in Russian).

Verter, U, Berman E. and Vaskonselyoz E. *Budushchee tekhnologicheskogo menedzhmenta* // [The future of technology management] // Technology-based firm: management and marketing. – M.: ANH, 1997 (in Russian).

Vitt, U. *Ekonomicheskaya teoriya i ekonomicheskaya istoriya – evolutsionnyiy peresmotr* [Economic theory and economic history – evolutionary revision] // Economic Bulletin of Rostov State University. Vol. 2. – 2004. – No. 3. – pp. 10–16 (in Russian).

Glazyev, K. *Krisis, antikrizisnyie mery i strategiya innovatsionnogo narodnokhozyaystvennogo razvitiya v zerkale teorii dolgosrochnoy megatekhnologicheskoy dinamiki* [Crisis, crisis intervention and strategy of innovative economic development in the mirror of the theory of long-term megatechnological dynamics]. // Rossiyskiy Ekonomicheskiy Zhurnal. – 2008. – No. 12. – pp. 5–9 (in Russian).

Dementyev, V.E. *Dogonyayushchee razvitie cherez prizmu teorii "dlinnovolnovoy" tehnologicheskoy dinamiki: aspekt "okon vozmozhnostey" v krizisnykh usloviyakh* [Catching-up development through the prism of the theory of "long-wave" technological dynamics: the aspect of "windows of opportunities" under crisis conditions] // Rossiyskiy Ekonomicheskiy Zhurnal. – 2009. – No. 1–2. – p. 35 (in Russian).

Federal State Statistics Service. *Rossiyskiy statisticheskiy ezhegodnik* [Russian Statistical Yearbook] – M.: FSSS, 2018 (in Russian).

Ivanova, E.V. *Tekhnologizatsiya natsionalnoy ekonomiki i eyo regionalnyi aspekt* [Technologization of the national economy and its regional aspect] // Rossiya: Tendentsii i Perspektivy Razvitiya. Yearbook of RAS, INION. – 2017. – Issue 12, Part 3. – pp. 327–333 (in Russian).

Ivanova, E.V. *Tekhnologicheskoye razvitiye rossiyskoy ekonomiki: problemy i perspektivy* [Technological development of the Russian economy: problems and prospects] // Teoreticheskaya Ekonomika. Academic Electronic Economic Periodical – 2018 – No. 4 (46). – pp. 68–76.

Izmailov, M. *O vozrastanii roli chelovecheskogo kapitala v ekonomike znaniy* [On the increasing role of human capital in the knowledge economy] // Problemy Teorii i Praktiki Upravleniya. – 2018. – No. 6. – pp. 95–105 (in Russian).

Kirdina, C.G. *Rossiyskoye litso evolutsionnoy ekonomiki.* [The Russian Face of Evolutionary Economics] // Economic Bulletin of Rostov State University. Vol. 1. – 2003. – No. 4 (in Russian).

Klochkov, V.V. *Ekonomicheskiy potentsial mirovogo khoziaystva: prirodnye i trudovye resursy i ikh optimalnoe ispolzovanie* [Economic potential of the world economy: natural and labor resources and their optimum utilization] // Mirovaya Ekonomika / Under the editorship of Nikolaeva, I.P. – M .: YUNITI, 2005. – pp. 10–16 (in Russian).

Moskovskiy, A. *Institutsionalizm: teoriya, osnova priniatiya resheniy, metod kritiki* [Institutionalism: theory, decision-making basis, critique method] // Voprosy Ekonomiki. – 2009. – No. 3. – p. 54 (in Russian).

Programma, "Tsifrovaya ekonomika Rossiyskoy Federatsii" [Program "Digital Economy of the Russian Federation"]. Approved By Decree of the Government of the Russian Federation of July 28, 2017 No. 1632-r., available at: http://www.government.ru/rugovclassifier/614/ (in Russian).

Pulayeva, V.N. *Uroven' razvitiya chelovecheskogo kapitala strany kak indikator effektivnosti ekonomicheskogo kursa Rossii* [The level of development of the country's human capital as an indicator of efficiency of the economic policy of Russia] // Ekonomika. Biznes. Banki (appendix). – 2018. – Vol. 4. – pp. 96–103.

Rodina, G.A. *Vverkh po lestnitse, vedushchey vniz, ili vniz po lestnitse, vedushchey vverkh?* [Up the stairs going down or down the stairs going up?] / International Research-to-Practice Conference "Russian Mittelspiel: Economics, Technogenesis, Geostrategy": Collection of abstracts / Under the editorship of Osipov, Y.M., Nip, S.S., Sukhina, T.S. – M.: Faculty of Economics, Lomonosov Moscow State University, 2018. – pp. 48–50.

Rodina, G.A. *Trudovoy faktor proizvodstva: prolegomeny k analizu kachestvennykh izmeneniy v XXI veke.* [Labor factor of production: prolegomena to the analysis of qualitative changes in the XXI century] // Nauchnyie Issledovaniya i Razrabotki. Ekonomika. – 2017. – No. 4. – pp. 4–8 (in Russian).

Sato, S., Kumamoto, H. *Reinzheniring okruzhayushchey sredy* [Environmental Reengineering]. – St. Petersburg: Biznes-Pressa, 2002 (in Russian).

Shedrovitskiy, G.P. *Metodologiya i filosofiya organizatsionno-upravlencheskoy deyatel'nosti: osnovnye poniatiya i printsipy (kurs lektsiy)* [Methodology and philosophy of organizational and managerial activity: basic concepts and principles (series of lectures)]. Vol. 5 ORU (5). – M.: Put', 2003 (in Russian).

Smirnova, I.A. *Global'naya ekonomika XXI veka: tendentsii i protivorechiya* [Global economy of the XXth century: trends and contradictions] // Problems of configuration of the global economy of the XXI century: the idea of social and economic progress and possible ways of interpretation. Collection of scientific articles. Vol. 1 / Under the editorship of Doctor of Science, Economics, Professor Alpidovskaya, M.L., Doctor of Science, Economics, Professor Tolkachev, S.A. – Krasnodar, 2018. – pp. 235–242 (in Russian).

Smirnova, I.A. *Obostrenie sotsial'no-ekonomicheskikh posledstviy globalizatsii: sistemnyy podkhod* [Exacerbation of the socio-economic consequences of globalization: a systematic approach] // Global economy in the XXI century: dialectics of confrontation and solidarity. Collection of scientific works / Under the editorship of Doctor of Science, Economics, Professor Sorokin, D.E., Doctor of Science, Economics, Associate Professor Alpidovskaya, M.L. – Krasnodar, 2017. – pp. 73–76 (in Russian).

Valentina Bondarenko, Ivan Aleshkovski, Ilya Ilyin

6 The Human Role in Achieving a Balance Between Technological and Socio-Economic Transformations

Introduction

Most countries are currently committing their future to the use of Industry 4.0 technologies seizing the benefits of the digital economy for development (Schwab, 2017). In doing so, they have to cope with ever-increasing crisis situations. The lack of balance between technological and socio-economic transformations is an objective basis and source for absolutely all crises and negative phenomena, economic and sanctions confrontations, natural anomalies and catastrophes, terrorism, irregular migration as well as for diplomatic, trade, information, cyber and real wars with casualties and material losses. And again, they are considered mainly as a technical and technological problem for processing data sets, growing incredibly fast (Big Data) and within the same paradigm of the human community development with all the negative consequences that were mentioned by us in a number of articles (Bondarenko et al, 2008; Bondarenko et al, 2017; Aleshkovski, Bondarenko, Ilyin, 2018). It should be emphasized that such a balance has never been reached: whether we refer to the times of the first three scientific and technological revolutions or to the current time of the rapidly developing fourth revolution.

All the above testifies to the fact that similar to the lack of fundamental understanding of the consequences for introducing the achievements of scientific and technological progress (STP) of the first three revolutions, still there has been no such understanding of the consequences for introducing high, digital or any other technologies of Industry 4.0.

The USSR experience also shows that there was no theoretical justification for the need and understanding of the consequences for introducing scientific and technological progress and automated control systems (ACSi) in various industries in the 1980s. Despite some attempts, under the influence of these achievements, there was no realizing of the need for the simultaneous transformation of socio-economic relations commensurate with these technologies.

The study of the USSR experience demonstrates that at the end of the 1960s, the idea of forming a digital economy was flashed for the first time in the works of Professor Anatoly Kitov, a Soviet scientist. He then posed the question to the top

Valentina Bondarenko, Institute of Economics, Russian Academy of Sciences, Moscow, Russia
Ivan Aleshkovski, Ilya Ilyin, Lomonosov Moscow State University, Moscow, Russia

https://doi.org/10.1515/9783110636147-006

USSR leadership and scientific community about the need to manage economy at national level on the base of the widespread use of computers. Referring to the possibilities of such management, Anatoly Kitov, in particular, wrote, "*[i]n industry, digital machines are used to automatically control individual units, machines, and production lines, and even entire automated factories. The use of electronic digital machines ensures the reduction in the number of service personnel, saving materials and energy, increasing production speeds (increasing the pace of work), improving product quality and reliable control over the course of production . . .* " (Kitov, 1956). In Kitov's articles, the entire Soviet economy was interpreted as "a complex cybernetic system that includes a huge number of interconnected controlled cycles". To optimize it, Kitov justified the need to create a national automation system for managing the national economy based on the Unified State Network of Computing Centers. The similar ideas were vigorously discussed not only in the Soviet Union, but also abroad. In particular, in the USA, a well-known journal Operations Research (Vol. 11, No. 6) published an extensive positive review of such proposals. From 1962, Kitov's idea was further developed by Academician Viktor Glushkov, Director of the Institute of Cybernetics at the Academy of Sciences of the Ukrainian SSR. He reconsidered Anatoly Kitov's project, intensifying the research on the creation of automated control systems, and the so-called "OGAS" system (National automated information accounting and processing system). The system was intended for automated control of the entire economy. Academician Viktor Glushkov was the pioneer of this research (Glushkov, 1975, 1987). But the idea of OGAS was not implemented. A deeper insight into this research showed the rationale behind the negative outcome. What is the reason things did not work out? What was this result about?

The study revealed that the more STP and ACSi achievements had been introduced into the national economic complex, the greater and stronger the imbalances in the economy would have been. That is, the acceleration of technological processes in production, in the wholesale trade and, at the same time, keeping the focus on producing consumer goods for an abstract consumer slowed down all processes in retail trade. So it happened. As we wrote at that time, this would lead to a crisis in the economy in the rigidly centralized model of the state management and planning system that prevailed in the USSR. It became much worse for a particular person (Bondarenko, 1983). That is, the system was non-cybernetic, without any feedback from a specific person and without a clear and unambiguous understanding of the development goal in relation to that person. Therefore, the USSR, even with the OGAS implementation, was not protected against the emergence of imbalances and problems in the socio-economic growth of social production. It was like this despite the fact that the very system of economic and mathematical models became a theoretical basis for OGAS functional structure and it was understood as an important part in the performance of OGAS functions. The main methods of modeling such as brainstorming, extrapolation method, variants of multi-factor regressive and correlation models, and others were taken. All the above methods, in the absence of an unequivocally accepted goal, contributed to the fact that the development of the USSR was planned to be carried out and was carried out by a "trial and error" method.

Since 2000, the era of building the information society has begun in Russia. Nowadays, the digital economy (DE) is being shaped and expanded. And again, they are considered mainly as a technical and technological problem for processing data sets, growing incredibly fast (Big Data) and within the same paradigm of the human community development with all the negative consequences that were mentioned by us in a number of articles (Aleshkovski, Bondarenko, Ilyin, 2018). No one has considered the problem in a comprehensive, holistic, systemic and interdisciplinary insight, taking into consideration the search of a unified development goal. A large number of very different goals are being set but none of them is being achieved. Therefore, the methodological approach of "trial and error" to the development of the human system has completely exhausted its creative function.

It should be said here that even in the late 1960s, the Club of Rome, an international non-governmental organization, which was created at the initiative of the Italian economist Aurelio Peccei, put forward a program for studying global problems and set a goal – to give society a method that would allow for a reliable analysis of all the "difficulties of mankind". Since 1968, more than forty reports have been issued on behalf of the Club of Rome. The Club of Rome's report "Come on!" was released at the end of 2017. The concepts outlined by E. Weizsäcker and A. Wijkman on 220 pages of the book require de facto the change of the entire mode of production and consumption of modern humanity, but do not answer the question of what the purpose of changing the mode of production is and how to do it (Weizsäcker and Wijkman, 2018).

The World Economic Forum in Davos, along with the Club of Rome, is considered to be a leading think tank. In January 2018 the 13th Global risks report that identified the most likely risks for the global economy, was presented at this forum. The risks included: 1) extreme weather events; 2) natural disasters; 3) cyber attacks; 4) data fraud or their theft; 5) inability to cope with the adverse effects of climate change; 6) large-scale forced migration; 7) man-made natural disasters; 8) terrorist attacks; 9) illegal trade; and 10) bubbles in the asset markets of key economies (The Global Risks Report, 2018).

In January 2019, The World Economic Forum presented a new report on global risks. The common thing in these reports is that the statistical and empirical information of the past is analyzed with the help of various mathematical models; the fact of increasing risks is stated; and research surveys are applied in order to understand what to do in the future. Thus, the report presents the results of the latest Global Risk Perception Survey, in which almost one thousand decision-makers from the public and private sectors, academic and civil societies empirically assess the risks facing the world. Nine out of ten respondents expect sharpening economic and political confrontations between the major powers in 2019. But, nevertheless, despite such a detailed analysis, the global society of people, from their point of view, still seems to be a probabilistic, not strictly predictable and controlled society, and is characterized by a high level of uncertainty in the future with a rapid increase of other risks (The Global Risks Report, 2019).

The situation in Russia also demonstrates the need to find and implement another development model that is not at odds with the use of Industry 4.0 technologies. These are not only the problems of developing the digital economy and the construction of "smart cities", but also the opportunity to provide a comprehensive link between solving all problems with each other and with the tasks outlined in the May 2018 president's decree, and especially to ensure that each individual strategy is linked with other strategic documents. After all, today, in accordance with the Federal Law of June 28, 2014 No. 172-FZ "On Strategic Planning in the Russian Federation", at least 23,200 strategies of different levels are being developed and scheduled for implementation at the same time in Russia. Each of these strategies has its own goal, its own indicators and its own criteria for evaluating their achievement. This is completely contrary to the systemic, holistic, and integrated view of development.

A similar situation is observed in all other countries of the world. We are witnessing more and more strategies. But a single unified strategy with a single unified development goal has not yet been defined. Therefore, there is reason to assert that no strategy will be implemented either in Russia or in the world. Therefore, it should be emphasized that fundamental science already has a methodology for solving all the problems of the development of Russia and the world through finding common goals for all strategies and projects.

New Methodological Toolkit

The proposed new methodological toolkit for solving problems in ensuring the development of Russia and the world without crises on the basis of achieving a balance between technological and socio-economic transformations is a result of the authors' multiannual empirical, political, economic and ideological research, in which four tasks were solved:

- The *first task* that needed to be solved was to define a common goal for the development of Russia and the world. The task was solved after realizing, whether we like it or not, that the vector of the human community development is aimed at the implementation of one single goal that is set objectively. Moreover, within the framework of human existence on Earth, this is a goal that cannot become a sub-goal of a higher order goal. Irrespective of our wish, it objectively turns out that a single unified goal setting is to satisfy the highest need of each particular person to become perfect in the physical, intellectual, spiritual sense, to become a person with a high level of consciousness.

- The solution of *the second task* showed that all the problems of development should be viewed from the position of integrity, comprehensiveness, and system, with all the sciences and spiritual knowledge being integrated into a unified interdisciplinary, or rather, transdisciplinary knowledge. And through this whole complex of knowledge in unity, there should be determined the path to achieving an objectively set goal. The practical use of this approach has shown that only in this case chaos, complexity and uncertainty in understanding development problems are not simply eliminated, but search for answers to all time requests is minimized in time and space. Indeed, until now, interdisciplinary research has been understood as solving problems of a particular science with the methods of another science. Or a set of simultaneous solving of separate systemically unrelated, for example, socio-economic, financial, demographic, environmental-climatic and other tasks and processes has been solved by methods of various sciences in the development of certain aspects of development.
- According to the conditions of *the third task*, it was necessary to find such an indicator, with the help of which it would become possible to measure and to compare all the processes and phenomena, again in relation to the development goal that is objectively set. The task was also solved. It turned out that this can be done only with the help of the only indicator – "time"!
- The fourth task was solved based on this single indicator – "time". The task was aimed at finding the criterion for the effectiveness of the human system development, again with the understanding that development should bring the entire community at all levels in time and space close to satisfying the highest human need. The answer to this condition was to obtain a single unified criterion of efficiency for the system as a whole and any subsystem and for each individual person – this is the "time between" the achievement of an objectively set goal and the reality in which we exist.

This makes it possible to understand that if the "time between" decreases and approaches zero without returning back (meaning without crises), this indicates that Russia and the world are objectively getting closer to achieving the goal and every single state, company and every person are beginning to be fully aware of this goal. And if it grows, and grows for everyone in different ways, then this means that the whole community, all its parts and all people are in different temporary spaces "between" and it is not possible to come to an agreement with each other. This is inevitably followed by the growth of conflicts until the emergence of real wars. Now the world is at the top of such a relationship. It is not possible to ensure universal security under these conditions.

The solution of all four tasks as a whole made it possible to understand that for the first time in science a new methodological toolkit was obtained for solving all aspects of the human system development and for the first time in history to create conditions for achieving a balance between technological and socio-economic transformations (Aleshkovski, Bondarenko, Ilyin, 2018; Bondarenko, 2018b).

The conditions for Achieving a Balance Between Technological and Socio-Economic Transformations

With the help of the new methodological tools, it became possible to do the following:

- To identify the patterns of development of the human community and to understand on this basis the nature of the systemic crisis as well as to realize that there have existed only two development paradigms on our planet in the entire history of human development. One of these paradigms is characterized by crises, while in another paradigm all conditions can be created to determine the path of development without crises;
- To form a new paradigm for forecasting the future from the future, that is, from the future when an objectively set goal is achieved and the "time between" approaches zero (Bondarenko, 2014). And this means that returning from the future, from this zero time to the present, it becomes possible to select only the projects and make only the decisions that ensure the achievement of this future, in which a person becomes perfect physically, intellectually, spiritually, and reaches a high level of consciousness and Higher Mind;
- Having predicted the future from the future, it is becoming possible to eliminate all the risks and threats to the economic security of Russia and the rest of the world not only in the near future, but for the whole prospect until reaching the goal and closing all projects in integrity with minimum resources and time, as well as to attain the objectively set goal – to become perfect for every person. And this will only be possible when elaborating a single unified development strategy for Russia, as well as for the whole world.
- The mechanism for the implementation of a single unified strategy for the development of Russia and the world will be obtained if, under the conditions of the rapid introduction of digital technologies of Industry 4.0, the economy develops by way of coordinating the interests of the state, business, and society with the interests of a particular person (Bondarenko, 2018a). It also can be obtained provided that this mechanism of coordination of interests with their maximum diversity will be implemented: in real time; at each local level in the regime of self-government; for example, with the help of additive technologies of personalized production upon its request, excluding the production of an unnecessary product.

Thus, we get the basic conditions for solving all problems. We are not elaborating a development strategy for 2025 or 2030, but for the entire long-term perspective, until the goal is reached. And only in this way a balance of technological and socio-economic transformations can be achieved, and safe development can be ensured with a precise understanding of goal setting for the whole system and each individual person living in the whole space not only of Russia, but of the rest of the world.

Nowadays, through the prism of a new methodological toolkit, it became clear that in the conditions of the technological revolution of Industry 4.0 and the absence of a single unified strategy in all countries, three models of the development of the human system are possible. They will build the relations between the state (government), society, business, and a specific person differently depending on the choice of development goal (Bondarenko, 2018).

In the first possible model, society and different groups of individuals consciously or unconsciously declare each their own development goals. As a rule, these goals are multidirectional. That is, based on a systematic, holistic and comprehensive understanding of development, none of these goals will be fully achieved, because development will go by the method of "trial and error". In such a development model, the future is uncertain, its achievement will be very long in time, and the use of Industry 4.0 technologies working at an incredible speed will increase the number of human and resource losses at the same rate, which is likely to lead to an apocalypse. That is, the moment of reaching the singularity as a point of no return in achieving different development goals and transition to a new socio-economic model may not come (Aleshkovski, Bondarenko, Ilin, 2018a).

The second possible model is characterized by development under the conditions of the paradigm existing today, but it is understood in the interests of a narrow group of people and the goal they have adopted and the values they profess. In this model, artificial intelligence and digital, biological and other technologies are the basis for the emergence of a steady trend of manipulating and controlling the human mind and controlling the entire world in order to extract maximum profit. The technological singularity is synchronized with the formation of such a model, in which the risks for all increase catastrophically, and the apocalypse becomes the inevitable final. Consequently, the transition to a new paradigm of socio-economic development becomes impossible, since it intensifies such processes as crisis and negative phenomena, economic and sanctions confrontations, natural anomalies and catastrophes, terrorism, irregular migration and diplomatic, trade, information, cyber and real wars with human and material losses. It is becoming even more possible the emergence of such phenomena as the ideology of the so called "Islamic state". That is why the values it shapes are so attractive to many, especially to young people. That is why present conditions have arisen when the digital revolution and other high technologies of the 21st century, in addition to their positive sides, carry enormous threats, even threats to the existence of humanity.

And only *the third model* has a dominance focusing on conscious development with a single unified goal-setting, in the interests of specific people, and here we talk not only about people living in Russia, but also in other countries and throughout the global world, as well as harmonizing their quite diverse interests in real time. It is only in these conditions that a foundation will be prepared for solving all problems. Orientation in this model to the interests of a particular person due to use of digital technologies in production at their request, allows us not to produce too much, but to keep resources in pristine condition, to solve all environmental problems and free the time for the perfection of each individual person. All this will be the only possible condition that can motivate every person, especially a young person, to put all their new knowledge into ensuring accelerated and sustainable development in relation to the goal. It is only in this way that conditions will be created so that the technological (digital) singularity is synchronized with the singularity of the formation of new relations between people and their awareness of the need to bring evolutionarily, without returning back, the moment of achieving the goal both in each individual country and at the level of global development.

The world is now closer to the second model, the ultimate goal of which is the control over the whole world and each person. The authors have already mentioned the consequence. Risks will increase, and the states themselves may disappear.

Therefore, it becomes critically important that the top leaders of all states for their own preservation and preservation of their citizens, for ensuring universal security and transition to sustainable development in relation to the goal should attend to the task of forming a third development model and a strategy for achieving it in the future understood and accepted by all.

Conclusion

Under the conditions of the technological revolution of Industry 4.0 and the rapid introduction into life of the various digital devices generated by it, artificial intelligence, the Internet of things, bio-, neuro- and other technologies of the 21stcentury, different countries may have different relations between the state, society, business and a specific person, depending on the choice of development model and its purpose. Research through the prism of a new methodological toolkit shows three possible models for the development of human system. And only one of them will achieve a balance between technological and socio-economic transformations, since development will not proceed by “trial and error”, but consciously, with an understanding of the future from the future and its final goal.

Focus on the interests of a particular person through the implementation of digital technologies to production at their request will help not lead to the excess of production over consumption. It will also allow preserving many resources in their original state and freeing the time for human improvement. All this will be the only possible condition that can motivate every specific person in any country of the world, especially the young one, to ensure accelerated and sustainable development in relation to the goal. As a result, in this model, the digital singularity is synchronized with the singularity of the formation of new relations between people and their awareness of the need to approach evolutionarily, without returning back, the moment of achieving the goal of global development in a clear and understandable future.

Acknowledgments: The following study was funded by RFBR, according to the research project No. 19-010-00809.

References

Aleshkovski I.A., Bondarenko V.M., Ilin Ilya (2018), *Rossiya v usloviyakh tsifrovoy transformatsii: vozmozhnyye modeli sotsial'no-ekonomicheskogo razvitiya* [Russia in the era of digital transformation: possible models for social and economic development] // Information Society, Vol. 6, pp. 145–152 (in Russian).

Bondarenko V. M. (1983), *OGAS v sisteme khozyaystvennogo mekhanizma vzaimosvyazey proizvodstva i potrebleniya* [OGAS in the System of Economic Mechanism of Interlinkages Between Production and Consumption] // All-Union Conference on OGAS, RASU and ACSs, dedicated to the 60th anniversary of academician V.M. Glushkov. Kiev: IK. 97 p (in Russian).

Bondarenko, V. (2008), *Prognozirovaniye budushchego skvoz' prizmu novoy metodologii poznaniya ili prognozirovat' budushcheye mozhno tol'ko iz budushchego* [Forecasting the future through the prism of the new cognition methodology, or future can be only forecasted from future] // Forecasting the future: A new paradigm / Ed. G.G. Fetisov and V.M. Bondarenko. Moscow: Ekonomika. pp. 220–270 (in Russian)

Bondarenko, Valentina M. (2014), Transition to Crisis-Free Development: a Myth or Reality? // World Futures, Volume 70, No. 2. pp. 93–119.

Bondarenko, Valentina M., Ilyin, Ilya V., Korotayev, Andrey V. (2017) Transition to a new global paradigm of development and the role of the United Nations in this process // World Futures, Volume 73, No. 8. pp. 511–538.

Bondarenko V.M. (2018a) *Usloviya realizatsii tseley ustoychivogo razvitiya* [Conditions for the Implementation of the Sustainable Development Goals] // UPF Today, No. 1. pp.12–13 (in Russian).

Bondarenko, V.M. (2018b) *Strukturnaya modernizatsiya v usloviyakh formirovaniya tsifrovoy ekonomiki* [Structural Modernization in the Conditions of the Formation of the Digital Economy] // "MIR" (Modernization. Innovations. Development), Vol. 9, No. 2. pp. 172–191. DOI: 10.18184 / 2079- 4665.2018.9.2 (in Russian).

Glushkov, V.M. (1975), *Makroekonomicheskiye modeli i printsipy postroyeniya OGAS* [Macroeconomic Models and Principles of OGAS Construction]. Moscow: Statistics. 160 p (in Russian).

Glushkov, V.M. (1987), *Osnovy bezbumazhnoy informatiki.* [Fundamentals of Paperless Computer Science. 2nd edition, revised]. M.: Science, 1987. 552 p (in Russian).

Kitov, A.I. (1956), *Elektronnyye tsifrovyye mashiny* [Electronic Digital Machines]. M.: Soviet radio. 358 p (in Russian).

The Global Risks Report 2018, 13th Edition, published by the World Economic Forum. Published January 15, 2018. Electronic resource: http://www3.weforum.org/docs/WEF_GRR18_Report.pdf [Accessed 01.04.2019].

The Global Risks Report 2019, 14th Edition, published by the World Economic Forum. Published January 15, 2019. Electronic resource: https://www.weforum.org/reports/the-global-risks-report-2019 [Accessed 01.04.2019].

Weizsäcker, E.V., Wijkman, A. (2017), "Come On! Capitalism, Short-termism, Population and the Destruction of the Planet". A Report to the Club of Rome. Electronic resource: https://batrachos.com/sites/default/files/pictures/Books/Weizsacker_Wijkman_2018_Come%20on.pdf. [Accessed 01.04.2019].

Schwab, K. (2017), "The Fourth Industrial Revolution". Translated from English. M.: Eksmo.

Nina L. Rumyantseva, Viktor P. Rumyantsev

7 Creativity of Human Future in Two Paradigms: Creation of Objects or Creation of Oneself?

Introduction

It has already become a tradition to raise the question of Russia's future from an economic or socio-economic perspective. The advantage of setting the problem of the future at this conference "Man and Scientific and Technical Progress in the Socio-Economic Paradigm of the Future" can be considered the inclusion of human problems in socio-economic issues: "The problem of human self-realization as a creator, a generator of ideas and their realistic implementer in the economy of the future has confronted the society of the present". However, this formulation of the problem of the future raises a number of questions.

The first group of issues: What does "society of the present" and "economy of the future" mean? The statement of problems at this conference does not share cultural-historical types, but speaks about the future of a single world civilization, in which Russia is included. Can we talk about a unified society of the future, about a single human civilization? We, the Russian people and the whole society – are we the same as the West? Are we just backward in a single process of scientific and technological progress? Yes – the majority of economists and political economists, who associate civilization with scientific and technical progress, answer. However, such an answer is controversial.

The other group of issues refers to the image of man, to the "problem of human self-realization as a creator and generator of ideas and a realistic implementer of them in the economy". What is the highest goal of human development – is it self-realization? One's creativity process? If so, what is the object of the process? What ideas and things? This study is dedicated to finding answers to these questions.

Methodology

The research method is systematic-dialectic. Systematic means the consideration of society as a system and a person as an element of the system, which it forms. Dialectic means that we will look for the answer to the questions posed not in

Nina L. Rumyantseva, Russian State Academy of Intelectual Property, Moscow, Russia
Viktor P. Rumyantsev, Institute of Intellectual Cybernetic Systems, Moscow, Russia

https://doi.org/10.1515/9783110636147-007

phenomena, but in the initial foundations that form human communities, civilizations, Russian civilization, first. The dialectic method of such research involves the identification of cause-effect relationships and, through them, the essence of the studied phenomena.

Results

Let us start with our geography. The geographical and geopolitical factors that determine the foundations of the social structure of Russia include: a vast territory (approximately 1/7 of the earth's territory of the entire planet); heterogeneity of the territory and living conditions on it; Russia's median geographic location between East and West; the length of the borders and the need to reflect constant raids; vast natural wealth in the earth and on its surface; harsh climate with cold, flooding, drought; mostly poor and infertile soils; the insignificance of maritime boundaries, hence the underdevelopment of international relations and trade.

It can be noted that these factors distinguish Russia from the West. Each of these factors played a role in the history of Russia, in the formation of Russian statehood and relations with other ethnic groups and religions, in the formation of the Russian mentality, the Russian cultural and spiritual code. So, a huge and heterogeneous territory makes it necessary to have a strong centralized management, such a power that A. Fursov called auto-subjective, which can, if necessary, make any decision that is not even provided by law. Otherwise, it is impossible to maintain the unity of such a territory – an area with a more favorable natural environment will strive for autonomy, will object to an increased contribution to the common pot, to which in any other region in any situation could not be filled, but only pilfered. Further, in our vast territory, resources are in most cases removed from the centers of their use, and therefore the production of goods is more expensive than in a small country, etc. The survival of the people, and not just survival, but the preservation and development of Russian civilization and the people in such conditions was possible only in the culture that it formed, in its values, which shaped the way of life of the people. This culture can be called collectivist (communal, conciliar and communist) it forms a collectivist society, in contrast to the individualistic culture of the West, which forms an individualistic society. What is the difference between them?

Russian civilization is based on Russian culture with such priorities: *spiritual over material* (which becomes possible when there is wealth in the family, because wealth, not the luxury, is the goal of economic activity in the Russian family tradition), while spiritual is determined by I. Ilyin as “a sincere desire for perfection” (Ilyin, 1957); *common (or collective) over personal (or individual)* – the basis for building an integrated system at all levels from family to nation, all humanity, when there is a threat to the existence of this level of the system; *morality (conscience, justice) over the law*, which becomes the basis of the behavior of Russian people, who act according to conscience, not being interested in the law "we can do without written laws when they are written in our hearts" – (Lobachevsky, 1990); *obligations over rights*, which creates a system of stability at any level – from family to state, the future (i.e., the lives of children, grandchildren, clan) over the present (own life) – the basis for the preservation of the Russian family and the reproduction of the clan and people, the truth. These values are not random in Russian culture, they are the product of a centuries-old history, in which the foundations of the existence of the Russian people were formed and its geographical and related political conditions were determined, as mentioned above. This collectivist culture ensured the life of the people in these conditions, became the spiritual means of the people's survival.

Other geopolitical conditions formed the Western model of society; limited territory and natural resources, but the prevalence of maritime borders, a mild climate and the absence of a communal environment (Kirdina, 2014) contributed to the development of trade and private initiative, created opposing value priorities, which became the basis of the ideology of Western civilization: here the material is higher than spiritual (priority of the economy based on private property); the individual is higher than the general (the priority of the rights and freedoms of the individual); the law is higher than morality (everything that is not prohibited by law is allowed, but "You're not a thief till you're caught", that is, you can even steal, you can kill, but you cannot leave evidence and witnesses, and we see this in the US, for example, three presidents were killed); the future (the life of children, grandchildren) is not as important as the present (own life, its duration); and the truth is replaced by the fulfillment of social roles, which was also noted by the European Shakespeare: "the whole world is a theater, and the people in it are actors".

The main value that forms the Russian society can be considered the value of collectivism or conciliarity as a priority of the whole, its interests, before the part, private interests. This value is the opposite of the main value of Western civilization – the value of individualism as a priority of private interests (individual, company, corporation, etc.) over the interests of the whole. But the value of collectivism is universal, only it can save the life of the "whole", humanity on the planet, and not those "universal human values" in which the priority of individualism, the rights and freedoms of the individual. Why is it "universal"? Because a system with a property of integrity, its steady state is built on the relation of the priority of the whole to the part in the systems approach, and this is the difference of the system approach to the formation of society from the reduction approach (on the principle "if everyone is good, then everyone is good") a society with the value of individualism, i.e. with the priority of private interests. But the reduction approach, which emerged (as a principle of superposition in mechanics) during the period of the formation of a mechanistic picture of the world, works in mechanical systems and does not work in organic systems – the emergence property does not appear. Building a social system on it leads to its unstable state and, as a result, destruction. And we see that there is an extinction of the peoples of Western Europe: "for all European countries (except Muslim Albania), the birth rate is lower than the reproduction level . . . If the current birth rate is maintained, by 2100 the population of Europe will be less than 1/3 of the current one" (Buchanan 2007).

The value of the collectivism of Russian culture corresponds to the systemic principle of the organization of society, in which the whole forms parts, and not vice versa – this has been proven for thousands of years of the existence of Russian civilization, which no external forces could conquer and subjugate to themselves, it only grew and revived to the enemies, building up its statehood. Thus, one can see the role of the model that Russia can play in shaping the world-system.

So far this has not been realized in Europe, although there are exceptions. For example, the German V. Schubart writes about Russia: "Russia possesses the forces that Europe has lost or destroyed in itself . . . Therefore, only Russia is able to inhale the soul into the human race dying from lust for power, subject to business excellence . . . Russia is the only country that can save Europe . . ." (Shubart, 2000/1938).

In two types of society, in two types of ideologies there are two human images: in any society a little man is born a small animal, but with the makings of a man, and what makings develop, he becomes such. In an individualistic society, man is an individualist, whose nature differs little from the instinctive nature of the animal, which develops intelligence (understood as the ability to overcome difficulties, to adapt to new conditions of life, which is inherent in animals). This intellectual animal should, while socializing, learn to live "according to the law" and decently "fulfill social roles". The ideal here is a person who has achieved self-realization and success; this is a creative intellectual. The problem of self-creation (as humanization) is not solved and is not even posed in an individualistic society; rather, this problem of self-creation is posed as a problem of personal success ("Cleansing" of all other human relationships that interfere, "litter" the road to success) which leads to dehumanization. In the individualistic ideology, now imposed on Russia, a person seeks not to self-improvement, but to increase consumption and comfort, but at the highest point of the pyramid of needs – to self-realization, to creative and well-paid activity. At the same time, the customer determines the success of an activity; it is beyond the criteria of good and evil, the creation and destruction of the life of a people, humanity.

There is another image of a person in a collectivist society: the concept of intelligence is different – the ability of thinking. But the main thing in this image is collectivism as a property of a person, defined as "awareness and perception of oneself as a part of the whole, generating behavior that contributes to the preservation of this whole", where the whole is hierarchical: from family, ancestry, circle of friends to ethnicity, nation, the whole humanity, all life. This property is inherent in human nature only as a deposit, and it may develop into the ability of the surrounding human social and cultural environment and then into a need, or it may not develop. The collectivist environment fosters such development, the individualistic one does not. Russian culture (both pagan, and Orthodox, and Soviet) sets such an ideal for collectivism, to the highest levels of which it is necessary to rise in the soul's constant work: ". . . the soul must work day and night. Both day and night!" (Zabolotsky, 2013), in self-knowledge and self-improvement. "Judge the people not by what they are, but by what they would like to be" (Dostoevsky, 1981/1876). Russian culture sets the path of humanization through repentance in pagan Russia (Mironova, 2014), confession (in Orthodox Russia), reflection (in Soviet Russia), through self-knowledge and self-improvement. The purpose of development, the ideal of a person is a person intellectually, spiritually and physically developed, and the idea of a person who can rise to the ideal, humanize, and only then self-realize. The humanization, first of all, is reflected in the human relations expressed in Christian "love thy neighbor . . .", in Russian, in the Soviet (collectivist) society "man is a friend, comrade and brother to man". This ideal and culture of the Russian people developed as a way of survival in the geographical environment in which it lived. We are the people who rose surviving all the ages under harsh geopolitical conditions, having managed to develop a communal culture and lifestyle, develop and preserve in fairy tales and epics, our values and the image of the ideal to which one aspired. In addition, we found in his environment such model of the avant-garde that succeeded in doing it, and we were ready to go after it. Now the contradiction of the Russian collectivist culture and the individualistic ideology imposed on Russia is the source of the destruction of the Russian man and the critical state (bifurcation) of society.

In both types of society, a person develops. But if in an individualistic society the mass rises to an existential level, where it "creates ideas and things", in a collectivist society, culture "pushes" him to the reflexive, and then to spiritual levels (Rumyantseva, 2014), to the "self-creation" and thus to the creation of things and ideas. The problem of creating ideas and things in an individualistic society is solved outside the criteria of good and evil, the preservation and destruction of life. What are these things?

Until the middle of the last century, the market economy of an individualistic society worked to satisfy human needs. But the "second generation of human rights", which was formed in the countries of Western civilization as a result of the global economic crisis and under the influence of economic success and social policy of the USSR, led to the transformation of the capitalist countries into "social states". As a result, the vital needs of the population of these countries were satisfied, and the market economy of these countries saturated the world market with essential goods and products. How was the further growth of the economy ensured and, in general, the existence of the capitalist system? The required growth in sales is now ensured by reducing the service life, reducing the reliability of the goods produced. Thus, the reduction in the cost of the materials from which, for example, the aircraft is made, reduced its protection from lightning strikes, and the decrease in the thickness of the metal on the car body, or on the roof of the house, or on the fence, etc. reduced their lifespan. Lifetime and other goods that meet the vital needs of a person – clothes, shoes, dishes, household appliances, etc. – began to decline rapidly, and in some cases, to strive for one day, one-time dishes, containers, shirts, etc. appeared. In many cases, such a reduced service life is not declared, but is specifically incorporated into the production technology. For example, for sewing clothes for this purpose, thin and fragile threads were used, the material used for the production of many goods (men's trousers and suits, women's tights, etc.) became thinner; on clothes with a rubber band (underwear, etc.) it is sewn so that it could not be replaced, and its shelf life falls; The parts of household appliances that are subject to wear, which are generally made of metal, are not made of metal, but of plastics etc. The share of the hidden market (drugs, weapons, etc.) that kills life is growing, and products and objects unnecessary for the preservation of human life and development (toys, various trinkets and decorations, perfumes and cosmetics, etc.) are beginning to occupy an increasing share of the open market, as well as the ideas how to sell them profitably (for example, using neuro-linguistic programming) develop. Man has become a slave to the financial and economic system, but with the appearance of the free creator of "ideas and things" of scientific and technological progress, and the Earth's resources are rapidly being turned into waste.

In a collectivist society like the USSR, the work of the Soviet person was directed by the social system for the common good, for the survival and development of the people.

Conclusion

Summing up, it can be said that an individualistic society loses the values of a culture that denies selfishness and does not form an integral personality. Rivalry intensifies the activity of a creative person, but scientific, technical and production activities become destructive for humans and for the Earth's biosphere. Scientific and technical progress is transformed into a spiritual regression and leads the "creative" individual to an existential vacuum, and the whole to self-destruction. Nations that are building civilization on the values of individualism are dying out. Humanity is no longer faced with the question of "to have or to be?" (Fromm, 1998/1976), but the question of "being or nothing"? (Kutyrev, 2010).

Only the culture of collectivism and the person formed by it is able to resist this tendency of destruction. Such is the culture of the Russian civilization.

References

Buchanan P. (2007) *Smert' Zapada.* [Death of the West] – M.: Pub. AST-Moscow, pp. 24–43.

Dostoevsky F. (1981) *Dnevnik pisatelya 1876 – T.23.* [Writer's diary 1876 – Vol. 23]- Leningrad, Science, Leningrad branch, available at: https://libking.ru/books/prose-/prose-rus-classic/163194-fedor-dostoevskiy-tom-23-dnevnik-pisatelya-1876.html (Accessed 24.04.2019).

Zabolotsky N. (2013) *Sbornik stikhov N.Zabolotskogo* [Collection of poems by N. Zabolotsky] – URL: http://userdocs.ru/literatura/110867/index.html (Accessed 24.04.2019).

Ilyin I. (1957) *"O Dukhovnosti instinkta" v Put' k ochevidnosti* ["On the Spirituality of Instinct" in The Path to Evidence] – Münhen, available at: http://rumagic.com/ru_zar/sci_philosophy/ilin/a/j9.html (Accessed 20.04.2014).

Kirdina S.G. (2014) *Institutsional'nyye matritsy i razvitiye Rossii: vvedeniye v KH-Y-teoriyu* [Institutional Matrices and the Development of Russia: An Introduction to the X-Y-Theory]. Ed. 3rd – S-Pb.: Nestor-History, available at: http://viperson.ru/wind.php?ID=255210 (Accessed 10.05.2015).

Kutyrev V. (2010) *Bytiyye ili nichto* [Being or Nothing] – S-Pb.: Aletheya.

Lobachevsky N. I. (1990) *Iz rechi "O vazhneyshikh predmetakh vospitaniya" v Antologiya pedagogicheskoy mysli Rossii vtoroy poloviny 19 – nachala 20 v.* [From the speech "On the most important subjects of education" in the Anthology of Pedagogical Thought of Russia in the second half of the 19th – early 20th centuries]. – M.: Pedagogy, p.176.

Mironova T. (2014) *Bronya geneticheskoy pamyati* [Armor of genetic memory] – M: Algorithm, available at: http://royallib.com/book/mironova_tatyana/bronya_geneticheskoy_pamyati.html (Accessed 24.04.2019).

Fromm E. (1998) *Imet' ili byt'?* [To have or to be?] Tran. from English – Kiev: Nika Center, (original: Erich Fromm "To Have Or to Be?" 1976).

Rumyantseva N.L. (2014) *Sotsialnaya evolyutsiya cheloveka. Sistemno-dialekticheskiy podkhod* [Social evolution of the person. System and dialectic approach] – M.: Book house of "LIBROKOM".

Shubart V. (2000) *Evropa i dusha Vostoka* [Europe and the Soul of the East]. Tran from Ger. – M: The Russian Idea Almanac (Issue 3), (Walter Schubart Europa und die Seele des Ostens – Luzern: Vita Nova, 1938).

Mayya V. Dubovik

8 From "Homo Economicus" to "Homo Digital": Challenges and Prospects

Introduction

When A. Smith introduced the new hero Homo Economicus into the economic literature in 1776, he did not even suspect that he laid the groundwork for a new classification of human species. Nowadays, a digital man (Homo Digital) has appeared. Who is he/she? What is he/she like? Can this person handle the responsibility, assigned to him/her? Will the human principle remain in him/her, with the universal digitalization of life?

The consequences of digitalization for a person are multifaceted. Thus, according to the surveys of respondents, the positive characteristics include innovativeness, speed and mobility, the ability to multitask. Among the negative factors are the growth of social inequality, artificiality in everything, difficulties in communication, communication in virtual reality, memory deterioration, loss of skills. There are uncertain prospects for a new legal space for a person in a digital economy.

The article studies the behavioral models of a man in economic and social life, considers both the real driving motives of human behavior and households, as well as the fictional characteristics of such behavior, in order to inscribe a person in one or another theory.

Methodology

Homo Economicus vs Homo Sapiens

In popular economic literature, it is assumed in a simplistic manner that A. Smith in "An Inquiry into the Nature and Causes of the Wealth of Nations" introduces the human model (Homo Economicus), who in his/her behavior was guided primarily by rationality, maximizing only own selfish gain. "It is not from the benevolence of the butcher, the brewer, or the baker that we expect our dinner, but from their regard to their own interest. We do not appeal to humanity, but to their own egoism and never tell them about our needs, but only about their benefits" (Smith, 2007). However, in his other work, "The Theory of Moral Sentiments", A. Smith writes

Mayya V. Dubovik, Russian Economic University named after G.V. Plekhanov, Moscow, Russia

https://doi.org/10.1515/9783110636147-008

about a softer concept – "prudence", which is based on "self-control" and a balanced and conscious understanding of one's needs (Smith, 1997). In the future, based on the model of Homo Economicus, the principles of equilibrium and completeness of information is based on the whole classical and further – neoclassical economic theory. The founder of utilitarianism, Jeremiah Bentham, proposed to consider the principle of maximizing pleasure and minimizing suffering at the heart of human behavior.

A. Marshall, in the study "Principles of Economics", extended the concept of rationality from consumer behavior to producers. Consumer behavior is determined by diversity, the desire to attract attention and the thirst for recognition, and manufacturers seek competition and satisfaction from the realization of their abilities and the instinct to acquire power. Motivation is determined quantitatively by the amount of money that people are willing to pay for the goods or get for their work. Earlier, Marshall wrote that "in addition to personal affections, a person has ideas about duty and devotion to high ideals" (Marshall, 2007). However, it should be noted that the pure rationality of Homo Economicus is feasible only in a completely ideal competitive market. Perfect competition and rationality, in the behavior of a person, according to L. Von Mises, mutually correlate with each other.

In his work "On Ethics and Economics", Amartya Sen emphasizes the need to include moral principles in the process of making economic decisions. "The mixture of selfishness and selfless behavior is one of the important characteristics of group loyalty" (Sen, 1996).

J. M. Keynes, in contrast to the classical approach, which hard core is a rigid rationality of behavior, contrasts the "psychological law of behavior". In addition to consumer and producer behavior, Keynes drew attention to the behavior of other economic entities – investors, and financial market participants operating under conditions of high uncertainty (Keynes, 2013). In the book "A Treatise on Probability", he suggested that probability should be viewed not as a characteristic of real events, but as a measure of the logical relationship between judgments expressed by the degree of rational faith, or reasonable certainty of a certain judgment (Keynes, 1921). Keynes associates the behavior of people not only with the whims and short-term impulses, but also with the currently available summary information. Forecasts and expectations with the arrival of new information change in the direction of reassessing the probability of events, while the behavior itself does not necessarily change.

This idea of J.M. Keynes resonated in the 1950s, in the concept of limited rationality of G. Simon. The limited resources such as information, its asymmetry, as well as the mental abilities of a person, do not allow us to really be guided only by rational maximization. In reality, the situation is much more complicated, and the decision is made on the basis of the ratio of the costs of obtaining additional information and the expected benefits.

In his study "The End of Laissez-faire", J.M. Keynes emphasizes the need for a rational combination of rational and irrational principles in the behavior of consumers and entrepreneurs, analyzing the best alternatives. In order to prevent mistakes and pessimism, to overcome uncertainty, to solve the problem of asymmetry of information about future events, Keynes considers the state intervention to be important, which can "guide society in a reasonable way". As far as the basic psychological law is concerned, Keynes explains with its help the causes of the economic crisis: with an increase in total income, consumption grows at a slower rate, aggregate demand is reduced, production and output are curtailed (Keynes, 1926).

In sociology, Homo Sociologicus appeared, having combed the philosophical, economic and anthropological models of a man. This character is closely related to Marx's theory of classes and a human being. K. Marx saw the mission of a person not in the manifestation of selfish qualities, but in the need for self-development of the individual in the interests and for the benefit of the whole of society. Behavior is determined not only by economic factors, the will and consciousness of economic actors, but also by social institutions (Marx, 1971).

The economic man changed from one economic school to another, but always remained within the framework of economic activity and economic decision-making. For example, in marginalists' opinion, he/she maximized another abstract subjective characteristic – utility. Neoclassicists tried to combine a human-optimizer and a social person. J.M. Keynes supplemented behavior with psychological subjective preferences – inclinations and motives of behavior. In neoclassical synthesis, P. Samuelson proposed to abandon the optimal choice of a behavioral solution and limit oneself to a set of selected preferences (Samuelson, 1938). According to G. Simon, human behavior is regulated by limited rationality (Simon, 1993). H. Leibenstein stands for a variable rationality depending on the person's own efforts dedicated to choosing.

Akerlof and Shiller in "Animal Spirits: How Human Psychology Drives the Economy, and Why It Matters for Global Capitalism" describe Homo Physiological and put forward five manifestations of "spiritus animalis" that destroy the foundation of classical economics – the perfection of the market mechanism, adding elements to it psychological impact on the behavior of economic actors (Akerlof, Schiller, 2009).

First, the concept of "trust" acquires an economic meaning, distances from an interpersonal, subjective relationship between people. As soon as crisis periods in the economy come, the media actively campaigns for the population to show confidence in the government. However, people behave irrationally, guided by their own faith. "Economists have only partially grasped what is meant by faith and trust. They assume that trust is rational: people use the information available to them to make a forecast, and then make a decision based on it". The authors propose to evaluate this behavior using the "trust multiplier", which shows how income will change if the level of trust changes by one percentage point. This procyclical indicator with some advance reflects the cyclical nature of trust: a growing economic activity is associated with its growth, and it slows down with a fall.

Another motive for irrational behavior is associated with the moral concept of "justice", which depends on trust, faith, and the ability to cooperate. Using the disclosure of the economic aspect of equity, the authors explain the pricing in commodity markets and the labor market, the ratio of inflation/GDP.

Another aspect of irrational behavior is the "vicious circle of abuse and bad faith". The reasons for the financial crises of 1990–1991, 2001, 2008–2010 lie in that there were financial abuses that led to a decline in confidence, a change in the perception of punishment, subsequent abuse and a slowdown in economic development in general.

The authors called the fourth characteristic the "monetary illusion". Prior to this, J. M. Keynes wrote that inflation should be taken into account when discussing wages and mortgage rates, concluding labor contracts and financial contracts (Keynes).

Fifthly, *susceptibility to stories* affects irrationality. Rumors of success, like a contagious disease, obscure rational considerations and motives.

According to Akerlof and Shiller, the state should level out "spiritus animalis" that negatively affect the behavior of economic agents, while creating conditions for "smart laissez faire".

An attempt to describe the dynamic model and the moment of a qualitative change in human behavior in the 1970s of the 20th century was taken by William Merkling and Karl Brunner who proposed the REMM model – "Resourceful, Evaluating, Maximizing Man". Human ingenuity means not only creative and experimental detailing, but also resourcefulness in adapting a person in a social and cultural environment, sometimes even associated with opportunistic behavior. Evaluation refers to asymmetry and imperfection of information, time constraints and associated transaction costs, the nature of preferences and their structure, the value of personal interest and selfishness. Evaluation can be both quantitative and qualitative. In this case, the evaluation becomes more subjective, it is based on simplifying the choice, which brings his behavior to the model of limited rationality of G. Simon.

To simultaneously take into account the individualism of Homo Economicus and the network social interdependencies of Homo Sociologicus, O. Neuloh combined both of these extreme types in Homo Socioeconomicus (Neuloh, 1980).

The forerunner of behavioral economics is the theory of perspectives proposed by Daniel Kahneman and Amos Tversky, based on the empirical patterns of individual choice (Kahneman, Tversky, 1979). Richard Thaler proposed to combine psychological and economic motives in consumer behavior with the help of the so-called mental or psychological accounting. He showed that the "price" of regular income for a household is higher than spontaneous income in the form of bonuses, bribes, gifts or winnings (Thaler, 1985). According to Thaler, a consumer can be controlled by automatically including and forcing the "silent people" to do prudent actions using the methods of libertarian paternalism, the main feature of which, unlike marketing strategies, is the preservation of individual freedom of action. (Thaler, Sunstein, 2008). In another study, a more delicate way is suggested – an individual is not forced, but is pushed towards the right choice.

Thus, it is possible to form a set of economic endogenous and exogenous factors that determine, according to various authors, the behavioral model of a particular individual or household in economic activity. The first group includes current and permanent income, accumulated wealth, the second – the cycle phase, investment climate, interest rate, tax system, inflation rate. Since it is impossible to disregard the social and biological components of a person, behavior is also influenced by such social factors as inclusion in social networks, the opinion of the reference group, consumption standards, religious norms and psychological – the system of values and beliefs, moral values, propensity to risk, optimism/pessimism.

The Homo Economicus model allowed to let go the internal – spiritual – and external – social – aspects of a person, to simplify the behavior to the maximum. However, this model, despite its sketchiness, from the point of view of methodological status is an "ideal type" with significant heuristic value. On the one hand, this is a purely theoretical model with anthropological limit characteristics. On the other hand, it can be considered as a type of person with an appropriate character, behavior, values, which is sometimes used as a common noun.

Challenges from Homo Digital to Homo Sapiens

The wave of digital technologies that has swept the entire world is transforming the behavior patterns not only of individuals, but of business, government, and society. Such deep and large-scale technologies like artificial intelligence, robotics, the Internet of things, wireless communication and a number of others are called cross-cutting, as they cover all spheres of life, create a new environment for humans. This environment differs not only in what a person does, but also in those who are this new person – Homo Digital – and what their behavior is in the conditions of the fourth industrial revolution based on digital technologies.

Human abilities that are less easily replaced by digital technologies are creativity, comprehensive problem solving, emotional intelligence, building relationships and making choices in the face of uncertainty, critical thinking, negotiation, complex cognitive skills, responsiveness, empathy.

On the other hand, a number of Homo Sapiens skills, under the influence of numbers, are at risk and are subject to partial replacement and/or destruction. These include such skills as identifying decisions necessary for human intervention, shaping moral principles in accordance with standards, laws, rules, ensuring balance and lack of bias in terms of decision-making, ensuring transparency and interpretation for immediate results. More specific types and areas of activity are administration, registration and reporting, information gathering, standardization, forecasting, physical labor, routine operations, quality control, driving and driving. In general, digitalization leads to the dehumanization of labor, its rationing, reducing the use of creative thinking, patience and open thinking.

Homo Digital is transforming under the influence of digital technology and, according to psychologist and writer Douglas Lyle, falls into the "pleasure trap". This is reflected in the reduction of exercise of both the brain and the body, since "smart numbers" reduce a person's contact with the natural environment, reformat the neural networks, destroy the habit of concentrated thinking (Carr, 2009).

However, the most important negative consequence of digitalization is informational and, as a result, economic, social and other types of inequality. This new phenomenon became widespread and is characteristic not only of developing countries in the 1990s with the wide penetration of the Internet in all areas and countries. The causes of informational inequality lie in the inequality of opportunities and access to educational, medical and other technologies, information. The Internet, therefore, along with the benefits, contributes to the deepening of inequality.

The Internet of things implies connection to the network, availability of modern technologies, possession and existence of the corresponding equipment. The absence of these opportunities leads to serious consequences: either the worldview of inferiority is formed, or the expectation of instant reward. In healthcare, the inaccessibility of new technologies limits the application of methods for the early diagnosis and treatment of many diseases, shortens life expectancy in poor countries. In education, the possibilities of augmented reality are available to the digital community to a greater degree, which also leads to a deepening of inequality and creates "vicious circles of poverty". It should be noted that distance learning is not conducive to the development of creativity and thinking. In medicine, remote treatment is also possible in standard form. This confirms the view that rich families will continue to teach their children in the classical form in contact with the teacher and receive medical care by contacting a doctor directly.

Another threat to the real relationship between Homo Sapiens is seen in the loss of communication skills, since everywhere a smartphone becomes the main means of communication. With the immersion of a person in virtual reality, digital absent-mindedness appears; a clip, superficial perception of information is being developed; attention time is reduced; a significant part of life goes on Facebook or Twitter; ability for critical thinking, reflection is reduced; multitasking prevents people from deeper perception of information, thinking.

Due to the fact that the international legal field has not been created with respect to digital technologies, human rights are vulnerable in the digital space, and the credibility of the digital environment is low. There are threats of cyberterrorism, information wars, cybercrime and cyber espionage, the compression and disappearance of traditional markets. Complications arise when something illegal in one country, may be acceptable in another, when the confidentiality of user information is violated. The main problem is to maintain a balance between risks and fundamental rights and freedoms of a person.

In Russia, the concept of digital economy is defined by two main aspects. On the one hand, this is the economy of a new technological generation (Presidential Address,

2016). On the other hand, it is a business activity based on digital data (Strategy for the Development of the Information Society of the Russian Federation for 2017–2030). Prospects of the development of the digital economy are designated as one of the national development goals. To achieve it, the following tasks are set:

- an increase in domestic spending on the development of the digital economy at the expense of all sources (by share in gross domestic product) by at least 3 times compared with 2017;
- creation of a sustainable and secure information and telecommunications infrastructure for high-speed transmission, processing and storage of large amounts of data, accessible to all organizations and households;
- the use of primarily domestic software by government agencies, local governments (Decree, 2018).

It is possible to ensure the solution of these ambitious tasks subject to the conditions of business and society's readiness for digital transformation, the presence and maturity of the high-tech sector, and the growing public demand for digital technologies.

Conclusion

In conclusion, the author can agree with the opinion of Sherry Tarkle, who believes that technologies are necessary to protect the modern man, where he/she is vulnerable, to give him/her speed. However, the digital person supports several behavioral myths of the modern person. A digital person lives by feeling that he is concentrating attention, on what interests him and controls what he wants. It seems to a person that when he spends his life in social networks, others hear him, empathize and sympathize with him. Leaving into virtual reality, according to the digital person, saves from loneliness, helps to find friends. However, all these fantasies are easy to destroy. It is known that S. Jobs and other prominent people from the digital world for their children prefer live communication and reading books to using gadgets, which they reduce to a minimum.

The digital economy opens up additional opportunities for personal development, and the significant gap between the beneficiaries of the industrial revolution and those segments of the population who cannot use them due to lack of competence or material wealth is widening. On the one hand, due to the growth of labor productivity, there is more time for improving human capital, new creative fields of activity, flexible forms and types of employment are emerging. On the other hand, the total rationalization of all aspects of life, the standardization of human behavior, the formalization of decision-making procedures and the depersonification of the processes taking place in the economy are approaching. There is an increase in the struggle between the privileged and those left on the fringes, and the demographic differentiation is deepening.

And the words of L. N. Tolstov remain classical: “When living with people, do not forget what you learned in solitude. In solitude think about what you have learned from communication with people”.

References

Address from the President of the Russian Federation to the Federal Assembly of December 1, 2016. URL: http://www.consultant.ru/document/cons_doc_LAW_207978/.

Akerlof G., Shiller R. Animal Spirits: How Human Psychology Drives the Economy, and Why It Matters for Global Capitalism. Princeton University Press, 2009. 230 p.

Carr H. (2009) Empty Shell. What the Internet Does With our Brains, / URL: https://readli.net/pustyishka-chto-internet-delaet-s-nashimi-mozgami/.

Decree of the President of the Russian Federation of May 7, 2018 No. 204 “On the National Goals and Strategic Objectives of the Development of the Russian Federation for the Period up to 2024” URL: // https://www.garant.ru/products/ipo/prime/doc/71837200/.

Kahneman D., Tversky A. Prospect Theory: An Analysis of Decision under Risk. Econometrica, 1979, vol. 47, no 2, pp. 263–292.

Keynes J.M. A Treatise of Probability. London, Macmillan & Co., 1921, 494 p.

Keynes J.M. The End of « laissez-faire », Hogarth Press, July 1926. (Russ. Ed.: Keynes J.M. Konets Laissez-faire, Moscow, 2001. 437 p.

Keynes J.M. The General Theory of Employment, Interest and Money / J.M. Keynes. Selected Works. M., 2013, 402 p.

Marshall A. Principles of Economics. London, McMillan and Co., 1890 (Russ Ed.: Marshall A. Osnovy ekonomicheskoi nauki, Moscow, Eksmo, 2007. 832 p.)

Marx K., Engels F. Collected Works. Moscow, 1971. Vol. 3.

Neuloh Otto: Soziologie für Wirtschaftswissenschaftler Homo socio-oeconomicus. Kurzlehrbuch für Studium und Praxis der Volkswirte und Betriebswirte. 1980, S. 14–15.

Presidential Decree of May 9, 2017 No. 203 “On the Strategy for the Development of the Information Society in the Russian Federation for 2017–2030” URL: // https://www.garant.ru/products/ipo/prime/doc/71570570/.

Samuelson P. A note on the pure theory of consumer behavior // Economia. 1938. № 1. P. 61–71.

Schiller R. The Crisis of Trust: The Irrational Man // Vedomosti. March 12, 2009. No. 43 (2313).

Sen A. On Ethics and Economics. M., 1996. 160 p.

Simon H. Rationality as a Process and Product of Thinking // THESIS Almanac, 1993, Vol. 1, Issue 3, pp. 16–38.

Smith A. An Inquiry into the Nature and Causes of the Wealth of Nations. M., 2007. 956 p.

Smith A. Theory of Moral Sentiments. M., 1997. 351 p.

Thaler, Richard H., Sunstein. Cass R. Nudge: Improving Decisions about Health, Wealth, and Happiness (Yale University Press, 2008)

Thaler, Richard H., “Mental Accounting and Consumer Choice.” *Marketing Science*. 4 (1985): 1999–214.

Nina O. Voskresenskaya

9 Digital Man and Digital Society from the Standpoint of Historical Science and Foresight: Regularities, Randomness and Limits of Growth

Introduction

Significantly faster than before – compared to the very recent past – the pace of scientific and technological progress brings us to the fact that "the future is getting closer to us": an increasing number of scientific discoveries and inventions which are being made per unit of time now, are implemented into practice faster and faster, and their aggregate influence on the life of a man and society turns out to be more and more powerful. What might be the way of the further evolution of humanity under the impact of digital technologies from the standpoint of foresight? Do the possible ways of the development of humanity in the "digital future" contradict the fundamental laws of our historical past? What sciences are likely to be crucial for our existence in digital and information society? What dangers and limitations can await humanity in the near and distant digital time? These problems which are evidently of great importance for us to understand who we are and where we are going to, are discussed in this chapter.

Methodology

Historical Science and Foresight in the Exploring "Digital Man" and "Digital Society" of the Future

Working out "images of the digital future" is based on linear extrapolations of the past and present trends into the future. Accepting possible reproaches that, as applied to such complex systems as human beings and human society, linear extrapolations might not be sufficiently reliable and not always able to take into account all possible "jumps", "discontinuities" and "bifurcation points", we have to admit that super-complex problems often exceed the cognitive abilities of modern science

Nina O. Voskresenskaya, Financial University under the Government of the Russian Federation, Moscow, Russia

https://doi.org/10.1515/9783110636147-009

(Kazyutinsky, 2013). However, even simple and straightforward linear predictions can be reasonable and useful: corrected with the help of "refinement factors", they can be used as a possible basis for creating "nonlinear forecasts".

History teaches us that linear trends anticipating the future are steadily detected at each stage of the development of human society. Thus, the signs of future transition from the nomadic hunter-gatherer society to agrarian one based on the domestication of various plants and animals could have been clearly seen long before the formation of an agrarian society really took place on the Earth; The situation was similar with the emergence of industrial and post-industrial societies. It is but the historical patterns and trends in the development of mankind (Malkov, Grinin, and Korotaev, 2016) and some signs of our current existence that necessarily lead us to the conclusion that the most likely future of our world is a digital society.

If the role of historical science – relevant to the problem – is to accept or refute the possibility of forming a digital civilization on Earth, basing on the trends in the development of society in the past, then the task of "researching the future" is to foresee what this future might be; The main methods to implement these tasks are forecasting and foresight (Voskresenskaya, 2012). "Future studies", describing the possible ways of future development, focus on different scenarios for the future, which can be ranging from the most negative to the most desirable ones; futurologists determine the degree of probability and possible consequences of scenarios, trying to anticipate their main characteristics, regularities and irregularities, and limits of growth. Combining all the "individual" spheres of life and giving them a "common denominator" in terms of goal-setting, these scenarios are necessary for developing national strategies for the society, and, like historical investigations, contribute to the rationalization and optimization of the functioning of society in the present. It is fundamentally important that our interest in the future is the basic feature of a human being: the essence of people is that they have goals and strive to realize them (Von Mises, 1966), and the sphere of "dwelling" of our goals is only the future. Human nature itself dictates us to be orientated towards the future: it is well known that human brain is mainly occupied with reflections on the "day of tomorrow", this is precisely what the main part of its energy goes to (Schwartz, 2012).

From the standpoint of "studies of the past and the future", the most probable transformation of modern society and a man as "Homo Sapience Ordinary" into digital society and a man as "Homo Sapience Digital" will be the movement of humanity along the path of gaining more and more complete and accurate knowledge of the world, strengthening the power of the human race and the extension of human life. Let us consider them in relation to the near future, limiting it to the middle of the current century, and in relation to the more distant future.

Early Digital Society: The Science

If we assume that one of the key characteristics of the digital society is producing information, which being presented in the digital and more and more complete form will cover all spheres of human life, as well as collecting information, its storage, processing and usage, then it would be logical to agree that the progress of all sciences, as the highest form of information (Ageev, Averyanov, Evtushenko, and Kochetova, 2017) will go much faster than now. Advances in the information technologies should lead us to breakthroughs in various branches of scientific knowledge. One of the most relevant research areas is brain research.

Understanding how the brain, the main organ of our exploration of the world, works, and what thought is, and how it is formed, is vital for the progress of all spheres of human life without any exception; A science of consciousness has all reasons to become the most important science of the near digital future. One of the obvious successes of brain research carried out by the hundreds of scientific organizations in dozens of countries around the world nowadays is the creation of working memory models as repositories of information. However, some other tasks, including the creation of functioning models of brain, and the technical reconstruction of emotional experiences and volitional personality characteristics, the achievement of which have been optimistically expected by 2021, are evidently being postponed indefinitely.

Maximum attention will be paid to artificial intelligence research as well. Already now artificial intelligence makes decisions for us in many areas. Neural networks, which have a fundamentally important characteristic of their ability to learn and, therefore, for self-improvement, successfully replace scientists in a growing number of scientific fields: neural networks formulate and test hypotheses, identify and analyze patterns, and incredibly quickly and accurately, even in comparison with mathematical methods simulations, process huge amounts of data. It is obvious that these scientific directions will continue to develop in the near future.

Less obvious, but not less desirable will be the appearance of certain new sciences, the need for which has always been huge, but which could not have appeared due to the lack of the necessary databases and corresponding methods of analysis. Among them there is a science aimed of studying the fate of people, let us give this science the provisional name of "fateology". The prerequisites for its appearance have already been created: various facts of the life of people from different social, professional, cultural and ethnic groups are being recorded more and more thoroughly; big data arrays are being formed, they are necessary for researchers to capture obvious as well as hidden "turning points" in human life; And the process of digitization of all texts written in the history of mankind is under the way. The practical consequence of the analysis of the accumulated data by neural network will be the identification of general laws, regularities and irregularities, "key factor" and "turning points" in human life. Taken together they could be the proper base to work out the rational life decisions at the individual level. "Destiny" as a field of scientific research is able to lead us to the "science of happenstances", the creation of which humanity has also been approaching for a long time, but without significant results: academic science, recognizing the exceptional importance of "random events", has not been able to work with them up to now, due to the lack of adequate analysis tools.

Another fundamentally new area of scientific research might be a science under the conditional name "search for reasonableness". It is well known that not a man only is capable of learning the world: more than 9 million species of animals living on Earth also explore the environment, and not unsuccessfully, but only Homo Sapience is designed in such a way that he can constantly and purposefully search for the meaning of what is happening and catch the "manifestations of the mind" in the world around him. Modern science has already revealed those features of the world that allow us to recognize the presence of a rational beginning in it (Gordon and Dembski, 2011). So, the search for meaning in everything is likely to become the driving force of the entire socio-economic, socio-political and cultural evolution of digital society.

The core of science will also include the fundamentally new sciences of the "digital series" such as "Setleterics" as the science of transferring personality to digital media; "Virtual realityology" as the science exploring virtual reality; a "Theory of everything" will be developed, capable of combining not only all known types of physical interaction, but also all possible scientific directions: science will continue the movement in order to examine the world in its integrity.

Early Digital Society: Digital Man, Service Robots for Personal and Domestic Use and "Smart Environment"

The development of science, an indispensable condition for the growth of human race power, will contribute to the realization of people's long-held dream – to create an assistant "for the housework", as close to us as possible, that is, capable to think and feel. Many different robots are already working in different areas, a significant part of them are personal robots. (Litzenberger, 2018). In two or three decades, they will probably acquire a human appearance, and artificial, ultra-strong, self-regenerating skin has already been created for them (Yue Cao et al., 2019); they will consume human food, and special sensors will provide them with almost human tactile capabilities. Robots will be fluent in any languages and will take on many functions, from personal secretary to doctor. The laws, the adoption of which seems inevitable, will regulate the rights and duties of personal robots and their relationships with people, including, as expected, marital.

The power over the "humanized" robots will be complemented by the power over the industrial robots, which will provide humans with a smart living environment and smart production; By the middle of the 21st century, "smart devices" that control and optimize many branches of people's life will become a common fact in all spheres of people's professional and private life.

Early Digital Society: Digital Technology and "Virtual Reality"

Digital technologies can change and, of course, will change the balance between the real and the virtual in the human world, and this promises mankind serious changes in its existence. Virtual worlds, bright and diverse, given to a man as a three-four-five-dimensional space, with a complete imitation of the effect of presence, smell and touch, are very likely to push a certain part of society to the preference of virtual reality over ordinary one. A likely consequence will be changes in people's behavior and the emergence of virtual, that is, false memory. Since each "virtual man" will have his or her own memory, it will inevitably affect the functioning of the whole society.

Early Digital Society: Increasing Life Expectancy as the Main Goal of Mankind

The methods of modern "mass medicine" will be complemented by personal medicine capabilities, built on deciphering an individual DNA of each person and therefore much more effective than mass medicine. The neural network will make diagnoses and suggest optimal treatment options; genetic engineering will allow to correct any genetic "errors"; the use of medical nanorobots will lead to the most accurate diagnosis and effective "point-to-point" treatment. Sensors placed on the human body will monitor a man's health and record all vital indicators of his health in the nonstop and on-line mode. The predicted result will be a significant increase in life expectancy, especially in developed countries: by 2050, every fourth resident there will be over 60 years old (World Population Prospects, 2017), people will be able to live up to 100–120 years, and this first generation "C" in history will live the active life of middle-aged people.

The cloning techniques of natural human internal organs which have been already created, have excellent prospects to be developed; among them there are the teeth grown right in the mouth, however, so far only for mice, human lungs, and the ears. Successful work is being done to create artificial substitutes for human internal organs: artificial vessels, joints, heart, kidneys, liver, and bones that can grow together with tendons and muscles; a smart pancreas has been already created equipped with artificial intelligence and therefore able to calculate the required insulin dose for diabetics; on the agenda there is a creation of the retina. Printing human organs by medical 3D printers will make their production a routine procedure. The development of technologies for the creation of repeatedly updated human body claims the status of the leading national project, the importance of which is occasionally spoken by many Russian politicians.

Along with the gigantic opportunities that achievements in the field of medicine promise humanity, there are also obvious dangers and limitations. Drugs which can easily become a deadly weapon are worked out: they slow down the thought processes, violate speech and understanding, allow to manipulate the emotions and actions of people, including those for military purposes.

Early Digital Society: Bionic Man

Suppose, however, that the main possibilities for extending a person's life are now concentrated not in biological, but mainly in the technological sphere. The technology that can significantly increase the life expectancy of a person and fundamentally change the whole world is the production of cyborgs.

Mankind has already embarked on this path: cyborg, a symbiosis of biological man and electronics, has long been our reality (Kaplan, 2012). Immobilized patients with neurochips implanted in the brain can manipulate artificial limbs with the power of thought; implantation of special chips under the skin of hands which is practiced by some people even nowadays allows "modern cyborgs" to pay for purchases and pay bills with a simple touch to a reader, instantly open and close doors, manage a "smart" house. In the future the implantation of specialized microchips into the brain will allow a "bionic person" to create the personal virtual reality of "full immersion" for himself and contact the virtual world throughout his own nervous system without any additional equipment, and search for the necessary information using thoughts only, and receive the results of search queries by their live broadcast straight to the brain.

A fully digital version of the extension of life of a normal biological as well as a bionic man is based on the creation of his "electronic portrait". Since from the point of view of the duration of the subject's existence, the potential of digital technologies exceeds the potential of biological substance by orders of magnitude, and since the transfer of human consciousness to machines is a matter theoretically possible (Bamford, 2012) in principle, there will be no need or point in trying to save the brain and the human body as a biological object. Digital technologies of full copying of the brain are likely to be developed, and "recording oneself", that is, recording the full information about person's intellect, will and emotions can be done unlimited number of times. Computer avatar, filled throughout a man's life with any related information, such as photo and video documents, diaries, displacement maps, recording conversations on transmitting devices, data on search queries and Internet sites, habits, manners, passions, relationships with relatives, friends, opponents, his attitude towards events – all this is essentially an "electronic cast" of his personality. It is noteworthy that such projects are already common on the Web. These digital portraits will enable people of the future to communicate "live" with the computer counterparts of their ancestors. So, in the long run, it is the digital way of achieving immortality that seems most likely. On this way, people also face limitations and dangers: intruders can penetrate into other people's databases making possible their destruction, distortion and unfair sale.

Early Digital Society: Vectors of Development, Opportunities and Dangers

Digital technologies will lead to significant changes in society. Tremendous opportunities of the Internet and different social networks even now provide much higher than before the communication capabilities of people, and, as a result, new and more effective ways and levels of self-organization of human society. It is also obvious that digital technologies dictate the emergence of new legal relations: humanity goes and will inevitably come to the establishment of a regime of "total digitization", and there will be no place for "non-digitized objects" (Ageev, Averyanov, Evtushenko, and Kochetova, 2017) in the digital future world. Total digitization will also lead to the complete openness of one and all, and that will fundamentally change the everyday life of a man and society.

Even nowadays about 80% of the entire global industry is working to provide technical support for leisure and the creation of new forms of entertainment, and in the near future, fundamentally new markets will be created in the field of entertainment, tourism and sports, such as the "Adventure-for-Sale-Market", the "Who-I-Am-Market", "Peace-of-Mind-Market", "Market-of-Convictions", "Care-Market", "Spiritual-Intimacy-Market", "Friendship-and-Love-Market" (Shcherbina, 2006). A very likely consequence of the preference for "entertainment" over "work" will be a decrease in the cognitive abilities of a significant part of the population: if machines are physically and mentally working for people, and it is clearly going to this, then people trusting artificial intelligence might lose their analytic and decision-making skills (Kudryavtsev, 2012). However, the "creators of machines" will develop in the opposite direction. The probable result will be the emergence of the new classes of the digital society: its top will be formed by people capable of producing new knowledge, their main values will be intelligence and science; workers not capable for science as well as their descendants – due to the absolute inequality of the starting conditions – will not be able to enter the elite of the new society. Almost zero vertical social mobility is likely to lead to a tough polarization of digital society, sharper than ever before in the human history. It is important that this vector of disharmonious development of civilization is largely set by the imperfect human nature, with its inherent selfishness and aggressiveness (Dubrovsky, 2012). In any case, the growing complication of the Technosphere without "human becoming better" may entail the destruction of a significant part of humanity: in the near digital future the threat of regional and global conflicts with the use of weapons of mass destruction is quite evident; environmental crises and redistribution of the world, strengthening the struggle for the possession of energy resources can take place easily (Voskresenskaya, 2013).

Early Digital Future: The Most Sought-After Professions

Labor market trends indicate that in the foreseeable future, the list of the most sought-after professions will include medical workers, gerontologists, cognitive aging specialists, biologists, chemists, pharmacists, lawyers specializing in medical issues, and green technology experts. Specialists in the field of energy, as well as in the field of information technology: programmers, engineers, creators of robots, developers of computer games, mobile devices, network antiviruses will also be in great demand. Specialists in the field of leisure, sports, tourism, including space tourism, and entertainment, will be well-paid, too.

So, judging by the tendencies of the past and foresight forecasts, the appearance of a new coming society is clearly visible; It is crucially important that this nearest digital society is still "inhabited" by ordinary people, albeit largely "digital", and there is still no fundamental difference between people "digital" and "non-digital", for "digital people" differing from "non-digital" by the level of knowledge and opportunities in relation to the world around them, will still remain humans with the same human nature and ethical attitudes within which they have been existing since their appearance on Earth.

The situation with the "distant digital future" man and society looks quite different.

Distant Digital Future: Movement Towards Immortality, Omnipotence, Omniscience and "All-Unity"

Suppose that humanity continues to move along the path of acquiring knowledge, enhancing power and prolonging life; in relation to the distant digital future, we denote these goals as the attainment of omniscience, omnipotence and immortality. It is worth noting that it is with these properties that people have always endowed their gods. Suppose also that digital technologies, becoming more and more powerful, will be able to make a person more and more "digital" and "artificial". In this case, one should expect the most serious changes in the individual and social existence of people throughout human history: scientific and technical progress is highly likely to change one day the very nature of a man: the "bionic" person of the digital society will be fully transformed into the "electronic" person of the post-digital of society.

The existence in electronic form will open up truly incredible prospects for humanity. People will be able to overcome any distance by the power of thought, explore the world without the help of any external mechanisms; It will be easy for them to tolerate extreme environmental conditions, such as high temperatures, huge pressure, radiation, lack of oxygen and, therefore, post-digital people will be able to exist in open space. (Kurzweil, 2015). And, if the knowledge of the Universe is the true purpose of mankind, it is unlikely to be ever fulfilled without the "eternal" electronic being of a digital-post-man.

People will be able to operate the external environment with the power of thought; connect to remote databases, instantly receive any information they want; master the techniques of collective consciousness, will be able to communicate mentally at any distance. The turning point on this path will be the unification of "individual" brains into a single thinking network: it will be the first time in the history of mankind when a "single mind" will be created, the importance of which people have been thinking about since antiquity; the "process of thinking" will become collective and will spread to all of humanity. "Thinking together" will inevitably lead to the complete "dissolution" of the personality in other electronic entities: all of them, simultaneously thinking and having the same maximum abilities, can no longer differ from each other; and the concept of "human society", understood as a combination of individuals and connections between them, will be a thing of the past. So, there will be a world that is radically different from both the modern world and the "early" digital one.

Successes on this path will put humanity in the face of the need to answer the most fundamental questions throughout its history: if a person acquires all he wants, that is, immortality, omniscience and omnipotence, doesn't he completely lose his human essence? And won't his life lose its meaning as a movement towards a certain goal? (Enikolopov, 2012).

Conclusions

The main streamline of human development in the "digital age" is a steady and ever accelerating movement from the "biological nature" to an increasingly obvious "artificial state". The desire to create more and more powerful helpers for themselves, at first exclusively external, and then more and more tangibly present in the person himself, and the willingness to move along the path from pure "biology" through "bionics" to pure "digit" is paradoxically embedded in the original biological nature of man. In the near digital future, some of the things discussed will be implemented; in the distant future, subject to the preservation of linear historical patterns, everything that science predicts will be realized, whether we like it or not. Awareness of this fact is an emotionally difficult action that can cause a desire to impede human progress on the digital path. However, formal bans on the development of digital technologies are unlikely to prevent digital future but can make it unpredictable and therefor even more dangerous for technologies will go underground, and their development might come out of control.

So, the whole history of mankind looks like just a pre-history of the digital society, the historically predetermined transition to which begins before our eyes.

References

Ageev A.I., Averyanov M.A., Evtushenko S.N. & Kochetova E.Yu. TSifrovoye obshchestvo: arkhitektura, printsipy, videniye. // Ekonomicheskiye strategii. [Digital Society: Architecture, Principles, Vision. // Economic strategies], no. 1, 2017, pp. 114, available at: http://www.inesnet.ru/wp-content/mag_archive/2017_01/es2017-01-114-126_Ageev_Averyanov_Yevtushenko_Kochetova.pdf (Accessed 12.03.2019)(in Russian).

Bamford, S. (2012). A Framework for Approaches to Transfer of a Mind's Substrate, available at: http://www.sim.me.uk/neural/JournalArticles/Bamford2012IJMC.pdf (Accessed 23.03.2019).

Dubrovsky, D.I. (2012), Soznaniye i mozg: perspektivy preobrazovaniya prirody cheloveka [Consciousness and the Brain: Prospects for the Transformation of Human Nature], available at: http://gf2045.ru/read/156/ (Accessed 12.03.2019) (in Russian).

Enikolopov, S.N. (2012), Ideologiya bessmertiya: psikhologicheskiy aspect [The ideology of Immortality: Psychological Aspect], available at: http://gf2045.ru/read/149/ (Accessed 12.03.2019) (in Russian).

Gordon, Bruce L., Dembski & William A. (2011), The Nature of Nature: Examining the Role of Naturalism in Science. Wilmington.

Kazyutinsky V.V. Blizok li "Vek Nauki" k eye zavershеniyu? Voprosy filosofii, [Is the "Century of Science" Close to its Completion? Problems of Philosophy], 2013, no. 3 (in Russian).

Kaplan, A. (2012), Consciousness Control of the Brainwave, available at: http://gf2045.ru/read/139/ (Accessed 13.03.2019) (in Russian).

Kudryavtsev, A. V. (2012), Global'nyye tendentsii razvitiya tekhnologicheskoy tsivilizatsii – k svobode cherez rabstvo [Global Trends in the Development of Technological Civilization – to Freedom Throughout Slavery], available at: http://gf2045.ru/read/152/ (Accessed 24.03.2019) (in Russian).

Kurzweil, R. (2015), A True Story About the Future. The Singularity is Near, http://singularity.com/themovie/index.php#.XJZ4FpgzbDc (Accessed 24.03.2019).

Litzenberger, Gudrun. (2018), Automation Boom in Electrical /Electronics Industry Drives 30% Increase in Sales of Industrial Robots, available at: https://ifr.org/post/automation-boom-in-electrical-electronics-industry-drives-30-increase-in-sa (Accessed 23.03.2019).

Malkov S.Yu., Grinin L.E. & Korotaev A.V. (2016), Istoriya i Matematika: Analiz i modelirovaniye sotsial'no-istoricheskikh protsessov [History and Mathematics: Analysis and Modeling of Socio-Historical Processes]. Ed. 3, URSS (in Russian).

Von Mises, L. (1966), Human Action. A Treatise on Economics, Yale University Press Publ. Third Revised Edition. Contemporary Books, Inc., Chicago, pp.11–14.

Schwartz, Peter. (2012), The Art of the Long View: Planning for the Future in an Uncertain World. Crown Publishing Group, available at: https://books.google.co.in/books?id=T-r36bIZA44C (Accessed 22. 03.2019).

Shcherbina, A.V. (2006), Konkurentsiya kak proyavleniye agonal'nosti v ekonomicheskoy kul'ture: avtoreferat diss. . . . doktora filosofskikh nauk: Competition as a Manifestation of Agonality in Economic Culture: Author's Abstract of the Diss. . . . Ph.D.: 24.00.01, 09. 00.11/ Rostov-on-Don state university. Rostov-on-Don (in Russian).

Voskresenskaya N.O. (2012), Banki idey kak rezul'tat forsayta – nauchnoy metodologii informatsionnogo obshchestva, in Rossiya: tendentsii i perspektivy razvitiya [Banks of Ideas as a Result of Foresight – the Scientific Methodology of the Information Society, in Russia: Trends and Development Prospects.] M.: RAS INION. Pp. 333–338, available at: http://innclub.info/archives/2616 (Accessed 25. 03.2019)(in Russian).

Voskresenskaya N.O. (2013). Postchelovek i postchelovechestvo – budushchaya real'nost' ili utopiya? (nekotoryye global'nyye tendentsii razvitiya mira glazami uchastnikov Kongressa "Global'noye Budushcheye – 2045") in Global'nyye tendentsii razvitiya mira. Materialy Vserossiyskoy nauchnoy konferentsii. Moskva, 14 iyunya 2012 g., INION RAN. [Postman and Post Humanity – Future Reality or Utopia? (some global trends of the development of the world through the eyes of the participants of the Global Future – 2045 Congress) in Global Trends of the World. Materials of the All-Russian Scientific Conference. Moscow, June 14, 2012, INION RASM.: Nauchnyy ekspert]. M.: Scientific Expert, pp. 115–117, (2013) (in Russian).

World Population Prospects. The 2017 Revision, available at: https://esa.un.org/unpd/wpp/Publications/Files/WPP2017_KeyFindings.pdf (Accessed 23.03.2019).

Yue Cao et al. (2019), Self-Healing Electronic Skins for Aquatic Environments, available at: https://www.nature.com/articles/s41928-019-0206-5 (Accessed 24.03.2019).

Igor V. Bormotov, Maksim S. Zhuravlev, Natalia V. Ovchinnikova

10 The Human-Digital Environment System in the Socio-Economic Paradigm of the Future

Introduction

A modern man is an active or passive participant in various environments: natural, technological, social, digital, etc. Some of them (natural and social) are designed to create conditions for human existence, others (technological and digital) are formed by a person himself to ensure his life and satisfaction of his increasing needs. An important condition for their implementation in the future will be the socio-economic human activity in the development of the digital environment.

Its emergence is associated with a new industrial revolution, called Industry 4.0 (Industrie 4.0), reflecting the introduction of fundamentally new technologies to which modern people must adapt. Among them are the following:

- cyber-physical systems and neurotechnologies with a fundamentally new mechanism of human interaction and the machine (device) created by him (Syuntyurenko, 2015)
- global industrial networks using artificial intelligence (AI) and the wide distribution of the Internet of things (Internet of things)
- introduction of services for automatic identification, collection and processing of global databases (big data)
- cloud services (cloud computing)
- smart devices and industrial facilities (smart everything)
- development of social networks and various platforms and services in the digital environment of the Internet

The search and use of new technologies is necessary not only to cover all areas of human activity, but also to substitute the traditional areas of its existence, and this is a more ambitious task – creating a new person who can not only adapt to the digital environment, but also function effectively.

Igor V. Bormotov, Maksim S. Zhuravlev, Natalia V. Ovchinnikova, Tula Branch of Financial University under the Government of the Russian Federation, Tula, Russia

https://doi.org/10.1515/9783110636147-010

Methodology

Consideration of the problem of human interaction and the digital environment suggests the rationale for the following methodological principles:

- comprehensive study of the relationships and relationships between the individual and the digital environment, involving the distinction between external and internal aspects of this relationship, the essence of which is manifested in the disclosure of form and content, chance and necessity
- self-development of human relations and the digital environment, which are aimed at finding out the source and internal logics of development between them
- a specific historical approach examines the formation and development of specific forms of relationships between a person and the digital environment
- consistency considers the interaction of man and the digital environment, which are subject to the general laws of existence and evolution of any system objects

It should be noted that in the modern scientific literature this problem has become widespread, it is sufficient to list the following works: Glazyev, S.Yu. The Great Digital Revolution: Challenges and Prospects for the Economy of the 21st Century, 2018 (Glazyev, 2018); Goikhman, O.Ya. Social reality in terms of virtuality // Theses of the first Belarusian philosophical congress (October 18–20, 2017). – Minsk: Belarusian Science, 2017 (Goykhman, 2017); Narykov, N.V., Dementiev S.A. Man in the Information Environment of A Modern Society: Ambivalence of the Nature and Essence of the Information Man // Philosophy of Law, 2017. No. 1 (Narykov, 2017); Digital transformation of the economy and industry: problems and prospects / ed. Dr. Econ. sciences, prof. A. V. Babkina. – SPb.: Polytechnic Publishing House. Un-ta, 2017 (Babkin, 2017); Digital society as a cultural and historical context of human development: a collection of scientific articles and materials of the international conference Digital society as a cultural and historical context of human development, February 14–17, 2018, Kolomna / by total. ed. R.V. Ershova. – Kolomna: State Social and Humanitarian University, 2018 (Ershova, 2018); Chernyshev, A.G. Strategy and philosophy of digitalization // Power, 2018. No. 5 (Chernyshev, 2018); Schmidt, E. New Digital World. How technologies change people's lives, business models and the concept of states / Eric Schmidt, Jared Cohen; per. from English Sergey Filin. – M.: Mann, Ivanov and Ferber, 2013 (Schmidt, 2013).

Results

Any object can act as a system if it satisfies the following requirements:
- The whole is divided into interconnected and interacting parts or elements.
- Parts or elements have their own structure.
- Elements are divided into interconnected subsystems of the second and subsequent levels.

With regard to the "human – digital environment" system, these requirements can be used to analyze each element of the system separately. For example, a person can be considered as a biological and social system, have gender, national, social, professional and other differences. The digital environment can also act as a standalone system, including various components that perform functions and represent holistic entities. Finally, an important condition for their study is a detailed analysis of the determinants of the external environment.

Features of the Influence of the Digital Environment on the Natural (Biological, Physical, Psycho-Physiological) and Social Organization of a Person

Under the influence of digital technologies, a change in the natural (biological, physical, psycho physiological) and social human identity is carried out. Consider the directions in which the digital environment affects human identities.

The first direction is characterized by the influence of the digital environment on the human body organization. It is as follows:
- modifying the body organization under the influence of digital technologies that create new artificial bodies (avatar, robot), "managed through a neuro interface; transfer of the human brain to avatars or technical devices in the brain. The digital environment is viewed on a biological basis (as, for example, in genetic engineering); the basis of a combination of organic and inorganic – technosymbiosis (cybernetic approach); inorganic basis" (Khmelevskaya, 2018). This leads to unlimited longevity of a person, because an artificial body can be replaced with more up to date modifications (why not to recall the works of science fiction writers: Belyaev AV, Professor Dowell's head. – Moscow: AST Publishing, 2016; Gibson, W. Neuromat – M.: LLC Publishing Group "Azbuka-Atticus", 2015, etc.).
- empowering digital technologies in restoring lost human functions, which allows creating and implanting various devices to resume normal operation of human organs. Among these technologies, there are: exoskeletons, autonomous life support systems of the brain, personality "transplantation" into other data carriers, creation of holographic organs, etc.

- the influence of digital technology on the physical activity of a person who spends most of his time sitting in front of a computer monitor, tablet or gadget. This way of life leads to occupational diseases: organs of vision (dry eye syndrome, etc.), spine (pain in the area of the back, forearm and pelvis).

Thus, the formation of the digital environment may in the future contribute to the satisfaction of human needs for the reorganization of the world and the person himself or lead to the destruction of the natural organization of the individual, replacing it with an avatar, a robot.

The second direction is associated with the peculiarities of the impact of the digital environment on the human psyche. Computers, tablets, mobile phones acquire the features of a "psychic organ" that has been imposed outside; without them, it is impossible to imagine not only the fulfillment of the communicative function, but human existence. Digital media have a negative impact on such psychological processes of a person as: memory, attention, thinking (Mayer-Schönberger and Kukier, 2014). The consequence of their influence are errors and distortions in the perception of information, the state of psychological tension and anxiety. As an example, the emergence of such a state as "network pessimism". It is expressed in the socio-psychological attitude of a person towards the unreliability and harmfulness of the received digital information. The digital environment can be rated by users as harmful, aggressive and negatively affecting the human psyche.

Another form of influence of the digital environment on a person is the formation of clip thinking, which is distinguished by the brightness and availability of the information received, reflected on glowing monitors. Its main purpose is to replace the fundamentals of modern knowledge with symbolic reality.

The digital environment creates the conditions for the virtualization of interpersonal contacts. This leads to the fact that live communication between people through verbal and non-verbal communications is gradually becoming a thing of the past, replaced by social networks, online games, webinars, dating sites, etc.

The third area examines the impact of the digital environment on a person's social identity. In the modern society, the very approach to the acquisition of identity changes. If earlier it was formed under the influence of local traditions and customs, now, it is done under the influence of digital technologies. This concept is filled with new content and acquires the ability to interact with a variety of sources, i.e. takes the global form of its expression.

The interrelation of the "figures" and social anthropology is manifested in the fact that "modern forms of human self-determination are such forms as the global network and autonomous person. On the one hand, there is a new habitat for modern humans – global networks. And, on the other hand, it is possible . . . in reality such a reality as the trajectory of atomic personalities. On the one hand, an atomic person . . . is only deterministic, on the other hand, a network that acts as an analog of a fundamentally open world" (Smirnov, 2019).

The proposed interrelation of the digital environment and a person helps to understand that modern social reality turns into a global web woven from various networks into which a person falls, regardless of whether he wants it or not.

The impact of the digital environment on a person's social identity can be done in the following areas:

- represents access to knowledge, ideas, thoughts and various cultural, scientific, and informational means of cognition of the surrounding world. Thanks to digital technology, a person gets access to any information in real time, that is, a paradox arises – he is everywhere and nowhere.
- unites people around websites, online games, webinars through distance, anonymity, lack of social contacts. These features are a prerequisite for being in a digital environment. The manifestation of social identity of a person in these conditions is possible only through the assimilation of the values and meanings of human existence as an active subject of the digital world.
- forms a digital workspace around a person, which contributes to the growth of labor productivity, professional development, successful user experience in the workplace. The content of the concept of "workplace" itself changes, such characteristics as design, comfort, convenient office furniture, good lighting of the room, and equipment with modern digital technologies become real.

Human in the Digital Environment: Problems of Creation, Implementation and Regulation

A modern human lives in the world created by him or the "noosphere" (Vernadsky, 1988), which represents the sphere of intelligent human activity. An important indicator of its development is the creation by man of a digital environment, which allows him to multiply his opportunities in economics, medicine, household appliances, creating electronics with minimal electricity consumption, 3D-modeling technologies and other areas. All this taken together imposes new requirements on the quality of human material, which at present and in the future will create, use, implement and manage the world of digital technologies.

Consider how a person affects the digital environment.

Having created the world of digital technology, a man released a "gin from a bottle", which can radically change his life. In the near future, he is likely to lose his influence over the digital environment, which will interact not with the person, but with his "digital counterpart". A person's professional and business activity also moves into the digital space, where it acquires the features of a virtual activity.

Let us put the question: "Is a modern person able to take control over his creation – the digital environment or not?"

As a response, we should note that throughout the evolution of the human race, Homo Sapiens created a huge number of technical machines and mechanisms of different complexity, but none of them could replace a human being, his creative, extraordinary thinking, the choice of values and his determination to achieve the goals. The creation of digital technologies is necessary for a person to solve economic, social and everyday problems of not only the present, but also the future existence.

The modern economy cannot develop effectively without the introduction of digital technologies. This is because extensive production has already reached its limits, beyond which no development is possible. Therefore, in order to meet its growing needs, a person is forced to create and implement digital technologies that expand his capabilities in influencing various spheres of society (Schwab, 2016).

We define the most promising areas for the introduction of digital technologies:

- automation
- workspace
- management
- economy
- business
- industry
- education
- telecommunications
- the medicine
- army

Thus, the introduction of digital technologies is carried out in various areas of the modern society. In the future, they can push an individual out of such a humanized sphere as life, for example, a self-parking car or a refrigerator ordering the food for a household. This is no longer a fantasy, but the near future of mankind.

A person regulates the digital environment in the social and economic activities of the society by means of moral and legal norms. The legal regulation of the economic sphere is that the regulatory and organizational conditions outline the boundaries for the use of digital technologies in such innovative areas of economic activity as: finance, high-tech production, information systems management, digital platforms, digital trading platforms, etc. Human influence on the economy through the use of digital technologies contributes to the simplification of production activities, commercial activities, trade and banking operations on each phase of economic relations.

The moral regulation of digital technologies is associated with the development of the concept of human rights and the determination of its status, which must be rethought based on a new understanding of human nature in the digital environment.

The difference between the legal and moral regulation of the digital environment in social and economic activities is that legal norms are fixed in codes, acts, laws and regulations, that is, they exist as written rules, and moral norms mostly live in the public consciousness, are supported, approved or rejected by public opinion or by the person himself. It should be noted that the process of adopting legal acts and ethical codes that would regulate the use of digital technologies in these areas is still forming.

Among the main determinants that affect the "man-digital environment" system, the following can be singled out:

- the improvement of the economic and technological spheres, where the "person – digital environment" system could function effectively
- the creation and development of a legal framework governing the interaction of man and the digital environment
- the formation of the social sphere of the modern society, contributing to the creation of such channels of social mobility, which made it possible to select the most talented and capable people to work with digital technologies
- the formation of the social sphere of modern society, contributing to the creation of such channels of social mobility, which made it possible to select the most talented and capable people to work with digital technologies
- the development of the education system with the aim of training and retraining of diverse specialists who not only created and developed new digital technologies, but also engaged in their implementation and regulation in various fields of activity

Conclusions/Recommendations

Thus, the consideration of the problem of human interaction and the digital environment is the priority for the modern humanitarian science. This is manifested in the fact that digital technologies "capture" all new spheres of human existence, replacing, simplifying one's life in solving economic and social problems. The place and the role of a person in this relationship is manifested in the fact that he acts as the creator of digital technologies that he introduces into various spheres of society and regulates their functioning by means of moral and legal norms.

All this taken together will contribute to the development and optimization of the "man-digital environment" system in the socio-economic paradigms of the future.

References

Babkin, A.V. (2017), *Cifrovaya transformaciya ekonomiki i promyshlennosti: problemy i perspektivy* [Digital transformation of the economy and industry: problems and prospects], SPb, Publishing House Polytechnic Universiteta (in Russian).

Chernyshev, A.G. (2018), "*Strategiya i filosofiya cifrovizacii*" [Strategy and philosophy of digitalization], Power, No. 5, pp. 13–21 (in Russian). OOO "Redaktsiya zhurnala «Vlast'»

Ershova, R.V. (2018), *Cifrovoe obshhestvo kak kul`turno-istoricheskij kontekst razvitiya cheloveka: sbornik nauchny`x statej i materialov mezhdunarodnoj konferencii "Cifrovoe obshhestvo kak kul`turno-istoricheskij kontekst razvitiya cheloveka"* [Digital society as a cultural and historical context of human development: a collection of scientific articles and materials of the international conference "Digital society as a cultural and historical context of human development"], Kolomna, Russia, 2018 (in Russian).

Glazyev, S. Yu. (2018), *Velikaya cifrovaya revolyuciya: vy`zovy` i perspektivy` dlya e`konomiki XXI veka* ["The Great Digital Revolution: Challenges and Perspectives for the Economy of the 21st Century"] available at: https://www.glazev.ru/articles/6-jekonomika/54923-velikaja-tsifrovaja-revoljutsija-vyzovy-i-perspektivy-dlja-jekonomiki-i-veka (Accessed 04.04.2018) (in Russian).

Goykhman, O. Ya. (2017), *Social`naya real`nost` v usloviyax virtual`nosti // Tezisy` pervogo belorusskogo filosofskogo kongressa* ["Social reality in terms of virtuality", Theses of the first Belarusian philosophical congress], Belorussia, 2017, Minsk: Belarusian science, p. 640–641 (in Russian).

Khmelevskaya, S.A. (2018) *Chelovek kak bio-socio-tekhnicheskoe sushchestvo: vliyanie novyh tekhnologij na prirodu cheloveka* ["Human being as a bio-socio-technical creature: the in pact of new technologies on the human nature"], Digital society as a cultural and historical context of human development: a collection of scientific articles, under total ed. R.V. Ershova, Kolomna: State social and humanitarian university, 2018, pp. 407–412 (in Russian).

Mayer-Schönberger, V., Kukier, K. (2014), *Bol'shie dannye. Revolyuciya, kotoraya izmenit to, kak my zhivem, rabotaem i myslim* [Big data. A revolution that will change the way we live, work and think], Moscow, Mann, Ivanov and Ferber (in Russian).

Narykov, N.V., Dementiev, S.A. (2017), *Chelovek v informacionnoj srede sovremennogo obshhestva: ambivalentnost` prirody` i sushhnosti informacionnogo cheloveka* ["Man in the Information Environment of Modern Society: Ambivalence of the Nature and Essence of the Information Man"], Philosophy of Law, No. 1, pp. 123–127 (in Russian).

Smirnov, S.A. (2000), *Chelovek perekhoda* ["The Human of the Transfer"] available at: http://www.antropolog.ru.doc/persons/smirnow/persons_2 (Accessed 22.04.2019)(in Russian).

Syuntyurenko, O.V. (2015), *Cifrovaya sreda: trendy` i riski razvitiya* ["Digital environment: trends and development risks"], STI Ser. 1. Organization and methods of information work, No. 2, pp. 1–7 (in Russian).

Schwab, K. (2016), *Chetvertaya promy`shlennaya revolyuciya* [The Fourth Industrial Revolution], Moscow, Eksmo (in Russian).

Schmidt, E. (2013), *Novyj cifrovoj mir. Kak tekhnologii menyayut zhizn' lyudej, modeli biznesa i ponyatie gosudarstv* [New Digital World. How technologies change people's lives, business models and the concept of states], Moscow, Mann, Ivanov and Ferber (in Russian).

Vernadsky, V.I. (1988), *Nauchnaya mysl' kak planetarnyj fenomen* [Scientific thought as a planetary phenomenon], Moscow, Science (in Russian).

Ludmila Karaseva, Alexey Zinatulin

11 New Creativity and Rationality Towards the Socio-Economic Paradigm of the Future

Introduction

On the Threshold of New Creativity

In creative activity as a function of person's self-realization many people of different levels of the social hierarchy interact. This complex structure is becoming global in the modern world. But it is especially important that the birth of new creativity transforms the multilevel connections and relations between the subjects of creative activity, as new ideas come into contact with a number of variables.

This refers to the transformation processes taking place in the economy and associated with creative activity, which is beginning to play an increasingly important role in economic practice. Within the economic system a new quality of socio-economic relations is emerging. This process requires methodological and theoretical justification. Methodologically every nascent must firstly be considered in itself to understand its nature, the necessary and sufficient conditions of its existence, its internal life mechanism. And then it becomes possible to understand how this new can be integrated into a particular economic system. After this there is an opportunity to model the mechanism of functioning and realization of innovative potential, stages of its formation (in case of immature relation) and its development (in case of the mature phenomenon (Karaseva, 2018).

In the understanding of creativity, we start from the definition of notion "creative" not only as a unique or innovative result, but also as a phenomenon caused by a special type of process flow. According to V. M. Bekhterev, creativity is the creation of new one in a situation "when the problem-stimulus causes the formation of a dominant around which the stock of past experience necessary for the solution is concentrated" (Bekhterev, 1926).

For the consideration of the named topic, it is of fundamental importance that the new attitude can be realized only by submitting to the dominant socio-economic relations, taking adequate organizational, institutional forms of its implementation.

Creative activity is a historical and future-oriented process in which planned mechanisms and stimulations always take place. These are natural and consciously formed needs and constraints (Petrishchev, 2018). Therefore, under the domination of corporate capital, the contact between creative and economic generates "economization" of

Ludmila Karaseva, Alexey Zinatulin, Tver State University, Tver, Russia

https://doi.org/10.1515/9783110636147-011

human relations in the course of formal and informal creative practices, economization of non-economic by their nature activities.

Wendy Brown, Professor at the University of California, talks about such deformations in modern economics and economic theory.

Rather, the point is that neoliberal rationality disseminates the model of the market to all domains and activities – even where money is not at issue – and configures human beings exhaustively as market actors, always, only, and everywhere as homo oeconomicus (Brown, 2015).

The problem of rationality is increasingly becoming the subject of research of philosophy and social sciences, including economic theory (Agafonova, 2008). The content of the term "rational" is a subject of another revision, which is explained by the original historical and socio-cultural conditionality of this multifaceted concept. Since in modern society, economy and culture there are global technological, socio-economic and value changes, it appears that there is a need to clarify the concept of rationality (and as antitheses – of the concept of "irrationality").

In economic theory, rationality is traditionally correlated with activity, with the actions of an economic agent. Neoclassical interpretation of action is the behavior optimization. Then the economic-theoretical content of the notion of *rational* is the ratio of purpose and means. It is the search of the best option of their combination, with the emphasis shifted to the "target" characteristic. For example, in the design rational will be considered as to obtain a unique result as an outcome of the coordination of many complex processes and activities in the condition of limited time, resources and budget. The expert assessment of the strategy of territorial development of the Russian Federation, expressed by Vladimir Kvint, head of the Center for strategic studies of Moscow state University, is indicative in this sense.

In the development of any strategy, especially at the national and regional level, three important postulates should be taken into account: any strategy can offer to implement only priorities that reflect national and regional interests, and they must be fully provided with all types of labor, material, financial and infrastructure resources . . . (Kvint, 2019).

The subject aspect of research of the economic relations is actualized. This aspect assumes their implementation only through socio-economic activity of economic subjects. As a result, the functioning complex system and its rationality are under consideration.

Then we should recognize as productive an idea of "system rationality", expressed by the German sociologist Niklas Luhmann. His concept of complexity and rationality is based on the need to embed a functioning system into the external environment. This actualizes the analysis of it as a functional one. System rationality is understood here as the ability of a system to be sensitive to the world around it, "to experience disturbances and at the same time to have countermeasures or programs to handle them ready" (Luhmann, 2002).

The paradox of the problem in this context is that worked out solutions can act only within the framework of this system, but not the whole world around it. Methodologically, this means the need of a consistent inclusion of the system in the surrounding world and the opposite action that is turning it off from the environment. Then irrational actions at the system level from the position of the outside world can be quite rational. Through the evolution, this will lead to *"the existence of forms that function better and perhaps even better formalized in plans and projects than other forms"* (Luhmann, 2002).

The settlement of this paradox allows us to search for rational solutions of problems that affect different spheres of human activity, i.e. obtaining that unique creative result that we talked about at the beginning. In this case, the rationality of action can be considered on different criteria: economic, financial, commercial, value, etc.

In practice, the aspect approach leads to the activation and strengthening of a kind of "technocratism" in the socio-economic processes management. It is becoming popular the myth that legal, financial, economic and similar expertise is a panacea for all ills, that they can replace the scrupulous study of the sociality mechanisms, including in creative processes. Such ideas are especially dangerous in regard to creativity, which is non-standard, destructive (in terms of established norms) by its nature. This leads us to the idea that it is fundamentally important which criterion of rationality becomes the system-forming, subordinating the complex of other parameters.

In general, the problem of institutionalization of economic interests in the transformation of the economic system on the basis of creative breakthroughs is impossible without the study of socialization of motives of economic entities as the formation of their social form of existence (of certain economic interests). It is necessary to study the structure of the existing interests, its dynamics in order to offer an adequate mechanism of their institutionalization for the formation of motivational orientation of economic entities to certain transformations.

The Method of Structural Levels: Rising to the Implementation

The common methodological basis of the identified problems is the inclusion in the analysis of the study of the implementation mechanism of socio-economic relations. On this basis, it becomes possible to understand the nature and existence of new economic phenomena: subordination of relations between planning and the market, the process of creativity economization, the implementation of economic life digitalization, the introduction of cryptocurrencies.

Under the mechanism of implementation of socio-economic relations, we understand subordinated mediation (Figure 11.1) – in the course of the deep-level relations implementation – organizational and economic, institutional relations and their output to the surface of the actual economic level (transformation into subjective relations).

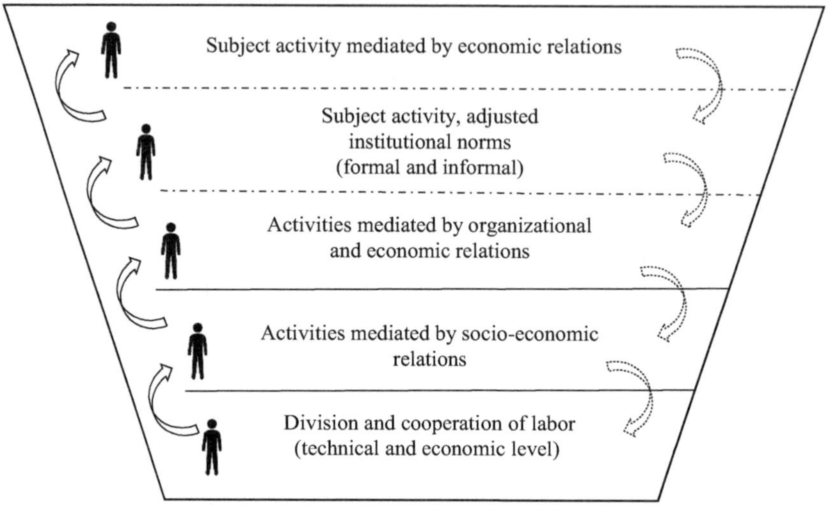

Figure 11.1: Mediation of creative activity in the subject section of the economic system.

It is important to stress out that these levels keep special "floors" of inclusion of other interests in the implementation of the creative process in the economy. The movement also has the opposite direction – economic entities through decision-making and their implementation in interaction affect the basic economic relations (the transition of the subjective into the objective).

This gives us the opportunity to trace theoretically the modification (deformation) of the economic entities relations in the transition from one level to another – "bottom-up" and purification, the movement to the essence – "top-down".

The key research problem is to answer the question how the objective becomes subjective and the subjective becomes objective, influencing and changing the socio-economic essence of the economic system (Karaseva, 2018).

Why is this approach important? Underestimation of the influence of subjective activity of economic entities, their subjective perception of the world, their motivational focus on deep processes, clarifying, developing social (including socio-economic) genomes leads to a simplified understanding of the mechanisms of creativity in the technological and socio-economic development of the modern world. Let us clarify that in sociology the social genome is understood as the main hypothetical particle of culture (cult, instruction, idea), which, like any gene in biology, is a unit of information transmitted to other generations (Teregulov, 2016).

The history of development of different economic systems shows us that breakthroughs in the productive forces were carried out. But, firstly, they often *didn't lead to the corresponding civilizational (in the broad sense of the word) development of the economic system. And, secondly, they were realized through the mechanism of "violence" in the literal and figurative sense of the word (depending on the instrument of violence).*

This is very important for modern Russia with its diversity, unequal distribution and development of productive forces, inhibition of socio-economic and social processes.

For example, taking into account the development of information technology, we can talk about the "new middle ages", where "digital feudalism" is dominating. Or we can discuss how in Russian culture, education and health care institutions the transformation of creative activity into appropriate services leads to their self-destruction and deformation of the vital infrastructure.

New Creativity: A Grain Metaphor

There is an experience of creative activity research in the Russian economic literature. It is enough to refer to the materials of A. V. Buzgalin and of his co-author on many works A. I. Kolganov. Let's stop on one work of Professor Buzgalin "Human or human capital?".

" . . . In the economy of the twenty-first century, Human increasingly acts as (1) a subject of creative activity, which at the same time (2) is integrally subordinated to the total market and capital, and therefore (3) acquires the visible form of 'human' capital" (Buzgalin, 2011).

But it is impossible to understand the mechanism of this subordination without developing the specific socio-economic nature of modern corporate capital through the mechanism of its implementation. Supporting the author opinion, we pay attention to two circumstances. Firstly, this process goes through the economization of the subject of creative activity at different levels of corporate capital functioning. And, secondly, the measure of the integrity of human subordination to corporate capital depends on the degree of capital maturity. It can take the form of feudalization and even slave relations. But in this case, the product of creative activity as a result of the order taken from the capital and its economization, alienating from its creators, can take a rational form of its existence for capital, but irrational – from the point of view of the society interests.

When and under what kind of conditions does the "concentration" of creative activity in the economic system occur? Why does the tension of the entrepreneurial field in the economy increase? How does creativity become an important element of the mechanism of economic development?

Since this multilevel process is organic by its nature, then for this model of new creativity we use the metaphor of grain and its structural elements – embryo, nutrient tissue and shell (Figure 11.2). Accordingly, creative ideas, their internal resource environment and institutional shell appear.

The source of the *new* can arise at different levels of economic relations implementation, depending on the degree of development of the economic system as a

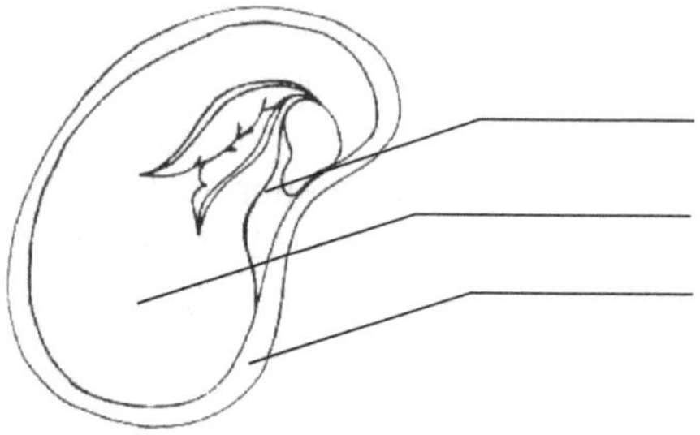

Figure 11.2: The structure of the grain of creativity.

whole and where the social order for non-standard solutions is formed. The economy creates prerequisites for the birth of new ideas necessary for it:
- *speculative* – as a reaction to the possibility of using "net market entrepreneurial opportunities"
- *product* – as a response to the dynamic growth of demand for new goods and services
- *technical and technological* – as a reaction to the possibility of mass introduction of technical and technological innovations in the system of social production
- *combinatorial* – as a reaction to the possibility of increasing production efficiency through innovative combination of production factors
- *managerial* – as a response to the fundamental challenges of the external environment at the organizational and economic, institutional levels
- *adaptational* – as a spontaneous reaction to optimize directly the economic conditions of activity

The accumulation of resource potential (*nutrient internal environment*) leads to the possibility of implementing of different types of innovative ideas that can change the management system as a whole: speculative and product for the traditional economy, technical and technological and combinatorial for the industrial economy; managerial and adaptational for the information economy.

Institutional shell necessarily performs a membrane function – on the one hand, formalizing the idea till its potential implementation, on the other hand – creating a protective and adaptive mechanism for the external implementation environment.

The study of the grain of new creativity takes into account the functional structure, the main part of which is associated with the mechanism of functioning within itself, and the other part – productive (as a result of implementation, as an activity implementation of this relationship) – characterizes the purpose of the system as a whole, interacting with the external environment. Then rationality can be interpreted in relation to the relation – as the adequacy of the forms of economic relations of their original form (grain). And if mediation does not correspond to the original form, there is an irrational form of existence of a creative product that takes an imaginary, deformed character.

Conclusions

The complexity of the modern Russian economy is that the institutional, organizational forms and norms imposed on it in the 1990s, taken from developed economies, could not work within the framework of the historically developed economic system. They were alien to it, giving rise to *an even greater deformation of economic relations*. At the same time, the concentration in the hands of the ruling elite of the bulk of resources and power does not give the opportunity to form institutionally to the other economic interests for their implementation, deepening institutional alienation, including representatives of creative labor.

In Russia, progress is possible only in the state of achieving the necessary depth of understanding of this movement goals, making changes for the sake of human and society development. This is the Russian genetic code.

References

Agafonova, E.V. Kontsept ogranichennoy ratsional'nosti v ekonomike i sotsial'noy filosofii [The concept of bounded rationality in economics and social philosophy]. Tomsk State University Bulletin. Philosophy. Sociology. Political science. 2008, no.3(4), pp. 21–27 (in Russian).

Bekhterev V.M. Obshchiye osnovy refleksologii cheloveka [General principles of human reflexology]. Leningrad: Gos. izd-vo, 1926 (in Russian).

Brown W. (2015), Undoing the Demos. Neoliberalism Stealth Revolution. New York: Zone Books, 2015. P. 17–45.

Buzgalin A.V. Chelovek ili "chelovecheskiy kapital" // Chelovek i ekonomika: spravedlivost' i bazisnaya demokratiya protiv totalitarizma rynka i kapitala [Man or "human capital" // Man and the economy: justice and basic democracy against totalitarianism of the market and capital]. Moscow: Ekonomika, 2011, 556 p (in Russian).

Karasëva L.A. Put' k integratsionnomu znaniyu: k voprosu o praktichnosti metodologii marksizma [The path to integration knowledge: the question of the practicality of the Marxist methodology]. Questions of political economy, 2018, Vol. 4, No. 4, p. 29–35 (in Russian).

Kvint V., Trushin A. Territoriya polupritsepov. Nuzhna li Rossii strategiya prostranstvennogo razvitiya? [The territory of semi-trailers. Does Russia need a spatial development strategy?] "Ogonok", No 10 of March 18, 2019, p. 8. (in Russ.).

Luhmann, N. (2002) Einführung in die Systemtheorie, Carl-Auer-Systeme Verlag, Heidelberg.

Petrishchev V.A. O neobkhodimosti uglubleniya soderzhaniya politicheskoy ekonomii [On the need to deepen the content of political economy]. Bulletin of Tver State University, A series of "Economics and Management", 2018, No. 4, p. 220–222 (in Russian).
Territoriya polupritsepov. Nuzhna li Rossii strategiya prostranstvennogo razvitiya? [The territory of semi-trailers. Does Russia need a spatial development strategy?] "Ogonok", No. 10 of March 18, 2019, p. 8 (in Russian).
Teregulov F.S. Ob obshchestvennom nasledovanii ili sotsial'nyy genom [About social heritage and social genome]. Historical and social-educational ideas, 2016, 8(2/1),pp. 114–123 (in Russian).

Dmitry P. Sokolov, Igor V. Astaf'ev

12 Social and Economic Reality: Digital Alienation

Introduction

The modern scientific community often discusses the so-called digitalization from the technical and economic standpoints: the application of technology in various sectors, changes in the markets or public administration due to the development of innovative goods. The core of the production relations is not the technical-economic (or organizational-economic) relations, but the socio-economic ones based on property as the dialectical unity of appropriation and alienation of production means, the labor results and labor force in the process of social reproduction (Al'pidovskaya and Sokolov, 2015). In the context of intensive development of new information technologies associated with bio-, nano- and cognitive ones and transformation of socio-economic situation owing to their introduction, it seems urgent to understand how social and economic relations transform, how a man changes and respectively his attitude to labor, nature, himself, and how these changes relate to the category of progress as commitment of human and mankind to a better, higher, more perfect development. A typical feature of the capitalist mode of production is the reproduction of alienation relations in the course of ensuring a high rate of return on invested capital. The research of the transformation hereof under the development of new digital technologies makes it possible to precondition the progress or regress of the fourth industrial revolution within the framework of the development of people and society.

Methodology

The category of alienation in the social sciences was introduced in the Modern Times by the adherents of the social contract theory T. Hobbes, J.-J. Rousseau, and J. Locke. This phenomenon was more directly investigated by disciples of German classical philosophy I. Fichte, G. Hegel, and L. Feuerbach. K. Marx was the first economic theorist who associated the issue of alienation with the reproduction and investigated the cause-and-effect relation between private ownership of production means and alienation.

Dmitry P. Sokolov, Financial University under the Government of the Russian Federation, Moscow, Russia
Igor V. Astaf'ev, Civil Society Development Fund, Kostroma, Russia

https://doi.org/10.1515/9783110636147-012

Karl Marx wrote in the Economic and Philosophical Manuscripts of 1844: "The devaluation of the human world grows directly with the value of the world of things. Labor produces not only goods: it reproduces itself and worker as a commodity . . ." (Marx, 2011).

According to Marx opinion, the general logic of alienation is the following: private property as the foundation of the capitalist system is based on the social nature of the production of goods under the private appropriation, which entails human alienation from the result of labor. Therewith, the production of a commodity that belongs no to the proprietor is alienation from the labor, which generates all other types. A human unable to fulfill himself in purely external labor is alienated from his essence and loses the self-identity. As a result, a human becomes alienated from society and nature, treating another human as a means but not as a purpose and acting against I. Kant's categorical imperative, i.e. reproducing exclusively commodity relations in the system of social ones. Erich Fromm wrote that the person can overcome alienation by means of free creative activity fulfilled through work and love (Fromm, 2011), which is prevented by the capitalist determinant of private profit maximization. The issue related to overcoming the alienation, dehumanization, and subordination to the machine for more than one decade has been acute in the social sciences. Today it is urgent due to intertwining nature hereof with our being.

Erich Fromm in the essay "Man Is Alone" emphasizes that alienation penetrates both production and consumption. "Our consumption is first and foremost the satisfaction of artificially created fancies detached from the true, real identity" (Fromm, 1966), which have researchers to think about the issue of virtualization of socio-economic relations caused by the development of digital technologies, in particular, augmented reality and consciousness control.

Results

The alienation and commodification in the conditions of modern scientific and technological development generate the virtualization of reality: a human alienated from work, himself, society and nature find the illusion of appropriating the alienated things in the virtual space, which occurs at purely personal levels or in groups and communities. The area of production met the development of alienation by establishing a market for simulacra. i.e. special goods with properties simulating true utility. The production of simulacra allows pushing the limits of capital accumulation in the real sector of the economy (Buzgalin, Kolganov and Barashkova, 2018) within tendency of the global return rate to zero in accordance with the economic law of the tendency of the return rate to fall statistically proved by Argentine economist Esteban E. Maito (Maito, 2014).

One of the researchers of the issue related to simulacra Jean Baudrillard argued that all modern socio-cultural phenomena have a simulation nature (Baudrillard,

2015). Then there is a question: is it possible a wide distribution of simulations in the appropriating society? Of course, in this context, it is not a society of gathering and hunting, but a hypothetical society without contradiction between appropriation and alienation, without exploitation; and step-by-step appropriation at the personal, collective and public level of the economic system. It is suggested that the simulation is detachment from reality, the next stage of alienation rise common to the mode of capital-based production.

The emergence of simulacra, i.e. signs of what doesn't really exist, is possible only in a society of alienation. However, one should not forget that in this system also there is subject of appropriation, which is inalienable from the actual reality and is an integral part of the dominant carrier of economic interests despite involvement in the virtual reality. Besides, the implementation of his economic interests is connected with the production and appropriation of the real manufactured product. And taking into account the dual nature of human being, it is appropriate to refer to Yuri Mikhailovich Osipov, a famous philosopher of household who distinguishes the household and the economy. Yuri Mikhailovich stresses that the economy has always been digital, that value and establishment of prices exist only in the people's mind (Osipov, 2017) and it means that the virtual image of the household has emerged at this level.

Thus, the term "digital" is construed in two dimensions. On the one hand, the digit is the basis of modern electronic data processing machines and corresponding technologies that drastically transform technical- and socio-economic relations of human. On the other hand, a digit as "it is" is a symbol and a sign, the main element in determining the efficiency and effectiveness of the human (and not only) activity. Although these aspects seem different, they mean the same, i.e. the creation of a virtual image of production, thinking, communication, and human labor. Based on the economic system, these images detach form its content but become factors of distribution relations.

In various analytical materials, statistical books or development programs we see the prevalence of value indicators over physical ones and at the same time the gap between the latter and real processes described by them. One of the most important objectives of the major actors of property relations is the development and introduction of such a coordinate system that ensure the complete fulfillment of economic interests, for example, the increasing growth rates of the economy attract investors even to risk-bearing sectors. Investments converted into physical and intellectual capital enter the economy due to annual GDP growth, a "digital" indicator that exists in people's minds and acting for double counting of revenue arising in the services sector of the so-called developed countries.

Therefore, arises a central problem related to goal setting. What system of needs constituted in economic interests is satisfied through the introduction of digital technologies? There can be only one answer to this question: the capital fulfills its own interests that recover the decline in the rate of return. As a result, the concept of a post-industrial society turned out to be future-oriented ideas in the style of

Owen and Fourier. Today, the mode of production doesn't change even under the apparent growing role of human and science capacity.

In the event of capital maintenance as a fundamental relationship, the modern geo-economic system, however, undergoes structural transformations. In particular, the Russian economist Mikhail Delyagin notes that the current trade opposition between the US and China evidences the trend of regionalization of the once global economic space (Delyagin, 2019). The collapse of the international economy into macroregions implies a contraction of the division of labor and a further drop of the return rate, which becomes a prerequisite for the intensification of alienation relations, including the deepening of the virtualization of the consumption.

As the Russian historian and researcher A.I. Fursov, the backbone of capitalism as a special historical system are the nation-state and the middle class with its economic and social forms (Fursov, 2014). Thomas Piketty points to a steady trend of wealth redistribution from the middle and upper middle class to the very rich (Piketty, 2015), which is a sign of ongoing removal of the middle class. Digital technologies make it possible to establish a system of relatively even distribution (with possible internal hierarchization – by analogy with the ideas of the Chinese social trust system) through the combination of real and simulated quality characteristics of consumer goods while maintaining and escalating social inequality between owners of key resources of the 21st century and the majority of the population.

The universalization of the production of consumer goods with their purely external customization allow providing the entire population with benefits of relatively low quality mitigated by the simulation component of their content and satisfaction of imposed needs and also intangible benefits and digital services in education, healthcare, art, literature, music and so forth. Besides, elite consumption remains analog and affordable for society due to enormously high value and even closeness.

The reverse effect of the ongoing transformation of the geo-economic system is a tendency to transition to the intensive exploitation of actors previously involved in capitalist relations. The combination of digital technologies, including big data, blockchain, and self-learning neural networks, promotes the unification of the majority of manufacturers and the population in big data arrays managed by both major TNC and national states. The preservation of capitalist relations as the dominant of the reproduction system subordinates the application of new technologies to the interests of profit maximization, including the household for which the logic of capital does not have a physical foundation, for intellectual property relations in particular.

As the digital economy develops, the area of information production both directly related to the production of real benefits and not related hereto becomes isolated. Information as a special object of appropriation and alienation allows for the multiple utilization without loss of utility, except for that consisting in owner's rental income. Private ownership of information does not arise from the intrinsic properties of information in contrast to limited tangible benefits and customized services but from simple extrapolation of ownership relations to the physical means of production to items of human intellectual and creative labor through the development of an artificial legal system on their restricted use. Such a feature of information the importance hereof in the productive forces of society is soaring can be interpreted as inconsistency between the productive forces and production relations, the dialectics hereof according to Marx' words forms the logic of social development. However, for barriers to the dissemination of information to be removed we have to drastically change the relations of intellectual rent distribution of (Al'pidovskaya, Gryaznova, and Sokolov, 2018).

Capital and society have both different economic interests and different basis for assessment of implementation thereof. In particular, the source of the expanded reproduction of capital in present conditions is both the real and the simulation components of the economy, whereas for society it's only the real economy but the simulation one acts as an imposed, on the one hand, and as a recovery of different levels of alienation, on the other hand. In this regard, there is the problem of assessing the effectiveness of the national economy due to the previously mentioned virtualization of performances. In the development of state programs and public assessment of their effectiveness, it is necessary to give a priority not to value categories, but to physical indicators showing changes in real, rather than simulated reproduction processes.

A bright example is the interpretation of the economic category of labor productivity in Russian legislation and national projects purely as a value indicator of the ratio between the added value of an enterprise (sector) to the monthly average number of employees within the enterprise (Decree, 2018). Thus, the economic content of labor productivity as the number of products manufactured by an employee per unit of time is blurred. Thus, the indicator of human activity becomes dependent not on the intellectual and physical abilities of a person, skills, the quality of labor management at the enterprise and factor endowment, but on the market value of the output, which often does not convey the real contribution of labor and capital to production.

Modern human finds himself in a digital trap: the pursuit of growth of digital indicators leads to alienation from creative labor and reproduction of performances solely for reproduction of performances (converted into an augmentation of cash flows of capital owners or rent recipients). It can be a focus on the number of publications to the detriment of their content, funding of rural schools without achievement of results, GDP growth gross with disregard of life quality of the country's population.

Conclusions

What is the recipe for appropriation? Surely, the process reverse to alienation is not possible in the conditions of the dominance of capitalist private property. It's more likely that a human will be alienated to such an extent that he will no longer be a source of profit for capital. Therefore, the capital will lose the foundation and will regenerate into a different social system. But now every human has the opportunity to acknowledge the current multi-level alienation and combat it. In the conditions of growing economic reductionism, an important role here is given directly to economic science. Eventually, the true purpose of the economic system is the fulfillment of the human need for free creative activity.

References

Al'pidovskaya M.L., Gryaznova A.G., Sokolov D.P. (2018) Regress Economy vs Progress Economy: Alternatives of Senses//Advances in Intelligent Systems and Computing, V. 622. pp. 638–646.

Al'pidovskaya M.L., Sokolov D.P. (2015) Property Relations in Modern Russia: Genesis, Problems and Prospects. Kostroma: KSU named after N.A. Nekrasov.

Baudrillard J. (2015) Simulacra and Simulation. M.: Ripol-classic.

Buzgalin A.V., Kolganov A.I., Barashkova O.V. (2018) Classical Political Economy: The Modern Marxist Direction. Basic Level. Advanced level. M.: Lenand.

Decree of the Ministry of Economic Development of Russia No. 748 as of December 28, 2018 "On Approval of the Methodology for Calculation of Labor Performances in Enterprise, Sector, Constituent Entity of the Russian Federation and Methodology for Calculation of Particular Indicators of the National Project "Labor Productivity and Employment".

Delyagin M.G. (2019) China will reprise with a yuan zone//Izborsk Club. URL: https://izborsk-club.ru/16994 (Accessed 03.05.2019).

Fromm E. (1966) Man is Alone // Foreign Literature, No.1. pp. 230–233.

Fromm E. (2011) Escape from Freedom Moscow: AST: Astrel'.

Fursov A.I. (2014) Farewell of Capitalism // Forecast World 2014. URL: https://www.mirprognozov.ru/prognosis/economics/proschalnyiy-poklon-kapitalizma-andrey-fursov/ (Accessed 03.05.2019)

Maito E. (2014) El capitalismo y su tendencia al derrumbe. En Defensa del Marxismo, No. 48. pp. 125–172.

Marx K. (2011) Capital: Criticism of Political Economy. V.1: [translated from German, French, English] M.: Eksmo.

Osipov Yu.M. (2017) New Economic Reality: Ontos and Gnosis (Philosophical Reminiscences) // Economic Strategies, No. 4. p. 110–121.

Piketty T. (2015) Capital in the 21st Century. Moscow: Ad Marginhem Press.

Lyudmila A. Murav'eva

13 The Role of Scientific and Technical Progress in the Formation of Industrial Society and Prospects for the Development of Modern Russian Economy

Introduction

The core of the modern post-industrial society is the transformation and processing of technological information and communication. Information technologies for the development of the modern world are the main source of improvement and progress. For the birth of an industrial society, such a source came from new types of energy, from steam and electricity to the emancipation of atomic energy. All the revolutionary technical changes taking place in society were based on scientific research and accumulated knowledge. (Tebekin A.V. On the Methodology of Analysis and Evaluation of Innovation Activity. // Economy. Entrepreneurship. Environment. M.: 2006. Vol. 4. No. 28. p. 25–33).

Methodology

History and Dynamics of Scientific Revolutions

The first scientific and technological revolution is dates from the end of the 18th and early 19th centuries. Its advance is impossible without previously made scientific discoveries. These include the doctrine of the heliocentric system of the world of N. Copernicus, which led to the conclusion that the universe is as infinite as the number of worlds that make it up. The most important discovery of modern times was the creation of classical mechanics based on experiment. G. Galileo's research on the principles of inertia and free fall of bodies, developed in the works of I. Kepler and R. Descartes on the laws of motion of the planets, lead I. Newton to the justification of the mechanical picture of the world and the discovery of the law of the universal gravitation. An important step was the development of natural science. I. Kant, P. S. Laplace, J. B. Lamarck, C. R. Darwin made an outstanding contribution to this

Lyudmila A. Murav'eva, Financial University under the Government of the Russian Federation, Moscow, Russia

https://doi.org/10.1515/9783110636147-013

field of scientific knowledge. Revolutionary discoveries in the field of science have added new breakthrough technologies that contribute to the improvement of weaving and spinning machines that sharply increased the productivity of weavers and spinners, and the invention of the steam engine, the main fuel for which was coal. Advanced positions in the use of new technologies were taken by England, which needed a large amount of metal to equip the army that used to lead constant wars. England begins to use coke instead of charcoal in metallurgical production.

In Russia, the extraction of coal began in the late 17th century. However, the production scale of this process was at the beginning of the 18th century. The large-scale transformations of Peter I, and above all, the creation of a regular land army and navy for offensive foreign policy and the development of trade relations, demanded an increase in the production of iron and cast iron. The development of a map of coal-mining areas begins and new deposits are opened. In the next two years, the country will celebrate the 300th anniversary of the opening of the Kuznetsk coal basin, which occurred in 1721. Over time, Russia has become the largest coal-producing country in the world. Coal mining in 1900 was 16, and in the middle of the 20th century 160 million tons per year, producing more than 18 million tons of steel. (Konovalov A. Industrial Heart of Siberia. // Literary Gazette. February 27 – March 5, 2019. No. 4 (6680). p. 29.)

The discovery and use of steam as a new type of energy was the innovation that provided an industrial revolution and gave noticeable dynamism to the development of world civilizations. The invention of the steam engine constituted the core of the first industrial process, which gave an acceleration to the development of production and the emergence of new types of transport.

In Russia, the first railroad appeared in the mid-1930s. of 19th century and at the end of the century the construction of the longest railway Trans-Siberian Railway has begun. The new railway connected the center of Russia with the Far East, which had not only transport and economic, but also military-strategic importance. The new Siberian route provided access to the Pacific Ocean and contributed to an increase in the population of Siberia and the Far East by 3.7 million people, the emergence of 10 cities and 18 villages, the development of the Kuznetsk coal basin and changed the scheme for the settlement of territories. Paris journalists declared the construction of the Trans-Siberian Railway the most outstanding event since the discovery of America. The organizers of the Paris World Exhibition in 1900 awarded the Grand Prix to the Siberian Railway Committee and the Ministry of Railways of Russia. (Korelin A.P., Stepanov S.A. Vitte S. Yu. – financier, politician, diplomat. M. TERRA – Book Club. 1996. – P.112–113.)

The second industrial revolution, which began about 100 years after the first, was based on the introduction of new electrical energy, the invention of an internal combustion engine and the creation of the chemical industry. If the first industrial revolution occurred in the UK, the second received a boost in the United States and

Germany. Electricity as the central force of the second scientific and technological revolution has changed transport, communications, factory production and life.

Finally, the third scientific and technical revolution of the second half of the 20th century based on the fundamental discoveries of nuclear physics and quantum mechanics, cybernetics, microbiology, chemistry of polymers and a high organizational and technical level of production.

Economists, government and party leaders of the USSR wrote and spoke of the need to combine the achievements of the scientific and technological revolution with production and the real economy in the 70s. of the 20th century. Such a breakthrough in science and technology was the construction of the Baikal-Amur Mainline. This year marks the 30th anniversary of the completion of the last great construction of socialism. 200 thousand builders of various specialties worked on the construction of BAM. This building has become truly national. It stretched for 3,819 km to the most remote and undeveloped corners of Eastern Siberia and the Far East. Foreign newspapers wrote about this construction site with enthusiasm. The true scale and significance of this grand and legendary construction in the economic sovereignty of our country has become particularly vividly understood and appreciated now. (Zamostyanov A. Necessity of BAM. // Literary Gazette. February 20–26, 2019. No. 7 (6679). P. 28; It Is. The Project of the Century. // Literary Gazette. February 27 – March 5, 2019. No. 4 (6680). S. 28.)

However, energy development had its costs. This circumstance prompted the intensive development of information technology.

Results: The Main Directions of Development of Modern Research and Production Activities of Russia

Modern technological innovations are not carried out in isolation. They are the result of a close interaction of various achievements based on clusters, which increases returns and provides a breakthrough based on the existing level of knowledge. These include the institutional and industrial environment, the presence of an innovative elite capable of posing and solving technological problems, a highly skilled workforce, able to introduce innovations into practice, an economic mentality that makes the invention profitable and a network of producers and users, whose interaction in exchange of experience in using and creating gives a cumulative effect.

Currently, a number of global industrialists and economists have started talking about the beginning of the fourth industrial revolution, which is also called "Industry 4.0". In their opinion, the new stage of development will be caused by the integration of information technologies, the so-called cyber-physical systems or CPS, into production processes. The world community talked about end-to-end digital processes based on a digital model of production and management. In the manufacturing sector, flexible interaction of all segments is provided based on the process of transforming global value chains and developing the technology of smart plants. Some productions still partially apply the technologies of the new generation and at the same time actively develop the cases of the new business model. Such programs are being developed and are beginning to be introduced into production practice in Germany, the USA, France, and the UK. In Russia, the foundations of this concept are reflected in the "Digital Economy of the Russian Federation" program, approved by a government decree in July 2017. The program document contains the main directions of development and state support for the introduction of digital technologies in the production and economic sphere. The main message of this program is "to increase the competitiveness in the global market of both individual sectors of the economy of the Russian Federation and the economy as a whole". (Program "Digital Economy of the Russian Federation". M.: 2017. – p.2) The combination of achieving competitiveness with management efficiency requires the development of a new theoretical substantiation and updating of the methodological apparatus and assessment and management methodology for implementation and practical use.

The basis of the modern concept is the philosophy of the "Internet of things", the essence of which is the ability of objects to independently collect data and exchange information without human intervention. For example, a car equipped with modernist technology will be able to collect information about the technical condition of assemblies and parts and inform the supplier about repairs and replacements. Since the technology of "smart parts" and "smart houses" has been introduced since 1999, the next step will be the emergence of a new generation of systems, as well as strategies and technologies aimed at optimizing labor and reducing costs. One of such business strategies is called a complex of technological solutions for product lifecycle management, also known as continuous information support for deliveries and product lifecycle. It systematizes and analyzes production processes from demand assessment to disposal. Its introduction now reduces the production time of the product by 1.5 times and leads to a reduction in costs by 50–80%. To further improve performance, continuous improvement of the Program at the state and sectoral levels, development of new pricing mechanisms, development of the regulatory framework, development of training programs for specialists, and diversity of technical support are required.

In the 1960s. of the 20th century the first business incubators and accelerators began to appear in the world. They became widespread at the beginning of the zero years. The average age of such formations in Russia is 7 years. Their main task is to implement innovative projects, monetize scientific developments, and support companies in the early stages of development. At present, a national technology initiative (NTI) program is being implemented in Russia, through which it is necessary to identify priority technologies for the industry of the future. Various tools have been developed, including the Generation 5 competition. In order to minimize the risks of modernist projects, they resort to applying the principles of venture financing. Create a special corporate venture fund to invest in high-risk projects. Such portfolio returns help to reduce the payments for failures through successful projects. Thus, venture capital funds allow conducting experiments without financial and organizational disruption, conduct business intelligence, which accelerates research in priority areas of knowledge, such as, for example, artificial intelligence. The scheme of the venture fund is built so that the money is not allocated immediately, but for a specific transaction. Technology companies participate in the fund as experts and partners, which allows creating test benches, testing and certifying start-up products on their sites. Such a combination of competences makes it possible to obtain high effect for small technology companies, whose philosophy of activity and management differs significantly from the large ones. With the described structure, management, responsibility for the result, participation in capital and profits are carried out simultaneously. A wide range of responsibilities, including financial responsibility, requires a serious attitude to the selection of qualified partners. Corporate accelerators can achieve the desired result in the search and selection of modern technological solutions in a short time and for reasonable money. (Collection of reports of the third conference "The economic potential of industry in the service of the military-industrial complex". M.: Financial University under the Government of the Russian Federation. 2017. – P.14.15.)

In recent years, the first analysis of the activities of business incubators and accelerators was carried out in Russia. According to the Russian Venture Company (RVC), "the study involved 59 university and 13 independent incubators. The analysis showed that Russian accelerators and incubators achieved great success in a short period of time and became an indispensable element of the ecosystem. They helped to create an average of 309 jobs in startups over the past five years". Despite the limited access to funds (4 times less than in European countries), on average up to 180 applications are made annually, which exceeds European figures by 18%. The results also showed that universities are beginning to play an increasing role in the socio-economic life of the region. Incubators and accelerators provide an environment for the creation, development and growth of companies. This work is especially active in Novosibirsk, Tomsk, Kazan, St. Petersburg and Moscow. (Strategy. 12.2016-01-2017. No. 4 (25). – P.60,61,62)

Conclusions/Recommendations

For further modernization, it is necessary to create an effective digital production strategy. This strategy also constitutes an important link in the fourth industrial revolution.

Digital technology is an integrated computer system that includes numerical modeling, three-dimensional visualization and engineering analysis. Vladimir Putin, President of the Russian Federation, speaks about the transition to a new economy:

"The digital economy is not a separate industry, but the basis for the development of the system of government, business and the whole society. This is a question of national security and independence of Russia in terms of the competitiveness of domestic companies!" For any modern high-tech enterprise, the transition to digitalization is a necessary process, since it will only allow a transition to a new level of management of the product's activity and economics, and an increase in the efficiency of all levels of production. In Russia, there are few examples of the use of such technologies and their scale is not wide. This is mainly engine and helicopter manufacturing. Currently, the rethinking of the principles of work organization is happening in the rocket and space industry. In this industry, there has been a transition to system engineering based on the principle of project management. The introduction of a system engineering approach will allow a transition to a "digital enterprise", and on its basis to a "smart enterprise of the future". Professor A.A. Romanov defines the term "Digital Enterprise" as "an organization that uses information technology as a competitive advantage in all areas of its business: development, production, supporting business processes, marketing, and interaction with customers". In a modern market economy, the main success of an enterprise's development is the speed of its development, which, in turn, depends on investments. Those enterprises and companies that have received good investments at an early stage of development win, as the initial costs are the highest. Consequently, in the level of business activity, a large proportion of finance is needed, so a new model of investment support is also required. A three-level investment model, including a system level, sectoral and regional levels and a micro level is considered to be the most optimal. An integrated approach makes it possible to take into account the whole diversity of factors, conditions, phases, growth rates and inflation at the macroeconomic and specifically regional levels. (Collection of reports of the third conference "The economic potential of industry in the service of the military-industrial complex". Moscow: Financial University under the Government of the Russian Federation. 2017. – P.45,39,47). Considering the traditions and specifics of the Russian economy and its enterprises in the real sector, it is advisable to focus on the digitalization of strategic industries for the production of durable, maintainable industrial products that can provide leadership in the global market and the needs of the domestic market. Since the domestic market is the first step for the growth of future digital leaders. (Digital Russia: A New Reality: Report of the Digital McKinsey Expert Group, LLC, McKinsey and the SIES Company. 2017. – p. 39.)

In the 20th century the most competitive and advanced associations in our country, USA, Germany and Great Britain were science cities. Gradually, they ceased to be the main generators of progress. There are several explanations for this, but there are two main reasons. Not all scientists want to do pure research work. Many seek to actively introduce their achievements in production. The science city does not provide such an opportunity. Another reason is the lack of researchers in one area. Clusters have come to replace science cities, which combine a diverse palette of qualifications and competencies. The mechanism for solving the tasks often becomes an effective cluster policy as the main indicator of regional innovation. Clusters can be with a special status or have a dual purpose. The structure of a cluster can be based on a diagram consisting of the following components:

- enterprises with state participation
- management company
- engineering centers engaged in technology transfer and the development of its special mechanisms
- centers of scientific and technical expertise. (Collection of reports of the third conference "The economic potential of industry in the service of the military-industrial complex" M.: Financial University under the Government of the Russian Federation. 2017. – P. 107)

In Russia, the policy of creating clusters began to operate actively in 2005. The Samara Region, which currently has 8 cluster associations, was the pioneer of this movement. Large agglomerations include clusters of Kaluga and Arkhangelsk regions, Bashkortostan, and Moscow. Tatarstan pursues active cluster policy. The most famous are its clusters Petrochemical and Kamsky. From 2015, a cluster in the Tomsk region began to operate, aimed at the effective interaction of science and business, the creation of comfortable living conditions. Clusters are developing most actively in such industries as chemistry and petrochemistry, information technology, tourism, nanotechnology, pharmaceuticals and medicine. To promote the effective innovative development of the participating regions, the Association of Innovative Regions of Russia (AIRR) has been created. The orbit of its activities includes 12 of the 27 innovative territorial clusters of federal significance. (Strategy. 12.2016-01-2017. No. 4 (25). – P. 139–142).

The Russian capital is not far behind. The most productive form existing in the megalopolis since 2014 is a technopark as a new way of organizing production, in which a cluster of several smaller ones is created on the basis of a large enterprise. Technoparks are equipped with modern high-tech equipment. Diverse ultramodern products are created on their base. Currently in Moscow there are 33 technoparks with 46 thousand jobs, the cost of one of them is up to 300 thousand dollars. Moscow's technology parks are the leaders of domestic import substitution and supply 22 world industries with world-class products. (Kolpakchi S. Enterprises of the New Economy. / / Literary Gazette. October 10–16, 2018. No. 41 (6662) .- P.22).

However, to date, narrow cluster specialization in a separate area does not meet modern needs. The system requires development, and it consists in creating innovative production associations at the junction of several industries. Such an innovative industrial cluster (IIC) will appear in 2019 in Moscow. Its activities will ensure coordination and interaction in the field of industry, science and education. The establishment of horizontal links will give a powerful synergistic effect. "The objective of the IIC is to promote the introduction of a new approach to the administrative support of the business environment in the capital, to establish inter-sectoral contacts, to stimulate new projects and to promote the commercialization of scientific research. All this will be built in the form of an IT communication platform that automates business processes". (Veselovsky V. Cluster for brilliant people and ideas. // Literary Gazette. December 5–11, 2018. No. 49 (6670). – p. 30).

The onset of the fourth revolution makes it necessary to introduce new technological advances in all sectors of the economy and training modern engineering personnel. The success and competitiveness of Russia in the international arena depends on it.

References

Kolpakchi S. *Predpriyatiya novoy ekonomiki*. [Enterprises of the New Economy]. // Literary Gazette. October 10–16, 2018. No. 41 (6662) (in Russian).

Konovalov A. *Industrial'noye serdtse Sibiri*. [Industrial heart of Siberia]. // Literary newspaper. February 27 – March 5, 2019. No. 4 (6680) (in Russian).

Korelin A.P., Stepanov S.A. *S.YU.Vitte – finansist, politik, diplomat*. [Vitte S. Yu. – financier, politician, diplomat]. M.: TERRA – Book Club. 1996. – 464 p (in Russian).

Programma "TSifrovaya ekonomika Rossiyskoy Federatsii". [The program "Digital Economy of the Russian Federation.]" M.: 2017. – 87 p (in Russian).

Sbornik dokladov tret'yey konferentsii "Ekonomicheskiy potentsial promyshlennosti na sluzhbe oboronno-promyshlennogo kompleksa". [Collection of reports of the third conference "The economic potential of industry in the service of the military-industrial complex.]" M.: Financial University under the Government of the Russian Federation. 2017. – 171 p (in Russian).

Strategiya. [Strategy]. 12.2016-01.2017. No. 4 (25) (in Russian).

Tebekin A.V. *O metodologii analiza i otsenki innovatsionnoy deyatel'nosti.// Ekonomika. Predprinimatel'stvo. Okruzhayushchaya sreda*. [On the methodology of analysis and evaluation of innovation]. // Economy. Entrepreneurship. Environment. M.: 2006.Vol. 4. No. 28. pp. 28–37 (in Russian).

TSifrovaya Rossiya: novaya real'nost': Otchet ekspertnoy gruppy Digital Mckinsey [Digital Russia: A New Reality: Report of the Digital McKinsey Expert Group], LLC, McKinsey and the CIS Company. 2017. -133 p (in Russian).

Veselovsky V. *Klaster dlya genial'nykh lyudey i idey.*[Cluster for brilliant people and ideas]. // Literary newspaper. December 5–11, 2018. Vol. 1. No. 49 (6670) (in Russian).

Zamostyanov A. *Neobkhodimost' BAMa*. [The necessity of BAM]. // Literary newspaper. February 20–26, 2019. No. 7 (6679) (in Russian). Same. *Proyekt veka*. [The project of the century]. // Literary newspaper. February 27 – March 5, 2019. No. 4 (6680) (in Russian).

Ekaterina Y. Charochkina, Yulia V. Vertakova,
Margarita A. Molokova

14 Human Capital: Efficiency of Formation in the Process of Global Transformations of Economy

Introduction

The researching of the nature and characteristics of the formation of human capital in the global transformation of the economy is a highly relevant issue. As a rule, the market economy does not imply the efficient formation of resources and creation in eliminating information asymmetry, a fair distribution of income, which argues the importance of researching the conditions and factors of creating and reproducing human resources and regulating human capital markets against the background of growing globalization. Due to crisis phenomena and external contradictions, majority of regions and countries are vulnerable to weak interest in development, economic and social passivity, low activity in business. These items negatively affect the competitiveness of the majority of the population, increasing new knowledge, the obsolescence of professional skills of the able-bodied part of the population (Crawford, 1991).

As the experience of developed countries shows, the quality of human capital directly depends on investments in human resources in the form of education, training, maintaining health, and improving the quality of life. The increase in the role of human capital and investment in human capital is especially evident in the context of globalization, which stimulates countries to create new production capacities, an efficient infrastructure for the reproduction of human capital and ensure a high level of capitalization of the economy (Hirst, and Thompson, 1999). The era of globalization, human capital acquires new competitive properties, such as: mobility, adaptability, increasing the rate of information transmission, innovation, narrowing of space and time, interactive communication. The globalization of human capital implies the acquisition of previously unknown knowledge and the transformation of this knowledge into qualitatively new equipment, technology, and materials with a high socio-economic value. The globalization of human capital will ensure the practical development of new high-tech products and incorporate them into the livelihoods of modern society.

Ekaterina Y. Charochkina, Yulia V. Vertakova, Margarita A. Molokova, Southwest State University, Kursk, Russia

https://doi.org/10.1515/9783110636147-014

Methodology

As the main factor of economic progress, human is a widespread category of economic knowledge, human potential is the main factor for the innovative development of society and economic growth. There are quite a lot of definitions of the essence of human resources in economics. Some researchers characterize them as a set of physical and spiritual abilities of a person (Becker, 1964), other scientists will define them through the working capacity of people of a certain age, or as human capital, human potential of society (Thomas, 2002 and Gabdullin, 2018). The multifaceted nature of human capital determines the existence of various theories and definitions. Thus, a number of researchers adhere to the view that human capital is the combination of all the productive qualities of an employee (Coleman, 1990, Nureyev, 2005). L. Turou defines human capital as "the ability of an individual to produce goods and services", "his productive abilities and knowledge" (Turou, 2014). The so-called "investment" definitions of human capital are also common. Thus, M. Blaug gives the most concise "investment" definition: "Human capital is the present value of past investments in people's skills, not the value of people themselves".

Speaking as an active resource, a person contributes to the unification, the proportional and synchronous development of all living conditions and the production of society, and the improvement of their use. Optimizing them quantitatively and qualitatively contributes to overcoming crisis phenomena and the scale of domestic and international labor migration (Pelikhov and Kushnikov, 2018).

However, each approach simplifies the purpose of the person in the aspect of the formation of a competitive society. Man as a resource includes many functions and qualities, abilities and talents. People are different in their perception of learning, genetics. Differences in the physical qualities of a person can affect the choice of specialty, employment, creativity (Soboleva, 2009). People have different abilities, inclinations towards building and strengthening families, raising children, maintaining discipline, public order and responsibility. The study of the totality of the qualities and abilities of people should be used to develop socio-economic programs for the activities of the population of the regions and countries. The level of human capital development is a crucial condition for the development of countries and regions.

Human capital has a certain structure and dynamics, which explains the need for a constant search for new ways and methods for their accounting and analysis, especially since many external and internal factors influence the level and composition of human capital, both relatively intensive and extensive. Usually, all these changes are useful, but they can also be negative. Therefore, it is necessary to provide continuing image monitoring of the assessment of the level of human capital development at all level of management. Modern theory offers a lot of various methods of quantitative and qualitative assessment of the human capital of countries, regions of the world community (Parushina, Lytneva and Semidelikhin, 2017).

However, it should be noted that none of their totality is not without certain disadvantages. In particular, they do not provide an opportunity to measure either quantitatively or quantitatively people's abilities, as a result, for a more complete assessment, it is necessary to use the entire set of indicators of both quantitative and qualitative assessments. This is a very laborious process not only at the macro level, but also at the level of individual business entities.

In the aspect of globalization of economic processes, the conditions and factors of the formation of human capital at the level of individual countries and regions, and highlighting the advantages and problems of its reproduction arouse the interest. Therefore, indicators of the social development of countries, which form the basis of the world ratings of socio-economic development, including human capital, are of great importance. The basis of these ratings are the indices of human capital development, which take into account a huge number of indicators of the socio-economic development of countries. In our opinion, an index approach for assessing human capital is the most optimal in terms of monitoring human development across countries and regions. Its main advantage can be considered the availability and uniformity of the required data and, as a consequence, the possibility of calculation for a wide range of countries.

Results

Cross-country differences in the qualitative and quantitative characteristics of human capital create the prerequisites for integration and cooperation in this area of entire countries and regions. It is obvious that the availability of goods, in particular a person with his abilities, is an indispensable condition for the formation of the market. The human capital market is forming at various levels, including the global one (Fedorova and Zueva, 2018). Their effectiveness lies in the accumulation and development of national and global potential, and competition stimulates the improvement of the quality of human resources.

The system of formation of human capital markets at the level of individual countries, including at the global level, traditionally depends on the formation of demand in commodity markets, which significantly reduces the possibility of forming an effective human capital structure. However, the experience of countries that manage to overcome these negative aspects and form an effective human capital structure suggests that these trends are completely predictable and manageable. That is important in improving competitiveness and efficiently organizing the process of human capital formation and reproduction (Gabdullin, 2018).

In this case, it would be possible to mitigate, and in some cases eliminate, some negative trends in the transformation of economic systems, their extreme differentiation in social and economic development, living standards of the population of countries and regions, compliance of training with current trends in demand formation in human capital markets. This problem is particularly acute for countries with a low level of human development, which are quite fall behind in the main indicators of human development from developed and developing countries. In many industries there is a shortage of highly qualified personnel who can develop, produce and operate new equipment and digital technologies. This situation is only one of the many negative characteristics that reflect the inefficient structure of human capital in some regions of the world.

A key tool in solving the problem of the formation and reproduction of human resources is to continuously monitor the demand and supply of labor, predict the trends of their changes in the global economy and develop directions for countries to adapt to modern conditions and the requirements of the global labor market.

As the experience of the developed countries of Europe and the West shows, human capital is the main factor in achieving qualitative and stable economic growth of the country in the context of increasing global transformations and competition. In the developed countries, the "knowledge economy" sphere became the main locomotive of socio-economic development a few decades ago. S. Kuznets, who for many years was in fact the scientific director of the main macroeconomic organization of the world (National Bureau of Economic Research (NBER)), made a great contribution to the understanding of this process. In his opinion, human capital is becoming the main source of socio-economic growth not only in developed but also in developing countries (Abel and Aganbegyan, 2017). According to expert estimates by the World Bank, the role of human capital has especially increased because of the transition of developed countries to a post-industrial economy, and at the present stage not only natural resources, but also fixed assets have replaced the importance (see Figure 14.1).

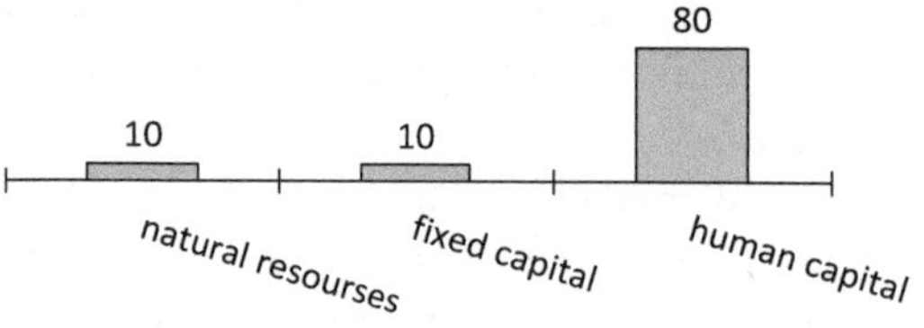

Figure 14.1: The structure of the national wealth of developed countries,% of GNP.
Source: Abel G. Aganbegyan C. The human capital and its main component is the sphere of "knowledge economy" as the main source of social and economic growth Economic strategies, 2017.

For comparison, in the structure of GNP of a number of developing countries, including Russia, human capital is no more than 50%, which is not enough to establish a competitive economic system corresponding to world trends.

According to the global development indices of countries, on average around the world only 62% of human capital is used. Figure 14.2 reflects the situation across regions, according to the survey, a serious lag in the effective use of human capital in the countries of South Africa and South Asia can be noted, and North America and Western Europe with the human capital reserve of 29 and 26 percent, respectively, are the most successful in this direction.

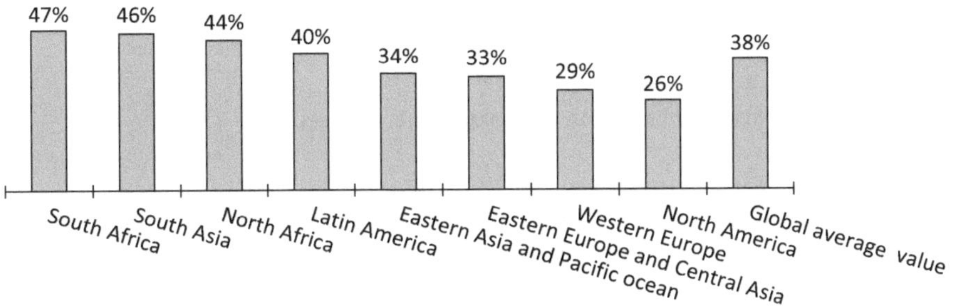

Figure 14.2: The potential for human capital development by region of the world.
Source: "Indices and Human Development Indicators: Updated Statistics 2018" available at: http://hdr.undp.org/sites/default/files/2018_human_development_statistical_update_ru.pdf (Accessed 30.04.2019).

In the context of global economic transformations, an important direction is the formation of a competitive global market for human capital. However, human capital markets are subject to external effects and have failures like any market. Traditionally, market failures are usually understood as the inability of the market to cope with monopolism, and lack of interest in creating public goods. The market is not interested in eliminating external effects and establishing a fair distribution of income, eliminating the asymmetric distribution of information, this situation is particularly acute in the trends of globalization. For example, in relation to the global human capital market, failures are manifested in the form of such trends as: a large gap between individual countries and regions in economic development; poverty of the majority of the world population leading to the deterioration of the reproduction of the human resource and its demographic structure, high international migration (Charochkina and Kashirtseva, 2014 and Pereverzeva, 2015).

At the micro level, the failures of human capital markets are also manifested in the weak development of the social sphere, in the growth of social conflicts, the reduction of human resources, the spread of diseases, the decline in the birth rate of the population and life expectancy. Market failures can be observed in the application of simple labor, where difficult labor is needed, in saving business to form an effective labor potential, in the trends of monopoly power development in trade union and other public organizations. Figure 14.3 outlines the main trends in the formation of human capital in the aspect of globalization.

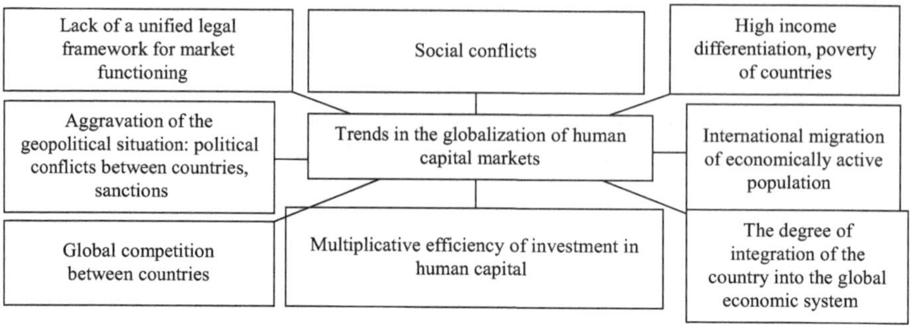

Figure 14.3: Main trends in the globalization of human capital markets.

Thus, the prevailing trends of globalization of the economy turn the process of formation and reproduction of human capital into an area under the influence of numerous factors of external order at the level of global political, legal, and psychological.

Conclusions

The inefficiency of the market mechanism is a serious problem for countries and regions in terms of social development and overcoming global transformations in modern society.

Historically, society for many centuries in these cases refers to government regulation, which pursues an active policy on social progress. Actual direction in the elimination of these shortcomings at the present time, can be attributed to the active participation of countries in solving geo-economic and geopolitical issues, the development of integration ties. Despite the fact that many countries are often interested in extracting current, short-term benefits from obtaining various kinds of interactions and preferential access to the world market, including the human capital market, an effective mechanism within a single global economic space should ensure the implementation of coordinated macroeconomic policies countries.

The development of common rules for regulating competition, organizing common resource markets, clarifying the legal status of migrants, coordinating issues of state support for developing countries, which today are the main source for reproduction of human capital in the global economy, seem to be relevant. The practical functioning of human resource markets, as well as other markets, requires the use of both socio-economic and institutional mechanisms to overcome market failures and government failures. In our opinion, in this system of mechanisms, first of all, a special place should be occupied by legal regulation and public investment. Macroeconomic optimization is also of great importance for regulating the reproduction of human resources, especially in terms of increasing the socio-economic efficiency of international relations. The analysis shows that the economics of human capital is a rather complicated system, differences in the technological base can be highlighted here; human resources; economic, social, institutional and organizational relationships. The interaction between them, as we have seen, also remains complex, they contain not only positive dynamics, but also failures, therefore mechanisms are needed for their coordination, both through free competition and state and public interaction. Some economists believe that this is genetically incompatible, however, the experience of developed countries demonstrates the opposite, relations arise about absolutely all products and resources, forming peculiar composites, which differ not only in their correlation depending on the level and nature of productive forces and the stage of development, but also the period of the industrial cycle. In modern economic theory, economics is often referred to as post-industrial; market; mixed social market; institutional economics. Taking into account the analysis, it is truer to call the modern world economy a system of state-market partnership; this definition reflects not only market and government regulation, their achievements, but also their failures, and finally, their synthesis. The theory of failures of the human capital market and failures of the state is also promising for further methodological progress in economics, solving complex practical issues, including in the context of global economic transformations.

References

Abel G. Aganbegyan C. *Helovecheskiy kapital i ego glavnaya sostavlyayushchaya – sfera "ekonomiki znaniy" kak osnovnoy istochnik sotsial'no-ekonomicheskogo rosta* [The human capital and its main component is the sphere of "knowledge economy" as the main source o f social and economic growth] Economic strategies, 2017, no. 3, pp. 66–74 (in Russian).

Becker, G. (1964), "Human capital", available at: http://www.econlib.org/library/Enc/HumanCapital.html (Accessed 11.04.2019).

CHarochkina E.Y., Kashirtseva A.Y. *Formirovaniye predprinimatel'skogo kapitala v usloviyakh globalizatsii mirovoy ekonomiki* [Formation of entrepreneurial capital in a globalizing world economy] Innovation and investment, 2014, no. 4, pp. 67–71(in Russian).

Coleman, J. S. (1990) "Fundamentals of social theory". Cambridge, MA: Belknap Press of Harvard University Press, pp. 241–527.

Crawford, B. (1991). In the era of human capital, New York, Harpercollins, 242 p.

Fedorova, O. I., Zueva, E. G. (2018). *Nakopleniye i realizatsiya chelovecheskogo kapitala v novykh usloviyakh: vozmozhnosti i ogranicheniya* [Accumulation and realization of human capital in new conditions: opportunities and limitations] Creative economy, Vol.12. Vol. 10, pp. 1649–1660 (in Russian).

Gabdullin N. M. Sovremennyye podkhody i metody izmereniya chelovecheskogo kapitala [*Modern approaches and methods for measuring human capital]* Issues of innovative economy, 2018, no. 8, pp. 785–798 (in Russian).

Hirst, T. & Thompson, G. (1999). Globalizatio in Question, Second Edition, Cambridge, England. Cambridge University Press.

Indices and Human Development Indicators: Updated Statistics 2018 available at: http://hdr.undp.org/sites/default/files/2018_human_development_statistical_update_ru.pdf (Accessed 30. 04.2019).

Nureyev, R. M. (2005). Development theories: new models of economic growth (contribution of human capital) / Economic Issues, vol. No. 9, p. 345.

Parushina N.V., Lytneva N.A., Semidelikhin E.A. *Metody izmereniya i otsenki chelovecheskogo kapitala (Nauchnyy obzor)* [Methods for measuring and evaluating human capital (Scientific Review)] Scientific Review. Economics, 2017, no 2, pp. 90–96 (in Russian).

Pelikhov, N. I. Kushnikov, E. I. K voprosu o faktorakh proizvodstva v sovremennoy ekonomike [*On the issue of factors of production in the modern economy*] Creative economy, 2018, Vol. 12. Vol. 11, pp. 1759–1770 (in Russian).

Pereverzeva, N. B. “Economic mechanism of regulation of market failures and the state in the human resources markets” Bulletin of the Kursk state agricultural Academy, no. 5, 2015, pp. 36–39.

Soboleva, I.V. *Paradoksy izmereniya chelovecheskogo kapitala: Nauchnyy doklad* [Paradoxes of measuring human capital: Scientific report] Moscow, Institute of Economics, RAS, 2009, 50 p (in Russian).

Thomas J Courchene (2002), “Human capital in the information age”, available at: http:www.jstor.org/stable/3552161 (Accessed 11. 04.2019).

Turou, L. *Upravleniye chelovecheskimi resursami* [Human Resource Management] Moscow, Yurayt, 2014, 150 p (in Russian).

Alexey Yu. Arkhipov, Elena V. Fomicheva

15 Human Development and STP: The Main Directions of the Economic Breakthrough of Russia

Introduction

The Russian economic system is going through difficult times of unstable development, which is affected by a huge number of factors, both internal and, to an ever-increasing degree, of external influence. The main trends and conditions of modern world economic development include the following: parallel development of globalization and de-globalization processes, scaling of globalization; multipolarity of development of the world economic system; a change in the ratio of the economies of the leading countries of the world (USA and China, the G7 and the 7 countries with emerging markets, BRICS – RIC and other formal and informal associations); economic instability and the formation of global imbalances: the gap between the financial and real sectors of the world economy; countries in which production is concentrated and countries with developed financial institutions; resorting, which is gaining momentum in a number of developed countries (USA, Germany, etc.) due to automation and digitalization of production on the one hand, and an increase in the cost of labor and the tightening of environmental standards, on the other; transformation of regional economic associations; the crisis of the European Union, associated primarily with the growing problem of adaptation of migrants, exacerbated by the relations between the countries of the Union, difficult passage of Brexit, etc.; the revival of protectionism, the unfolding of trade wars (a bright and not the only example is the confrontation between the US and China) and others (Arkhipov 2016, p. 50–51).

The level of development of the modern world economy, both the entire system as a whole and individual components, the multi-vector nature of its trends, the complication of cause-effect relationships, the multi-sphere and multi-factor nature of the models being implemented, predetermine a complex hierarchy of relations between its subjects, characterized by fierce competitive struggle, search for strategic partners, cooperative cooperation, competition for influence and access to markets and factors of production, geopolitical cooperation and confrontation, etc.

The format and direction of development of relations is determined by the system of economic and geopolitical interests of participants in international economic relations, the desire to increase the country's competitiveness on the world market

Alexey Yu. Arkhipov, Elena V. Fomicheva, Southern Federal University, Rostov-on-Don, Russia

https://doi.org/10.1515/9783110636147-015

and ensure its economic security. Changing the conditions for such interaction in the shortest possible time can both significantly strengthen the country's position in the system of international division of labor and create additional threats and sometimes act in both directions, taking into account the complexity and multilevel nature of the processes under consideration.

In the context of innovation growth and the creation of a single global economic space, the role of individual states, integration associations, multinational companies in the production of the global gross product and interaction in the international division of labor changes. The Russian Federation, due to a number of reasons, became involved in a number of geopolitical and geo-economic confrontations, projected both on positions in the world system, relations with international organizations and on the internal economic and development system.

The need to create objective conditions for the economic breakthrough of Russia is due to: insecurity before the world economic crises, insufficient development of the economic security system; the failure of the process of modernization of the economy (the task of overcoming the raw materials orientation of the economy and exports remains unsolved, as far as the backwardness in the development of the leading branches of the manufacturing industry, engineering, etc.); an unsatisfactory domestic financing mechanism; high levels of economic inequality and unresolved many social issues and a number of other equally significant problems.

Methodology

The systemic basis of this study is the modern Russian economy as a complex mechanism of subject-functional and causal relationships in the situation of the objective need to create the conditions, ways and institutions for implementing breakthrough economic development.

The focus of research is the development of human, human capital, and scientific and technological progress as reference points of Russia's economic breakthrough. In the opinion of the authors, the process of knowledge commercialization and technology transfer is of particular importance, increasing its efficiency can have a decisive impact on the development of both directions and cause a synergistic effect in the development of the Russian economy, which is critically necessary in the conditions of the negative impact of modern challenges of the world economy.

In the process of researching the chosen topic, based on the principles of the systems approach and general scientific methodology, the methods of logical, statistical and comparative analysis, synthesis and selective scientific abstraction were applied.

The information-empirical basis of the study was composed of data from statistical agencies, analytical reviews of Russian and foreign economic organizations, periodical materials, legal acts of the legislative and executive authorities, and results of studies by Russian and foreign economists.

Results

The main directions of Russia's economic breakthrough, through the stimulation and directional regulation of which we can achieve significant socio-economic results, can be the development of man and human capital and scientific and technical progress.

In the international ranking on the human development index (HDI), a comprehensive comparative indicator used, among other things, to assess the impact of economic policy on the quality of life of the population, published in 2018 based on the analysis of data for 2017, Russia ranks 49th out of 189 countries, hitting a group of countries with a very high level of human development. According to Table 15.1, one can trace the value of rating indicators and compare them with the data of the leading countries of the TOP-10, the USA, China, the EEU countries and some others. *(Human Development Indices and Indicators: Updated Statistics 2018)*

However, despite getting into the highest group in the rating table, Russia needs a comprehensive program to preserve, improve and build human potential,

Table 15.1: Rating of countries on the human development index – 2018.

Rating	Country	Human Development Index (value)	Life expectancy at birth (in years)	Expected study duration (in years)	Average study duration (in years)	Gross National Income (GNI) per capita (in US dollars 2011 PPP)
COUNTRIES WITH A VERY HIGH LEVEL OF HUMAN DEVELOPMENT						
1	Norway	0.953	82.3	17.9	12.6	68.012
2	Switzerland	0.944	83.5	16.2	13.4	57.625
3	Australia	0.939	83.1	22.9	22.9	43.560
4	Ireland	0.938	81.6	19.6	12.5	53.754
5	Germany	0.936	81.2	17.0	14.1	46.136
6	Iceland	0.935	82.9	19.3	12.4	45.810
7	Hong Kong, China	0.933	84.1	16.3	12.0	58.420
7	Sweden	0.933	82.6	17.6	12.4	47.766

Table 15.1 (continued)

Rating	Country	Human Development Index (value)	Life expectancy at birth (in years)	Expected study duration (in years)	Average study duration (in years)	Gross National Income (GNI) per capita (in US dollars 2011 PPP)
9	Singapore	0.932	83.2	16.2	11.5	82.503
10	Netherlands	0.931	82.0	18.0	12.2	47.900
...						
13	USA	0.924	79.5	16.5	13.4	54.941
...						
48	Oman	0.821	77.3	13.9	9.5	36.290
49	Russian Federation	0.816	71.2	15.5	12.0	24.233
50	Montenegro	0.814	77.3	14.9	11.3	16.779
...						
53	Belarus	0.808	73.1	15.5	12.3	16.323
...						
58	Kazakhstan	0.800	70.0	15.1	11.8	22.626
COUNTRIES WITH HIGH LEVEL OF HUMAN DEVELOPMENT						
...						
83	Armenia	0.755	74.8	13.0	11.7	9.144
...						
86	China	0.752	76.4	13.8	7.8	15.270
COUNTRIES WITH MEDIUM HUMAN DEVELOPMENT						
...						
122	Kyrgyzstan	0.672	71.1	13.4	10.9	3.255

as well as to improve the quality of life of the population and reduce its gap between segments of society. Human development requires promotion and assistance from the state in the following areas: priority development of education and health care; other person-oriented services; solving social issues; in general, man-centric development of the economy and society. The implementation of these areas has already been reflected in the Decree of the President of the Russian Federation dated May 7, 2018 "On the national goals and strategic objectives of the development of the Russian Federation for the period until 2024", in accordance with which it is necessary to ensure the growth of real incomes and pensions of citizens; halving the level of poverty in the Russian Federation; increase in life expectancy up to 78 years, etc. According to the set of tasks assigned to the ruling institutions one can understand that there are many problems in this area. The most acute problems can be recognized as falling real incomes of the population; natural decline in the population, once again put on the agenda; sharp differentiation of population and high level of poverty; unemployment among the young population; brain drain.

In the development of scientific and technological progress in Russia, we can state an unsatisfactory situation, as evidenced, for example, by such data, voiced by the Deputy Chairman of the Government of Russia on social policy, T. Golikova, as a reduction in the number of developed advanced production technologies from 1.53 thousand in 2016 to 1.4 thousand in 2017; reduction of used patented inventions from 527 in 2016 to 485 in 2017; introduction of 55% of developed advanced production technologies into the country's economy in 6 years or more and only 28% – within 3 years (Sukharev, 2018). The data in Table 15.2, which shows the positions of countries in the ranking of innovative economies of the Bloomberg Innovation Index 2019, with its positioning by its individual components, as well as the ranking positions of countries for the previous 3 years, in the period 2016–2018, also confirm this fact. In the 2019 ranking, Russia, being at the end of the third dozen countries, ranked 27th, between Malaysia and Luxembourg, shows its worst result for the period, moving from 12th place (falling by 15 positions), which it occupied in 2016. In the current ranking, Russia is in the top ten best economies (10th place) only in terms of the efficiency of higher education.

The aforementioned Decree of the President of the Russian Federation dated May 7, 2018 indicates: the tasks of accelerating the technological development of the country, increasing the number of organizations implementing technological innovations; accelerating the adoption of digital technologies; formation of high-performance export-oriented sector, based on the use of modern technologies, etc., whose solution is designed to improve the situation in this area. It remains only to find and implement tools effective in the existing conditions of development for the implementation of these tasks, both in the field of human development and in creating the conditions for scientific and technological progress in the Russian Federation. In accordance with this, national projects are being developed in the following areas: demography, health care, education, labor productivity and employment support, science, digital economy, etc. Obviously, their results can potentially appear over time. At the same time, the situation continues to deteriorate.

According to the RIA Rating, the first months of 2019 in the Russian industry show a decrease in growth rates with the strongest drop in production seen in mechanical engineering (according to the Ministry of Economic Development, in March

Table 15.2: Positions of countries in the ranking of innovative economies of the Bloomberg Innovation Index in 2016–2019.

Place in the ranking of 2016	Place in the ranking of 2017	Place in the ranking of 2018	Place in the ranking of 2019	Country	Points	Intensity of research and development	Added value production	productivity	High technology density	The effectiveness of higher education	Study Concentration	Patent activity
1	1	1	1	South Korea	87.38	2	2	18	4	7	7	20
2	3	4	2	Germany	87.30	7	3	24	3	14	11	7
7	5	7	3	Finland	85.57	9	16	5	13	9	8	5
5	4	5	4	Switzerland	85.49	3	4	7	8	13	3	27
11	10	10	5	Israel	84.78	1	33	8	5	36	2	4
6	6	3	6	Singapore	84.49	13	5	11	17	1	13	14
3	2	2	7	Sweden	84.15	4	15	9	6	20	5	25
8	9	11	8	USA	83.21	10	25	6	1	43	28	1
4	7	6	9	Japan	81.96	5	7	22	10	39	18	10
10	11	9	10	France	81.67	12	41	13	2	11	20	15
9	8	8	11	Denmark	81.66	8	21	15	12	19	1	28
13	12	12	12	Austria	80.98	6	11	12	24	8	9	18
16	13	14	13	Belgium	80.43	11	26	10	9	41	16	9
15	16	13	14	Ireland	80.08	32	1	1	16	15	14	38

18	15	16	15	Netherlands	79.54	16	29	21	7	42	12	12
21	21	19	16	China	78.35	14	13	47	11	6	39	2
14	14	15	17	Norway	77.79	17	49	23	15	17	10	11
17	17	17	18	Great Britain	75.87	20	45	26	14	5	21	19
20	18	18	19	Australia	75.38	19	56	17	20	18	15	6
19	20	22	20	Canada	73.65	22	39	27	22	31	19	8
			. . .									
25	23	26	26	Malaysia	67.61	23	9	46	21	37	40	41
12	26	25	27	Russia	66.81	33	37	51	25	10	24	30
35	34	32	28	Luxembourg	66.37	29	47	3	48	58	6	3
			. . .									

Source: According to 1) Bloomberg Innovation Index. 2016 // www.bloomberg.com/news/articles/2016-01-19/these-are-the-world-s-most-innovative-economies; 2) Bloomberg Innovation Index. 2017 // https://www.bloomberg.com/news/articles/2017-01-17/sweden-gains-south-korea-reigns-as-world-s-most-innovative-economies; 3) Bloomberg Innovation Index. 2018 // https://theworldonly.org/rejting-innovatsionnyh-ekonomik-2018/; 4) Bloomberg Innovation Index. 2019 // https://www.bloomberg.com/news/articles/2019-01-22/germany-nearly-catches-korea-as-innovation-champ-u-s-rebounds.

the decline was 4.3% in annual comparison, and in the first quarter – 7.7%), while the worst figures were recorded in the most high-tech sector – the aerospace industry (according to Rosstat, the production of aircraft, including space aircraft and the corresponding equipment, decreased in March 2019 by 30.8% in the annual comparison, and in the first quarter – 42.3%). (Economy in March: high-tech directions inhibit industry, 2019)

In accordance with the Strategy for Innovative Development of the Russian Federation for the period up to 2020, the main indicators of the transfer of the Russian economy to the innovative path of development are the increase in the share of Russia in the global markets for high-tech goods and services (nuclear power, aircraft, space technology and services, special shipbuilding, etc.) up to 5–10% in 5–7 or more target sectors and an increase in the share of Russian exports of high-tech goods in the total volume of world exports of high-tech goods to 2% by 2020 (Strategy for the Innovative Development of the Russian Federation for the period up to 2020). In line with this, an increase in the segment of non-primary supplies and, in particular, the share of high-tech products to foreign markets, is currently being implemented as one of the priority directions of state policy for the development and modernization of the national economy. In 2017, the Ministry of Industry and Trade issued an Order No. 672 dated March 10, 2017 "On the approval of the provision on high-tech products, works and services, taking into account the priorities of the development of the Russian economy", which secured the technology and technology of Russia. This document allows avoiding the misunderstanding of the concept of "Russian high-tech exports", and makes it possible to conduct a unified analysis of foreign trade statistics in order to determine the dynamics and trends in exports of domestic high-tech products.

Russia exports a relatively small number of high-tech products. The dynamics of the export of Russian high-tech goods in the period of 2000–2017, including in comparison with other countries of the world, can be traced according to the data of Table 15.3.

The scientific and technological inertness of the Russian economy, which is formed under the influence of fragmentary innovative development, curtailing research in a number of important areas of scientific and technical progress, the lack of effective bilateral ties between science and business, weak innovative activity of enterprises and lack of motivation for it and a number of other factors lead to an increase in external technological dependence (Fomicheva, 2018).

One of the important directions of enhancing scientific and technological progress in Russia is the development of the process of commercialization of knowledge and technology transfer. For the development of this direction, an important role will be played by both the establishment of direct interaction between institutes of the Russian Academy of Sciences and universities with Russian enterprises on the basis of bilateral trajectories, including first and foremost, in finding effective tools to overcome the "death valley" as the most difficult initial non-profit phase of a

Table 15.3: Ranked number of countries exporting high-tech products, billion USD.

	Country	2017	2016	2010	2005	2000
1	China	504.4	496.0	406.1	215.9	41.7
2	Germany	171.6	189.6	158.5	146.4	85.5
3	Hong Kong	141.7	0.4	1.1	2.5	5.1
4	Singapore	136.1	126.3	127.0	39.1	73.9
5	USA	110.1	153.5	145.9	145.4	197.8
6	France	98.7	103.8	99.7	70.5	58.7
7	Japan	83.7	92.9	122.1	125.4	128.9
8	South Korea	72.7	118.4	121.4	83.9	54.3
9	Great Britain	68.6	68.3	60.1	82.5	71.7
10	Netherlands	63.6	53.0	59.5	65.9	44.9
11	Vietnam	52.8	43.6	4.2	0.9	0.6
12	Mexico	50.4	46.8	37.7	32.4	31.1
13	Malaysia	41.1	55.6	59.3	57.7	47.0
...						
23	India	14.5	13.3	10.1	4.1	2.1
...						
28	Russian Federation	9.1	6.6	5.1	3.8	3.9
...						
41	Kazakhstan	1.7	2.1	2.3	0.4	0.0001
...						
54	Belarus	0.6	0.6	0.4	0.22	0.18

Source: 1) High-technology exports (current US$). The World Bank. Data // https://data.worldbank.org/indicator/TX.VAL.TECH.CD; (Accessed 30.01.2018) 2) Export of high-tech goods // https://knoema.ru/atlas/ranks/Экспорт-высокотехнологичных-товаров (Accessed 10.05.2019).

start-up, which is impossible to survive and reach the stage of mass production, according to various expert estimates, for up to 95% of new technologies, and the introduction of the "triple helix" concept on the basis of networking "institutes of the Russian Academy of Sciences, universities – state-business", in which each of the elements is designed to increase the efficiency of others and reduce the uncertainty of the implementation of innovative processes at various stages of its passage. The global experience of introducing this concept shows the dominance of the regional level of its implementation, based on the relations of scientific, government and business structures typical for this region. In this case, of course, it is necessary to take into account the qualitative and functional characteristics of potential participants in the interaction, their readiness to implement the goals and objectives set, the availability and development of the infrastructure for joint activities, etc. In this regard, the formation of innovative clusters can be a very important point: on the basis of universities and large, medium and small innovative enterprises, with the active support and coordinating role of the state. The data in Table 15.4 vividly characterize the level of differentiation of the Russian regions by the level of development of science and technology (a sample of ten leading and some regions are presented in accordance with the research interests) and, accordingly, the geography of the potential cluster formation.

As an example, let us consider the experience of interaction of universities with Russian enterprises in the Rostov region (Southern Federal District), which occupies

Table 15.4: The level of development of science and technology in the regions of Russia.

The subject of the Russian Federation	Index 2018		Index 2017	
	Index value	Ranking place	Index value	Ranking place
Moscow	86.64	1	82.11	1
Saint Petersburg	73.24	2	70.11	2
Republic of Tatarstan	67.64	3	64.93	3
Nizhny Novgorod Region	66.53	4	64.22	4
Moscow Region	65.31	5	61.51	6
Samara Region	59.63	6	61.65	5
Perm Region	56.27	7	56.31	7
Sverdlovsk Region	55.34	8	55.53	8
Tula Region	55.25	9	53.58	9
Tomsk Region	54.70	10	52.78	10
Rostov Region	51.31	14	50.58	14
Voronezh Region	50.76	16	50.01	15
Krasnodar Region	39.33	31	32.79	45
Volgograd Region	37.80	36	36.63	34

Source: The level of development of science and technology in the regions of Russia – rating 2018// http://riarating.ru/infografika/20181017/630109152.html.

14th place in the overall ranking of Russian regions in terms of the development of science and technology and has a leading position compared with neighboring regions.

"The Southern Constellation" Innovation and Technology Cluster, the creation agreement of which was signed on January 29, 2015, at the initiative of the Regional Development Corporation and the Southern Federal University, is aimed at shaping the global technological competitiveness of the Rostov region in the fields of aviation and radioelectronic industry, instrument engineering, electrical engineering and a number of other directions by promoting intracluster cooperation in the creation of high-tech production and the effective implementation of technological innovation. The structure of "The Southern Constellation" includes 20 actors, including JSC "Regional Development Corporation", which acts as a coordinator; South Federal University; PJSC "Taganrog Aviation Scientific-Technical Complex after G. Beriev"; PJSC Research and Production Enterprise for Space Instrument Engineering "Kvant"; PiezoTech LLC; South-Russian State Polytechnic University (NPI) after M.I. Platov; Chamber of Commerce and Industry of the Rostov Region, etc.

The Institute of High Technologies and Piezotechnics of the Southern Federal University carries out the production of piezoelectric elements using nanotechnology at the Priboy plant (Taganrog) to provide the element base for the production of acoustic devices. Applied technologies are already better than world analogues. New jobs are being created, production volumes are steadily increasing.

The basic Don State Technical University (DSTU) carries out various forms of cooperation with industrial enterprises, creates small innovative enterprises (SIE). So, SIE DSTU LLC "Enset" produces, according to the technologies developed by scientists of the university, machines for the production and repair of cardan shafts (UNIKAR-3000 stand), which are in demand not only at enterprises of our country, but also abroad: delivered to Germany, contracts are concluded with the enterprises of Spain, Italy and Poland. Negotiations are underway with companies from the USA, Hungary, Latvia, etc.

It is necessary to gain more of such examples. At the same time, it is very important for the initiative and interest to come from all sides of the potential "spiral" of innovative development, with the proper level of research, technology implementation and real results, representation of interests and the creation of infrastructure.

Conclusions

Improving production efficiency and increasing its innovativeness can be achieved through the search and revitalization of domestic resources, as well as by increasing the volume and financing of scientific activities (salary increases for employees engaged in research and development activities, the implementation of grants, the construction of new research centers and their equipment with innovative technology, the creation of reference points of scientific and technological development on the basis of federal universities, etc.)

The Russian Academy of Sciences, federal and supporting universities are an important part of the system of innovative transformations. To increase the efficiency of their functioning in this mechanism, it is necessary to increase efficiency, to transform the management of the RAS system (the ongoing reform has not yet given the desired results); optimize the interaction of scientific institutions and the state; to form a transparent and balanced system of indicators of the activities of a scientific organization and an individual scientist; to ensure the cooperation of academic institutions and universities.

Russia faces global challenges associated with the emergence of new markets, technologies and products, the transformation of traditional industries, the intensification of the flow of knowledge, technology, capital, human resources between science and business, companies, economic sectors and countries. The emergence and strengthening of positions in the international arena as an influential state sets Russia with the task of geopolitical and geo-economic positioning, corresponding to its capabilities and strategic interests and involving the definition of its place and "circle of power" in the geopolitical space, the choice of development benchmarks, the vector of external and internal policy.

References

Arkhipov A. (2016) Vzaimodeystviye i perspektivy razvitiya Evropeyskogo Soyuza i Evraziyskogo ekonomicheskogo soyuza (Interaction and development prospects of the European Union and the Eurasian Economic Union) // Philosophy of Economy. No. 5. p. 49–59 (in Russian).

Bloomberg Innovation Index. 2016 // www.bloomberg.com/news/articles/2016-01-19/these-are-the-world-s-most-innovative-economies; (Accessed 30. 04.2019).

Bloomberg Innovation Index. 2017 // https://www.bloomberg.com/news/articles/2017-01-17/sweden-gains-south-korea-reigns-as-world-s-most-innovative-economies (Accessed 30. 04.2019).

Bloomberg Innovation Index. 2018 // https://theworldonly.org/rejting-innovatsionnyh-ekonomik-2018/ (Accessed 30. 04.2019).

Bloomberg Innovation Index. 2019 // https://www.bloomberg.com/news/articles/2019-01-22/germany-nearly-catches-korea-as-innovation-champ-u-s-rebounds (Accessed 30.04.2019).

Ekonomika v marte: vysokotekhnologichnyye otrasli tormozyat promyshlennost' (Economy in March: high-tech industries slow down industry) // http://riarating.ru/macroeconomic_study/20190424/630124044.html (Accessed 08.05.2019) (in Russian).

Eksport vysokotekhnologichnykh tovarov (Export of high-tech goods) // https://knoema.ru/atlas/ranks/Экспорт-высокотехнологичных-товаров. (Accessed 10.05.2019) (in Russian).

Fomicheva E.V. (2018) Nauchno-tekhnologicheskaya inertnost' rossiyskoy ekonomiki kak ugroza ekonomicheskoy bezopasnosti (Scientific and technological inertness of the Russian economy as a threat to economic security) // Humanitarian and socio-economic sciences. No. 6. pp. 93–96 (in Russian).

High-technology exports (current US$). The World Bank. Data // https://data.worldbank.org/indicator/TX.VAL.TECH.CD; (Accessed 30.01.2018).

Indeksy i indikatory chelovecheskogo razvitiya: Obnovlennyye statisticheskiye dannyye 2018 (Human Development Indices and Indicators: Updated Statistics 2018) // URL: http://hdr.undp.org/sites/default/files/2018_human_development_statistical_update_ru.pdf (Accessed 17. 04.2019) (in Russian).

Strategiya innovatsionnogo razvitiya RF na period do 2020 goda (Strategy of innovative development of the Russian Federation for the period up to 2020) // http://government.ru/docs/9282/ (Accessed 20. 02.2019) (in Russian).

Sukharev O. (2018) Pochemu idei uchenykh ne vostrebovany v Rossii? (Why are the ideas of scientists not in demand in Russia?) // URL: https://ruskline.ru/news_rl/2018/11/30/pochemu_idei_uchenyh_ne_vostrebovany_v_rossii/ (Accessed 09. 01.2019) (in Russian).

Uroven' razvitiya nauki i tekhnologiy v regionakh Rossii – reyting 2018 (The level of development of science and technology in the regions of Russia – 2018 rating) // http://riarating.ru/infografika/20181017/630109152.html (Accessed 08. 05.2019) (in Russian).

Svetlana S. Gorokhova, Anna V. Popova, Marianna G. Abramova

16 Human Capital as Quality Indicator of Russian Economic Growth in the 21st Century

Introduction

The concept of "human capital" was defined in the second half of the 20th century, due to the emergence of the theory of post-industrial (information) society, whose main actor is a person and his intelligence, which serves the purpose of developing economic potential – homo economics. As modern economists believe, notably, this syntagma is an integral sum of health, knowledge, culture and individual freedoms and other intellectual components (Rimashevskaya, 2004). As E.A. Bondarenko underlines, human capital is, above all, a "concept" that not only defines the economic part of this notion, but also its legal, political, social and philosophical content (Bondarenko, 2013).

Why has the new vision of the concept of "human capital" appeared precisely in the post-industrial information society era (digital, in the modern interpretation)? The answer to this question lies in the interpretation of the "capital" concept. This is known to be the definition of Karl Marx, who explained it as a person's ability to work – productivity in the production of material wealth (Marx, 1960). Gradually, with the development of society, economic relations are becoming closely entwined with social relations, at a special stage of development of monetary relations, with the emergence of capital, as superprofits of the employer, resulting from appropriating the value of labor, representing a source of growth of social capital and social wealth, only partially reimbursed as salary. Thus, the sale of the labor force by an individual was accomplished in full accordance with the laws of the market, i.e. at the "fair" market price, when the employer, receiving superprofit, gave it to the employee in the form of wages. This trend continued throughout the 19th and 20th centuries, when the concept of human capital was directly dependent on each individual's ability to work, whose qualifications depended on professional skills, and to obtain a certain wealth, it was enough to master only one profession.

The 1960–1970s see the fourth industrial revolution begin, marking the transition to a digital economy, the development of information and telecommunications, which gives rise to a different interpretation of human capital. Now, the "one person – one profession" paradigm is not decisive simply because the technological

Svetlana S. Gorokhova, Anna V. Popova, Financial University under the Government of the Russian Federation, Moscow, Russia
Marianna G. Abramova, Moscow State Lomonosov University, Moscow, Russia

https://doi.org/10.1515/9783110636147-016

spectrum can no longer “fit” in one specialty. There is a need for multidisciplinary knowledge and skills, primarily in the field of information technology. There is a growing distinction between skilled and unskilled workers, the units of measurement of which are intended to become the new content of the human capital notion based on the different requirements imposed on it. Therefore, in order to achieve breakthrough growth of the Russian economy, it is necessary to create all conditions for the development and steady growth of human capital, based on a long-term and theoretically verified system of requirements for people employed in the economy.

The main component of human capital is the category of “human potential”, introduced into science by Theodor Schultz (Schultz, 1971) and defined by him as innate and acquired human qualities. This point of view was also developed in Russia, when in the monographic studies of the 1990s, human potential was interpreted as a certain characteristic of an individual in terms of his health, education, competences, motivation to work, personality and psychological characteristics, etc., which are important for labor productivity, and, therefore, one’s wages, in particular, and income, in general (Dobrynin, Dyatlov and Konnov, 1993). Therefore, health, education, culture capitals (Ilyinsky, 1996) should be included as individual elements in the content of human capital. At the present stage of development of the information society, human potential initially means the ability to learn, gain knowledge, the possibility of their creative use in the production of material and intellectual benefits.

Methodology

The solution of the research tasks of the analyzed topic is based on the use of hermeneutics, the interpretation of legal texts, as well as formal and logical tools in the system analysis of existing Russian strategic planning acts designed to coordinate the activities of economic entities and public authorities in the relevant direction; regulations that establish the legal, economic and institutional framework for promoting the development of human capital and human potential; as well as other legal documents determining the state policy of the Russian Federation in this area.

Results

The development of human capital by the development of human potential is the main task of the state policy in the field of economic security. By determining the ways and means of ensuring economic security, planning the tasks to be solved in the future, the "Strategy for Economic Security of the Russian Federation for the period until 2030" establishes the main directions of state policy in terms of human development among Russians. The need to improve the entire education system on the basis of modern scientific and technological achievements of modern civilization in the process of obtaining education by an individual, ranging from children's preschool institutions to master's degree programs, has been identified as a priority task aimed at developing human potential. Giving the first place to "education capital" is confirmed by the request of Russian civil society. According to the data obtained during sociological polls, the satisfaction of Russians with the quality of almost all levels of education is not high enough. Thus, according to the Levada Center, in recent years, the relative majority of respondents (38–49%) has not been satisfied with the education system as a whole, the percentage of satisfied people varied from 18 to 26, and from 26 to 39% could not give a definite answer (Avdeev, 2018). Researchers agree with society, pointing out that "the level of training continues to decline to unacceptable levels" (Britikova, 2015). At the same time, the main problems of education are: the corruption component in the educational environment, the low-quality level of teaching, the students' lack of interest in gaining knowledge and focus only on getting a degree certificate, a weak global rating of Russian universities. (Bobrova, 2018). In order to overcome these negative phenomena, a number of steps have been taken to develop a unified strategy for the development of education in order to create a unified system of upbringing and education worthy of being among the top ten in the world. (Kirillova, 2018).

After the improvement of the system of general and vocational education, the next task aimed at the development of human potential (capital) is the importance of the development of the system of continuous education. The recent changes in the Russian pension legislation, which extended the officially established period of work capacity of citizens for five years, are of particular relevance to this task. It is planned to organize events for vocational training and additional education for people of pre-retirement age within the framework of the National Project "Demography" and the Federal Program "Older Generation" from January 1, 2019. According to the Russian Minister of Labor and Social Protection M.A. Topilin, in six years they are planning to educate 450,000 people, 75,000 per year. In terms of the national project "Demography", 30 billion rubles are to be spent on it in 2019–2024. (Topilin, 2019). 1,530,000 thousand rubles are allocated on the creation of centers of continuous improvement of professional skills of teachers and accreditation centers of the education system in 2019, by the Federal Law "On the Federal Budget for 2019 and the 2020 and 2021 Planning Period".

The next task in order to ensure the development of domestic human potential, in subparagraph 3, paragraph 23 of the Strategy, is the improvement of the national system of qualifications. After all, the national system of qualifications is an object of coordination of the quality of qualifications of workers between employers and educational institutions providing training for them (Tashkinova, 2018). At the same time, by introducing and developing this system, it is proposed to solve the problem of inconsistency between the level of skills of new employees and employers' requirements. In order to do this, employers can directly influence the training of professional personnel by identifying the necessary knowledge and competencies in each specific professional area and consolidating them in professional standards. In 2016, the Federal Law "On Independent Qualification Assessment" was adopted in order to implement the national qualifications system. It establishes the procedure for compliance of an individual's assigned qualifications with those listed in legislation and other regulatory acts, as well as the professional standard of the necessary requirements for each individual category of employees. The independent assessment of qualification takes place in the form of a professional exam, the procedure for which is determined by the "Rules for the Center for the Evaluation of Qualifications of Independent Assessment of Qualification in the Form of a Professional Exam", approved by a Government Decree. According to its results, a certificate of qualification is issued to the applicant or his legal representative within thirty days, and if the professional exam has not been passed – instead of a certificate, recommendations in a special report form are given to the applicant.

It should be noted that the applicant independently initiates such a professional exam at his own expense or other individuals', including legal. Also, the articles of the Labor Code of the Russian Federation provide for the possibility of holding a professional exam by the referral of the employer. In this case, expenses for the exam are carried by the supervisor. The procedure of sending an employee to pass such an exam by an employer is defined as follows: firstly, the need to send workers is determined by the employer (paragraph 1 of the article 196 of the Labor Code of the Russian Federation), secondly, employees are given the right to obtain an independent assessment of qualifications, although not at the employer's expense, but their own (article 197 of the Labor Code of the Russian Federation), and, thirdly, workers can theoretically refuse to undergo an independent assessment of qualification, since, according to paragraph 2 of the article 196 of the Labor Code of the Russian Federation, the process of sending workers to undergo an independent assessment of qualifications is carried out by the employer with their written consent, in the manner determined by the collective agreement, and other local acts. That is, for now it is a question of a voluntary independent assessment of qualifications, based on the initiative of either an employee or an employer.

The following achievements can be noted within the framework of the development of the national system of professional qualifications: the Priority Program "Increasing Labor Productivity and Employment Support" was adopted; Passport of the Priority Project "Federal Center of Competence in the Sphere of Labor Productivity" was approved; the Federal Center of Competence was created; "Qualification Directory of Managers, Professionals and Other Employees" was edited; amendments have been made to the State Program of Russia "Employment Assistance to the Population", dozens of professional standards have been adopted or changed. It should be noted that the task of improving the requirements for professional qualifications of certain categories of workers, as well as informing about new professions and the state-legal development of Russia that are in demand at the present stage, is solved in the most intensive way, and how soon it will lead to the development of human potential of Russians, only time will show.

An important task for the development of human capital is the promotion of effective employment and labor mobility. The authors remind that the right to professional orientation has been reserved for Russian citizens for quite some time, and, although the Russian Constitution does not mention such a right, it is nonetheless enshrined, firstly, in the European Social Charter. Thus, article 9 of the European Social Charter states that in order to ensure the effective exercise of the right to vocational guidance, the Parties (the signatories of the Charter) undertake to provide (encourage) the provision of services that help all persons (including the disabled) to solve problematic issues related to individual choice of profession or raising the qualification level of citizens and employment opportunities for the population of the country. Such assistance should be provided free of charge to both young people and adults.

In accordance with the content of article 9 of the Law of the Russian Federation "On Employment in the Russian Federation", citizens have the right to receive free consultations, free information and services related to the choice of profession in employment services to determine the scope of activities, possible employment, as well as the availability of the necessary and additional education. The employment service authorities provide an opportunity for Russians to receive these services in electronic form in accordance with the law. In addition, the unemployed may be provided with free services for relocation to another area for employment, psychological support, vocational training and additional education.

The only noticeable difference, in our opinion, is that the charter mentions persons with disabilities, but the national law does not. On the other hand, Russian law goes further, imposing on the state the provision of free services to assist in relocation to another area for employment. In the Order of the Ministry of Labor of Russia "On the Approval of the Federal State Standard of State Services to Assist Unemployed Citizens in Relocation and Unemployed Citizens and Members of Their Families in Relocating to Other Area for Employment by Referral of the Government Employment Bodies" the employment service assumes the following functions: 1) informing an unemployed citizen about the availability of vacancies and vacancies in other areas; 2) selecting work options; 3) agreeing with the employer on the candidacy of an unemployed individual; 4) issuing an employment referral to a citizen; 5) designating financial support for relocation and resettlement, and transfer of funds to an unemployed citizen; 7) entering information about the results of the provision of public services in the register.

The next task aimed at the development of human capital, in general, and human potential, in particular, is associated with a reduction in the level of poverty and property inequality of the population. The admissible threshold at which it remains possible to ensure a tolerable existence for one and one's family (poverty line) is income which is not lower than the subsistence minimum, that from January 1, 2019, amounts to 10,451 rubles per capita, for the employable citizens – 11,310 rubles, for pensioners – 8, 615 rubles, children – 10,302 rubles. According to Rosstat 19 million Russians in absolute terms now have income below the subsistence minimum. The authors believe that the implementation of the analyzed task may face serious difficulties caused by objectively difficult internal and external economic conditions, which include the increase in geopolitical instability and unsustainable development of the global economy, anti-Russian economic sanctions, critical dependence on imports of a wide range of high-tech equipment, low productivity labor and other.

The list of tasks aimed at the development of human capital in Russia is concluded with the improvement of the mechanisms for ensuring environmental safety and maintaining a favorable environment. The environment, as the habitat of people, as well as the observance of the rules of ecological safety, as a guarantee of the preservation of this area, is an important factor, and at the same time a means of preserving and developing human potential. In December 2018, the Federal Law on Amendments in the Procedure for Conducting State Ecological Expertise was adopted, in accordance with which: 1) the period for conducting state ecological expertise was reduced from 3 to 2 months; 2) the procedure for the examination of project documentation of category I objects was clarified; 3) the design documentation of individual boreholes created on land plots provided to the subsoil user and necessary for regional geological exploration, exploration and production of oil and natural gas is excluded from the list of objects for examination; 5) provisions have been introduced relating to the removal of administrative barriers when applying for complex environmental permits for facilities of category I and the submission of declarations on environmental impact for facilities of category II.

Particular attention is devoted to the new system of handling municipal solid waste, which is defined in the Federal Law "On the Legal Regulation of Relationships in the Field of Production and Consumption Waste".

Authors believe that a lot has already been done in the framework of the implementation of the final analyzed task, and it is likely that the work will continue, and only time will show whether it leads to the development of human potential of the Russians.

Conclusion/Recommendations

Analyzing the practical implementation of the tasks aimed at implementing the direction of the state policy of the Russian Federation related to the development of human potential, the authors would like to emphasize that although the issues of education, obtaining a profession, and employment itself, occupy an important place in the life of every person, nevertheless our state, represented by its own government bodies, should not forget why every particular person needs to have this. After all, education – for the sake of education, and labor, for the sake of labor, a priori, cannot lead to anything good. One, at least, must be sure that he/she works, he/she will not be below the poverty line, and if he/she has still worked up to the statutory disability age, he/she will not become fully financially dependent on the Pension Fund payments and social assistance of the state.

Nevertheless, authors hope that the systematic solution of the tasks set by the Strategy, not only related to human development, but also others, aimed at ensuring the state of economic security of an individual, society and the state, in general, in the near future will contribute to an increase in economic ecurity of the individual, society and the state, and, ultimately, lead to a significant improvement in welfare and satisfaction of the population.

References

The European Social Charter (revised in Strasbourg, May 3, 1996), Bulletin of International Treaties, 2010, No 4, pp. 17–67.

"Labor Code of the Russian Federation" 30 December 2001 No 197-FZ (rev. 27 December, 2018), Collection of Legislative Acts of the Russian Federation, 2002, No 1 (Part 1), column 3.

Federal Law of 29.11.2018, No 459-FZ "On the Federal Budget for 2019 and the 2020 and 2021 Planning Period", Collection of Legislative Acts of the Russian Federation, 2018, No 49 (Part II), column 7531; (Part III), column 7531.

Federal Law of 03.07.2016, No 238-FZ "On Independent Assessment of Qualifications", Collection of Legislative Acts of the Russian Federation, 2016, No 27 (Part I), column 4171.

Act of the Russian Federation of 19 April 1991, No 1032-1 (rev. 11. 12.2018)"Employment of the Population in the Russian Federation", Collection of Legislative Acts of the Russian Federation, 1996, No 17, column 1915.

Decree of the President of the Russian Federation 13 May 2017 No 208 "Strategy for Economic Security of the Russian Federation for the period until 2030", Official Internet portal of legal information, http://www.pravo.gov.ru, 15 May 2017.

The Order of Ministry of Labor and Social Protection of the Russian Federation of 07.03.2013 N of 92 N (an edition of 16. 06.2017)"On the Approval of the Federal State Standard of State Services to Assist Unemployed Citizens in Relocation and Unemployed Citizens and Members of Their Families in Relocating to Other Area for Employment by Referral of the Government Employment Bodies", Russian Newspaper, No. 112, 28 May 2013.

Order of Ministry of Labor and Social Protection of the Russian Federation 12 November 2018 No 695n "On Establishment of Size of a Minimum Wage Per Capita and on the Main Social and Demographic Groups of the Population in General Across the Russian Federation for the Third Quarter of 2018", Official Internet portal of legal information, http://www.pravo.gov.ru, 30 November 2018.

Avdeev, S. (2018) "On the Way to Degradation. What is Happening to the Russian education system?" available at: https://samolet.media/posts/3242 (Accessed 16.03. 2019)

Bobrova, T.A. (2018) “Modern Higher Education System of the Russian Federation: Main Problems and Ways of Their Solution”, Young Scientist, No 45 pp. 127–130.
Bondarenko, E.A. (2013) “Concepts “Human Capital”, “Knowledge Society” and “Intellectual Property”: was K. Marx right?”, Scientific papers of the Belgorod State University, Philosophy series, Sociology, Right, No 23 (166), Issue 26, pp. 189–197.
Britikova, E.A. (2015) Modernization of Russian Higher Education Trend, Problem, Prospects (on materials of a comparative research of the state and commercial universities): abstract of dis. (. . .) candidate of social science: 22. 00.04/ Krasnodar University of the Ministry of Internal Affairs of the Russian Federation. Krasnodar, 2015.
The Number of the Poor Grows In Russia: Income of 19 Million People is Lower than Subsistance Minimum. Available at: https://2goroda.ru/infobar/v-rossii-vyroslo-chislo-bednyh-dohod-19-millionov-chelovek-nizhe-prozhitochnogo-minimuma (Accessed 16.03.2019)
Dobrynin, A.I., Dyatlov, S.A., Konnov, VA. (1993) Productive Forces of a Person: Structure and Forms of Manifestation, St. Petersburg: Publishing house of St. Petersburg University of Economics and Finance.
Ilyinsky, I.V. (1996) Investments Into Future: Education in Innovative Production, St. Petersburg: Publishing house of St. Petersburg University of Economics and Finance.
Kirillova, G.T. (2018) “The Short-Term Prospects in Education for 2019”, available at: https://nsportal.ru/npo-spo/obrazovanie-i-pedagogika/library/2018/12/24/blizhayshie-perspektivy-v-obrazovanii-na-2019 (Accessed 16. 03.2019)
Marx K. (1960) The Capital. Critique of Political Economy. Vol. 1, Marx K., Engels F. Compositions, Vol. 23, Moscow: Publishing house of political literature.
Topilin, M. (2019) “The Minister M. Topilin in an interview to Rossiyskaya Gazeta”, available at: https://git60.rostrud.ru/news/746550.html (Accessed 16. 03.2019)
Rimashevskaya, N.M. (2004) “Human Potential of Russia and Problem of Saving the Population”, Russian economic magazine, No 9–10, pp. 22–40.
Tashkinova N.A. (2018) National System of Qualifications: for Who and What for? We Understand: Information Materials and Methodical Recommendations, Tyumen: GAUK TO “TONB”, 2018.
Schultz, T.W. (1971a) Investment in Human Capital: The Role of Education and of Research, New York: The Free Press.

Elena G. Popkova

17 The Problem of Economization of the Non-Economic Spheres and Types of Activities Through the Prism of Paradoxes of the Economic Time

Introduction

A current tendency of the recent decades at the level of the global economy has been economization of the non-economic spheres and types of activities. According to the existing scientific and economic paradigm, this tendency is assigned the social nature – i.e., it is considered that it is caused by social reasons and leads to social consequences. That's why it is studied with the help of the tools of the neo-institutional economic theory through the prism of institutionalization of social practices.

The neo-institutional approach to studying the tendency of economization of the non-economic spheres and types of activities does not allow for quantitative measuring of this tendency and precise evaluation of causal connections of its manifestation in the modern global economy; also, it leads to a priori negative treatment of this tendency as a process of transformation of public benefits (widely provided by the principles of corporate social responsibility with minimum expenditures of society/state) into economic (with limited access, provided for obtaining profit with high expenditures of society/state) benefits.

Thus, there emerges a problem of fragmentary and unidirectional elaboration of the tendency of economization of the non-economic spheres and types of activities, which leads to its subjective (qualitative) treatment and complexity of its forecasting and management. The working hypothesis of the work is that the tendency of economization of the non-economic spheres and types of activities could and should be studied with the help of the neo-classical approach, which will allow solving the determined problem and will ensure the objective treatment of the tendency of economization of the non-economic spheres and types of activities and will allow for its forecasting and management in the interests of development of modern socio-economic systems.

The purpose of the work is to study the problem of economization of the non-economic spheres and types of activities with the help of the tools of the neoclassical economic theory through the prism of paradoxes of economic time. The purpose predetermined the structure and sequence of the research (its tasks). The conceptual

Elena G. Popkova, Plekhanov Russian University of Economics, MGIMO University, Moscow, Russia

https://doi.org/10.1515/9783110636147-017

foundations of studying the paradoxes of economic time are developed. After that, the paradoxes of economic time in the modern global economic system are determined. Finally, the tendency of economization of the non-economic spheres and types of activities through the prism of paradoxes of economic time (by the example of the sphere of higher education) is analyzed, perspectives of future development of this tendency are determined, and recommendations for its management are offered. The authors use the econometric tools: correlation, trend, and regression analysis.

Materials and Method

The problem of economization of the sphere of higher education is studied in detail in the existing publications, which include Ahlburg (2017), Bartl (2014), and Fischer et al. (2018). The performed content analysis of the above works allowed determining the following features of economization of the sphere of higher education, which are peculiar for most of the modern socio-economic systems, including Russia:

- reduction of the volume of state financing of universities and stimulation of their entrepreneurial activity (through establishment of the corresponding criterion during evaluation of their effectiveness)
- active involvement of universities in the process of commercialization of innovations as sellers of intellectual capital
- expansion of the universities' opportunities for provision of paid scientific and educational services and their pricing
- difference between the quality of provided research and educational services of universities, volumes of their state financing, and reputation in the market of educational services, market of innovations, and labor market (absence of guarantee of quality)

Studying economized universities as social institutes, some scholars – for example Huynh (2019) and Meza-Bolaños et al. (2019) – explain the process of their emergence with deregulation of the sphere of higher education (reduction of state interference), and other authors – Peter and Bröckling (2016) and Zou et al. (2017) – with the change of consumer preferences (reduction of quality of educational services and growth of demand for their prestige).

The above authors connect the consequences of economization of the sphere of education to reduction of accessibility of scientific and educational services in the short-term (in five years) and slowdown of the rate of economic growth and reduction of population's living standards – in the long-term (10–15 years).

However, all the above approaches to the conceptual treatment of the causal connections between economization of the sphere of education, the scientific positions are substantiated only by the authors' statements and suppositions, which leads to a multiple number of unproved hypotheses and absence of a common treatment, which would describe the studied tendency objectively and precisely. This gap in the existing scientific and economic knowledge should be filled by this work.

Results

The Conceptual Foundations of Studying the Paradoxes of Economic Time

Various aspects of the influence of the time factor on functioning and development of economic systems are studied within the separate spheres of scientific economic knowledge (concepts), in particular:
- the concept of economic cycles (Mohammadi et al., 2018)
- the concept of time rows (Shahbaz et al., 2018), (Güney et al., 2015)
- the concept of economic growth (Castaldo et al., 2017), (Gómez and Neves Sequeira, 2014), (Kupina and Salko, 2015)
- the concept of economic crises (Christakou, 2014), (Raźniak et al., 2018)
- the concept of lost opportunities (Stafford et al., 2011)
- the concept of economy of human labor (Hecht, 2018)
- the concept of growth poles (Jia et al., 2018)
- the concept of extrapolation (Pirker and Lichtenegger, 2018), (Mitrouli and Roupa, 2018)
- the concept of scenario analysis (Jalles, 2017)
- the concept of given indicators (Creemers, 2018)
- the concept of "underdevelopment whirlpools" Popkova et al. (2018a), Popkova et al. (2018b)

However, despite the high level of elaboration of the above concepts, the comprehensive Theory of time in economy is not yet formed. The authors offer and develop a new concept – the concept of paradoxes of economic time. The paradoxes of economic time are treated as economic phenomena and processes (scientific facts from experience/practice of economic systems) that contradict the traditional ideas of time in economy (contradicting or not confirming the adopted concepts). The paradoxes of economic time should be conducted with application of the econometric tools that include the methods of correlation, trend, and regression analysis.

Paradoxes of Economic Time in the Modern Global Economic System

As a result of a series of empirical experiments on verification of the adopted concepts of the influence of the time factor on functioning and development of economic systems, the authors determined two paradoxes of economic time in the modern global economic system.

1st paradox: absence of economic calendar with the modern economic systems. According to the concept of economic cycles, each economic system should be developing according to its own economic calendar (regularly repeating cycle). In this case, there should be a clear sequence of seasons in the development of economic systems. However, the performed analysis of time rows, which reflect the dynamics of the change of GDP per capita in the leading developed (G7 – according to the classification of the International Monetary Fund) and developing (BRICS) countries of the world for the recent 24 years (1995–2018), did now show any signs of their seasonality. The initial selection of the data is shown in Tables 17.1 and 17.2.

Based on the data of Tables 17.1 and 17.2, we calculated the coefficients of autocorrelation (r) and their standard errors (q). As the selection of the initial data includes 24-time rows (n = 24), the number of periods (lags) based on which the coefficient of autocorrelation was calculated does not constitute n / 4 = 6. Presence of the signs of seasonality requires the significance of the coefficients of autocorrelation, for which the standard errors should exceed the table value of Student's t-test (in this case – 2.17). The results of calculations are shown in Figures 17.1–17.12.

As neither of the autocorrelation coefficients was significant according to the Student's t-test (all standard errors are below 2.17), the studied time rows do not contain a tendency and cyclic (seasonal) fluctuations, but have only random (stochastic) component. Therefore, the modern economic systems do not have a clear economic calendar – i.e., they do not have regularly recurring cyclic fluctuations with predictable frequency and amplitude.

2nd paradox: difference between economic time and physical time – economic systems are in different economic time, which does not coincide with their difference in physical time. This paradox by the example of difference in the economic and physical time of the countries G7 and BRICS with Russia in 2010 I shown in Table 17.3.

Table 17.3 shows that in 2010 Russia was in the present economic time, and it is selected as a basis for comparison with other countries of the world. The countries of G7 are in the future economic time, showing higher level of GDP per capita, despite being in the past physical time. Brazil is in the same economic time as Russia (at present), but is behind the physical time by 6 hours.

China is in the past economic time (behind Russia by 6 years), but in the future physical time (+6 hours). India is behind Russia by more than 13 years and is in the

Table 17.1: Dynamics of GDP per capita in constant prices in countries G7 (Major advanced economies) in 1995–2018, USD.

Country	1995	1996	1997	1998	1999	2000	2001	2002
Canada	20,641.54	21,257.09	21,857.61	20,975.14	22,261.15	24,221.27	23,777.49	24,210.04
France	27,898.3	27,870.57	25,167	25,951.7	25,680.9	23,317.94	23,342.09	25,226.21
Germany	31,907.94	30,744.89	27,257.16	27,581.93	27,054.59	24,008.66	23,949.76	25,576.54
Italy	20,609.06	23,033.4	21,811.82	22,283.57	21,968.42	20,116.62	20,423.14	22,303.02
Japan	43,454.78	38,453.38	35,042.32	31,931.07	35,912.46	38,533.86	33,860.45	32,301.3
UK	22,759.46	23,974.94	26,366.88	27,769.02	28,159.95	27,828.38	27,296.67	29,654.24
USA	28,762.68	30,047.31	31,553.62	32,929.04	34,601.72	36,432.51	37,241.35	38,113.89
Country	**2003**	**2004**	**2005**	**2006**	**2007**	**2008**	**2009**	**2010**
Canada	28,242.19	32,075.36	36,315.73	40,441.77	44,599.15	46,660.87	40,831.1	47,512.68
France	30,808.71	35,153.79	36,209.52	37,900.03	43,155.5	47,273.32	43,234.25	42,249.06
Germany	30,785.6	34,657.52	35,239.9	37,020.35	42,531.38	46,681.07	42,576.34	42,641.68
Italy	27,527.38	31,319.73	32,066.38	33,486.01	37,890.2	40,953.86	37,130.15	35,969.19
Japan	34,844.66	37,701.44	37,228.23	35,464.64	35,342.48	39,453.5	41,014.19	44,673.61
UK	34,049.76	39,871.03	41,566.63	44,095.77	49,973.92	46,890.22	38,180.57	38,737.56
USA	39,591.87	41,838.46	44,218.31	46,351.67	47,954.53	48,302.28	46,909.42	48,310.34

(continued)

Table 17.1 (continued)

Country	2011	2012	2013	2014	2015	2016	2017	2018
Canada	52,143.84	52,577.39	52,494.13	50,509.59	43,349.62	42,210.13	43,611.26	44,649.65
France	45,430.28	42,333.09	44,104.92	44,413.12	37,612.91	38,127.65	37,294.72	38,087.37
Germany	46,853.22	44,089.69	46,545.09	47,978.61	41,197.41	41,902.28	41,243.88	42,196.07
Italy	38,379.31	34,918.74	35,706.62	35,456.7	30,032.11	30,507.18	29,747.13	30,260.04
Japan	48,168.81	48,632.91	40,490.16	38,143.11	34,513.36	38,917.29	38,281.58	39,308.31
UK	41,259.5	41,683.67	42,452.95	46,478.84	43,976.42	40,095.95	37,812.51	38,254.4
USA	49,733.88	51,403.39	52,741.73	54,559.86	56,174.94	57,436.41	59,609.07	62,001.97

Source: compiled by the authors based on International Monetary Fund (2019).

Table 17.2: Dynamics of GDP per capita in constant prices in the countries of BRICS in 1995–2018, USD.

Country	**1995**	**1996**	**1997**	**1998**	**1999**	**2000**	**2001**	**2002**
Brazil	4,950.301	5,273.89	5,394.64	5,197.032	3,552.143	3,778.965	3,183.794	2,859.599
China	608.375	708.58	780.839	827.643	872.222	958.564	1,053.145	1,150.213
India	391.249	418.602	434.737	432.225	462.133	463.118	471.311	492.234
Russia	2,271.31	2,842.858	2,944.467	1,975.972	1,432.661	1,905.949	2,259.023	2,556.64
South Africa	3,752.377	3,500.031	3,556.537	3,160.844	3,089.367	3,042.429	2,671.989	2,524.22
Country	**2003**	**2004**	**2005**	**2006**	**2007**	**2008**	**2009**	**2010**
Brazil	3,090.663	3,659.099	4,815.707	5,912.55	7,374.075	8,854.162	8,624.417	11,297.84
China	1,293.129	1,512.619	1,765.721	2,110.574	2,703.003	3,467.03	3,837.903	4,524.055
India	572.299	657.522	748.85	839.927	1,080.89	1,053.439	1,159.061	1,429.599
Russia	3,197.688	4,408.374	5,713.361	7,420.484	9,753.262	12,468.38	9,178.45	11,445.13
South Africa	3,775.557	4,870.662	5,412.37	5,635.287	6,117.192	5,793.118	5,914.136	7,361.936
Country	**2011**	**2012**	**2013**	**2014**	**2015**	**2016**	**2017**	**2018**
Brazil	13,242.49	12,367.14	12,295.09	12,112.57	8,810.496	8,726.901	10,308.81	10,699.6
China	5,582.887	6,329.464	7,080.828	7,701.691	8,166.756	8,113.257	8,480.654	9,146.854
India	1,497.401	1,470.732	1,475.168	1,594.317	1,615.789	1,723.301	1,850.226	1,998.255
Russia	14,187.19	15,145.38	15,558.8	14,388	9,521.081	8,928.697	10,885.48	11,248.33
South Africa	8,058.905	7,548.447	6,898.484	6,492.891	5,721.149	5,260.902	5,588.959	5,662.045

Source: compiled by the authors based on International Monetary Fund (2019).

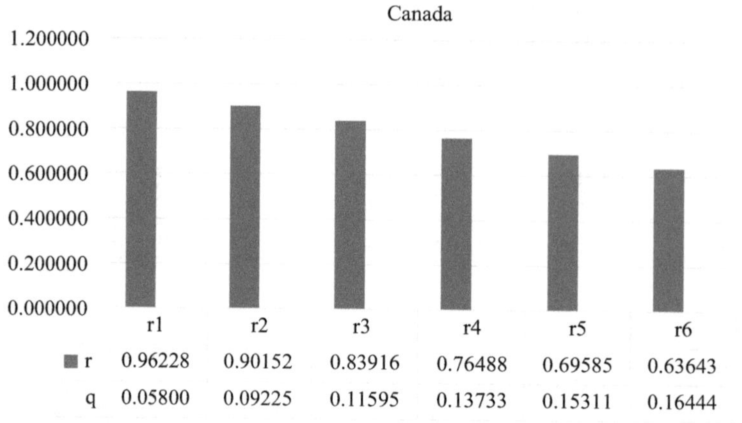

Figure 17.1: Correlogram of the time row of dynamics of GDP per capita in Canada in 1995–2018 and standard errors.
Source: calculated by the authors.

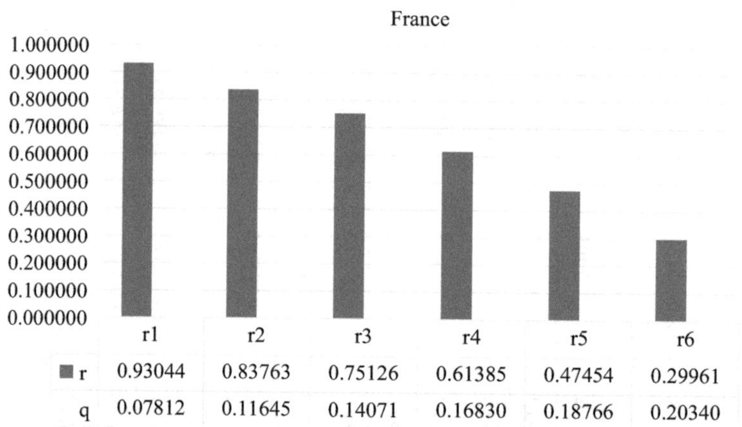

Figure 17.2: Correlogram of the time row of dynamics of GDP per capita in France in 1995–2018 and standard errors.
Source: calculated by the authors.

past economic time, but in the future physical time (+6 hours). South Africa is in the past economic and physical time, but with a large difference – underrun from Russia is 4 years, and physical underrun is only 1 year.

3rd paradox: inaccessibility of leveling the disproportions of the global economic system. According to the concept of economic growth, it is necessary to reduce the underrun of developing countries from developed countries as to the level

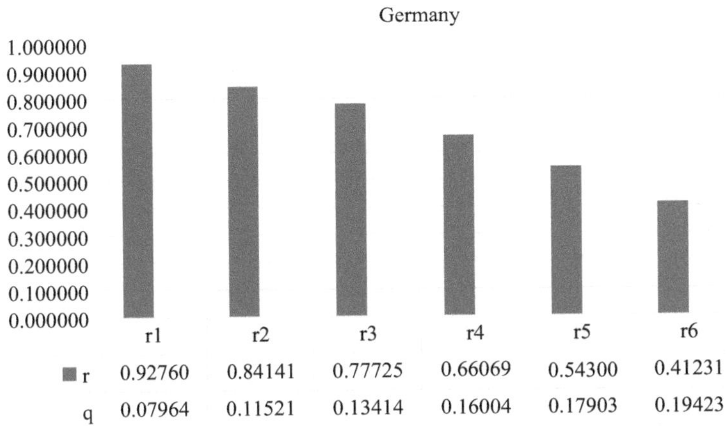

Figure 17.3: Correlogram of the time row of dynamics of GDP per capita in Germany 1995–2018 and standard errors.
Source: calculated by the authors.

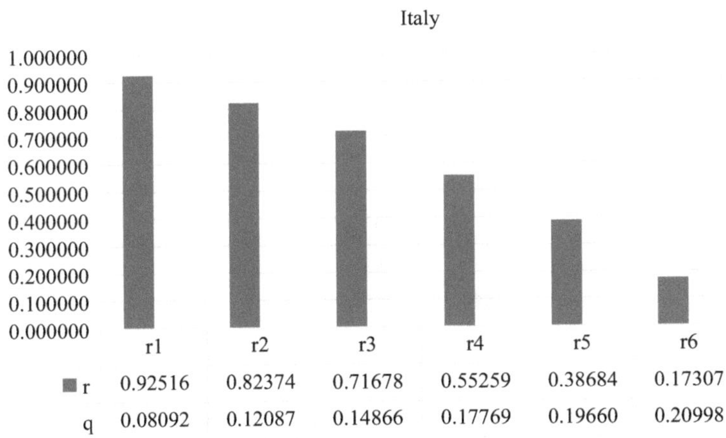

Figure 17.4: Correlogram of the time row of dynamics of GDP per capita in Italy in 1995–2018 and standard errors.
Source: calculated by the authors.

and rate of economic growth, which indicator is GDP per capita. Large efforts have been made in the recent decades for achieving the balance of the global economic system. Developing countries implement the models of economic growth, developed and tested by developed countries, and receive additional financing and non-financial support. It is supposed that this should lead to reduction of their underrun from developed countries (differentiation). Its dynamics is shown in Figure 17.13.

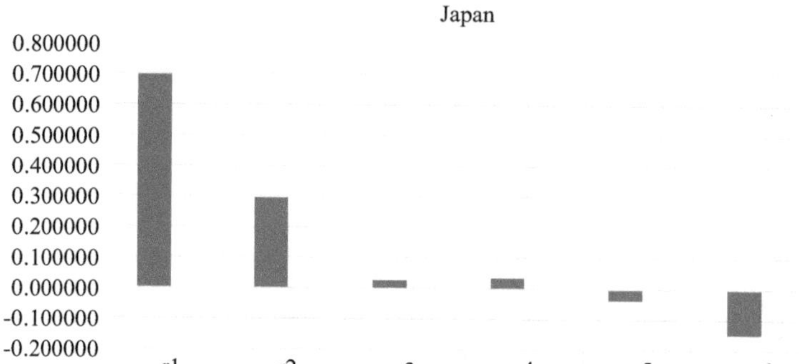

	r1	r2	r3	r4	r5	r6
r	0.69582	0.29446	0.02580	0.03487	-0.0350	-0.1490
q	0.15312	0.20374	0.21313	0.21307	0.21307	0.21082

Figure 17.5: Correlogram of the time row of dynamics of GDP per capita in Japan in 1995–2018 and standard errors.
Source: calculated by the authors.

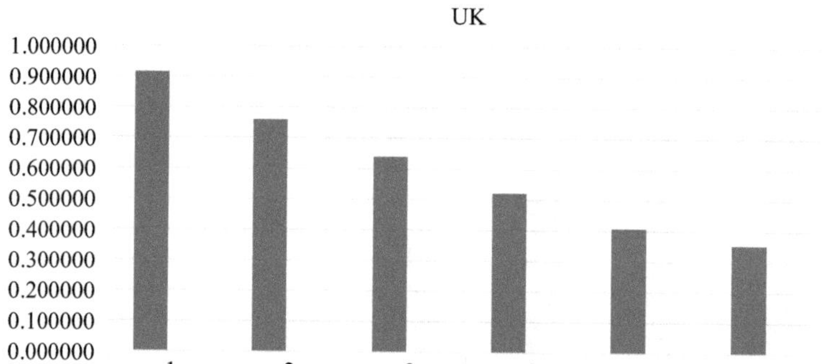

	r1	r2	r3	r4	r5	r6
r	0.91476	0.75869	0.63790	0.52132	0.40691	0.35387
q	0.08613	0.13888	0.16419	0.18193	0.19475	0.19940

Figure 17.6: Correlogram of the time row of dynamics of GDP per capita in the UK in 1995–2018 and standard errors.
Source: calculated by the authors.

Figure 17.13 shows that differentiation between the average level of GDP per capita of the countries of BRICS and the countries of G7 in 1995–2018 has not reduced, but only increased. In 2018 it grew by 34.15% as compared to 1995. This contradicts the provisions of the concept of economic growth regarding the balance of the global economy.

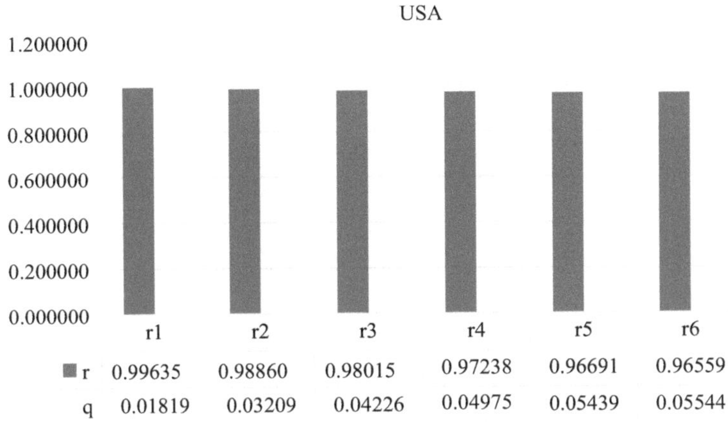

Figure 17.7: Correlogram of the time row of dynamics of GDP per capita in the USA in 1995–2018 and standard errors.
Source: calculated by the authors.

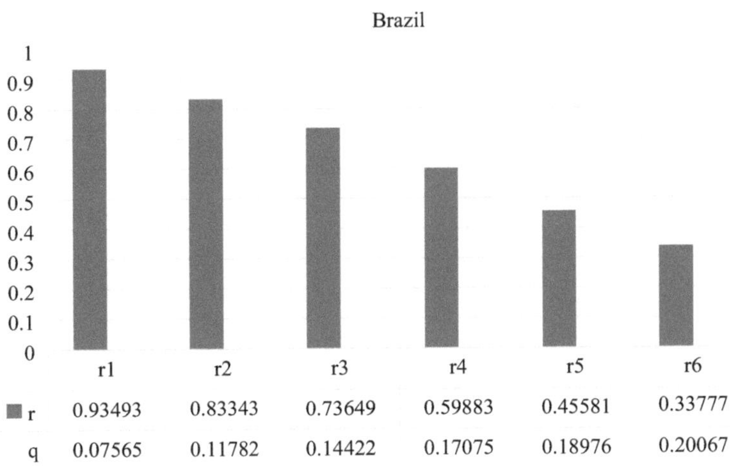

Figure 17.8: Correlogram of the time row of dynamics of GDP per capita in Brazil in 1995–2018 and standard errors.
Source: calculated by the authors.

The tendency of economization of higher education through the prism of paradoxes of economic time

Let us study the connection between the determined paradoxes of economic time and economization of higher education in the selected countries (by the example of G7 and BRICS). For that, we shall use the method of regression analysis, for determining

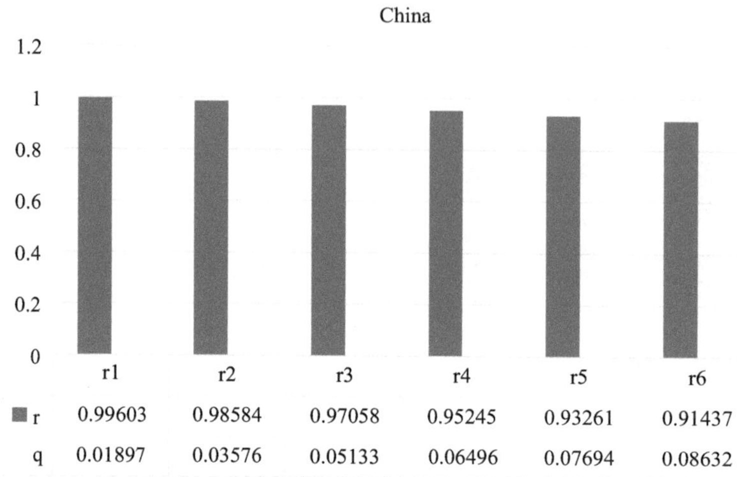

Figure 17.9: Correlogram of the time row of dynamics of GDP per capita in China in 1995–2018 and standard errors.
Source: calculated by the authors.

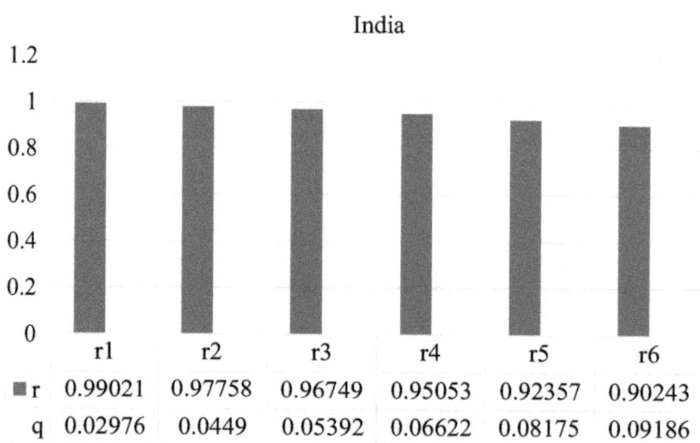

Figure 17.10: Correlogram of the time row of dynamics of GDP per capita in India 1995–2018 and standard errors.
Source: calculated by the authors.

the dependence of GDP per capita on the volume of attracted investments by the most economized (occupying the leading positions in the rating of attraction of investments) universities of each countries of the selection in 2018. The initial data are given in Table 17.4, and the results of the analysis – in Table 17.5.

The data from Table 17.5 show that growth of the volume of attracted investments in the most economized universities in the countries of G7 and BRICS by USD 1 leads to increase of GDP per capita in constant prices by USD 0.1347 (2018). As significance

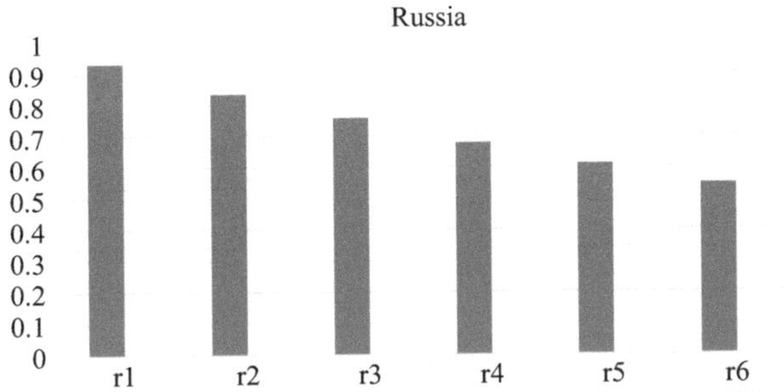

	r1	r2	r3	r4	r5	r6
r	0.93178	0.83325	0.75675	0.67649	0.60833	0.54485
q	0.0774	0.11788	0.13937	0.15701	0.16921	0.17878

Figure 17.11: Correlogram of the time row of dynamics of GDP per capita in Russia in 1995–2018 and standard errors.
Source: calculated by the authors.

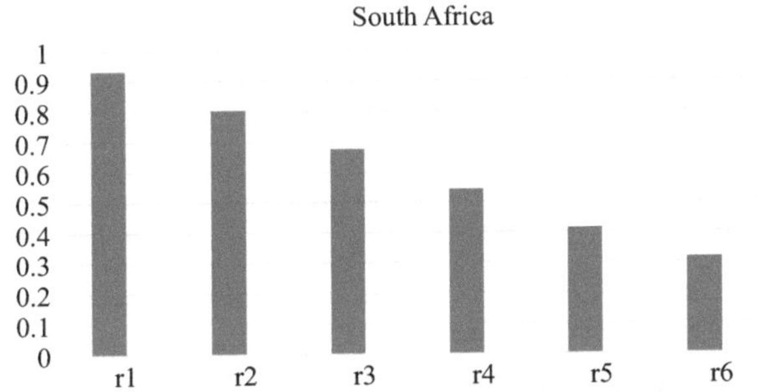

	r1	r2	r3	r4	r5	r6
r	0.93369	0.80322	0.6748	0.54206	0.41319	0.31527
q	0.07634	0.127	0.15734	0.17916	0.19415	0.20233

Figure 17.12: Correlogram of the time row of dynamics of GDP per capita in South Africa in 1995–2018 and standard errors.
Source: calculated by the authors.

F (0.0016) does not exceed 0.05, the established regression dependence is correct at the significance level $\alpha = 0.05$. The obtained value of the determination coefficient ($R^2 = 0.6453$) shows that the change of dependent variable by 64.53% is explained by the change of the independent variable.

Therefore, economization of the sphere of education stimulates the increase of population's living standards, which contradicts the offered hypotheses that state the opposite. This conclusion allows forecasting further development of the studied tendency under the influence of the natural market forces. As the volume of attracted investments is one of the criteria of evaluation of modern universities' competitiveness that determines their position in the global ratings, it is obvious that

Table 17.3: Difference in the economic and physical time of the countries of G7 and BRICS with Russia in 2010.

Country	GDP per capita in 2010, USD	Year with the similar level of GDP per capita in Russia	Difference in economic time, years	Difference in physical time (Moscow time), hours
Canada	47,512.68	after 2018	more than +8	−8
France	42,249.06	after 2018	more than +8	−2
Germany	42,641.68	after 2018	more than +8	−2
Italy	35,969.19	after 2018	more than +8	−2
Japan	44,673.61	after 2018	more than +8	6
UK	38,737.56	after 2018	more than +8	−3
USA	48,310.34	after 2018	more than +8	−8
Brazil	11,297.84	2010	0	−6
China	4,524.055	2004	−4	+6
India	1,429.599	Before 1995	more than −13	+2.5
Russia	11,445.13	2010	0	0
South Africa	7,361.936	2006	−4	−1

Source: compiled by the authors based on International Monetary Fund (2019).

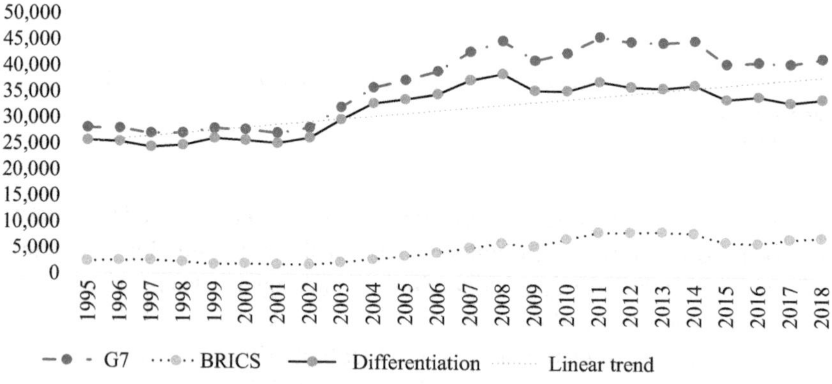

Figure 17.13: Dynamics of average GDP per capita in the countries of G7, countries of BRICS, and their differentiation in 1995–2018.
Source: calculated by the authors based on International Monetary Fund (2019).

Table 17.4: The volume of attracted investments (endowment) in the most economized universities and GDP per capita in constant prices in countries G7 and BRICS in 2018.

Country	The most economized university	Volume of attracted investments, USD	GDP per capita, USD
		x	y
Canada	University of British Columbia	1,269,851,000	44,649.6
France	Sorbonne University	22,127,751,425	38,087.4
Germany	Heidelberg University	24,514,794,726	42,196.1
Italy	University of Pisa	17,580,278,749	30,260.0
Japan	University of Tokyo	22,837,085,152	39,308.3
UK	University of Oxford	22,224,789,097	38,254.4
USA	Harvard University	36,021,516,000	62,002.0
Brazil	University of São Paulo	6,216,181,228	10,699.6
China	Peking University	5,314,079,348	9,146.8
India	Indian Institute of Science	1,160,933,106	1,998.2
Russia	Moscow State University	6,534,983,439	11,248.3
South Africa	University of South Africa	328,949,7832	5,662.05

Source: compiled by the authors based on International Monetary Fund (2019), The Best Schools (2019).

they will continue their economization for attraction of the larger volume of investments and strengthening of positions in the rankings.

Based on the above conclusion on the positive role of economization of the sphere of higher education for modern socio-economic systems, we offer the following recommendations for state regulation of the studied tendency:

- support for natural economization of universities: instead of creation of direct stimuli (requirements, norms, and standards of economization), indirect stimulation of this tendency through the normative and legal establishment of the necessity for universities to occupy certain positions in the global ratings that take into account the criteria of economization – this practice has been successfully applied in Russia in recent years
- social marketing of economization of the sphere of higher education through informing of all interested parties on the advantages of this tendency for formation of public support

Table 17.5: Characteristics of regression dependence of GDP per capita in constant prices on the volume of attracted investments in the most economized universities in countries G7 and BRICS in 2018.

Regression dependence						
Multiple R	0.8033					
R-square	0.6453					
Normed R-square	0.6098					
Standard error	12,037.3433					
Observations	12					
Dispersion analysis						
	df	SS	MS	F	Significance F	
Regression	1	2635712829.6259	2635712829.6259	18.1902	0.0016	
Leftover	10	1448976347.5059	144897634.7506			
Total	11	4084689177.1319				
	Coefficients	Standard error	t-statistics	R-Value	Lower 95%	Upper 95%
Y-crossing	8817.0577	5645.3447	1.5618	0.1494	-3761.5542	21395.6697
x	0.1347	0.0000003	4.2650	0.0016	0.000001	0.000002

Source: calculated and compiled by the authors.

Conclusion

Thus, it was shown by the example of the sphere of higher education that the tendency of economization of the non-economic spheres and types of activities could be studied with application of the neoclassical approach – through the prism of paradoxes of economic time – which ensures the objective treatment of this tendency and allows for its forecasting and management in the interests of development of modern socio-economic systems. The performed analysis of time paradoxes by the example of the leading developed (G7) and developing (BRICS) countries of the world showed that economic systems do not have an economic calendar (regularly repeating predictable cycle of development) but have a general trend – e.g., increase of population's living standards.

Secondly, economic systems are in different economic time, which does not coincide with their physical time and differences in physical time. It is shown by the example of modern Russia (its level of GDP per capita is the basis for comparison) that the countries of G7 (Canada, France, Germany, Italy, Japan, the UK, and the USA) are in the future economic time; Brazil is in the present time; and India, China, and South Africa are in the past economic time. However, from the physical point of view, Canada, France, Germany, Italy, the UK, the USA, Brazil, and South Africa are behind Russia (Moscow time) as to time, and Japan, China, and India exceed it. The differences between the countries as to the economic and physical times do not coincide either.

Also, leveling of disproportions of the global economic system cannot be achieved – despite the active efforts in this direction, the disproportions growth with time. A probable reason of this paradox is absence of the universal model of economic growth due to specific national peculiarities that transform the causal connections of implementation of any measures of state and corporate management. However, there are common vectors of development of socio-economic systems – e.g., economization of the sphere of higher education, which stimulates the increase of the population's living standards.

Concluding, economization of the sphere of higher education could be defined as a tool of accelerating the economic time of modern socio-economic systems. This means that the more active the economization of the sphere of higher education, the quicker the flow of time in socio-economic system (that is, the higher the rate of growth and development of the system) and vice versa. Based on this, state support for economization of the sphere of higher education is recommended.

The performed research by the example of the sphere of higher education showed that studying the economization of the non-economic spheres and types of activities through the prism of paradoxes of economic time opens opportunities for determining new vectors of economic growth and new tools of managing the development of economic systems. That's why further studies should focus on the modern experience of economization of other non-economic spheres and types of activities (e.g., healthcare and transport infrastructure) for specifying and developing the scientific and methodological foundations of the modern economic science.

References

Ahlburg, D.A. (2017). Is going to university in Britain a wise investment? Political Quarterly, 88(4), pp. 660–666.

Bartl, W. (2014). Economisation of the education system in shrinking regions? The demographic responsiveness of education demand and supply at different levels of the education system | [Ökonomisierung des bildungssystems in schrumpfenden regionen? Demografische reagibilität von bildungsnachfrage und -angebot auf verschiedenen stufen des bildungssystems]. Comparative Population Studies, 39(2), pp. 371–408.

Castaldo, A., Fiorini, A., Maggi, B. (2017). Measuring (in a time of crisis) the impact of broadband connections on economic growth: an OECD panel analysis. Applied Economics, 2(1), pp. 1–1.

Christakou, A. (2014). Present simple and continuous: Emergence of self-regulation and contextual sophistication in adolescent decision-making. Neuropsychologia, 65, pp. 302–312.

Creemers, S. (2018). Moments and distribution of the net present value of a serial project. European Journal of Operational Research, 267(3), pp. 835–848.

Fischer, B.B., Schaeffer, P.R., Silveira, J.P. (2018). Universities' gravitational effects on the location of knowledge-intensive investments in Brazil. Science and Public Policy, 45(5), pp. 692–707.

Gómez, M.A., Neves Sequeira, T. B.E. (2014). Phases of economic development of: Do initial endowments matter? Journal of Macroeconomics, 12(1),21.

Güney, P.Ö., Telatar, E., Hasanov, M. (2015). Time series behaviour of the real interest rates in transition economies. Economic Research-Ekonomska Istrazivanja, 28(1), pp. 104–118.

Hecht, J. (2018). Research and development of and labor productivity: do high-tech firms exhibit labor – or capital-saving technical change? Applied Economics, 50(16), pp. 1790–1811.

Huynh, T. (2019). What makes external financial supporters engage in university spin-off seed investments: entrepreneurs' capabilities or social networks? International Journal of Innovation Management, 23 (2), 1950010.

International Monetary Fund (2019). World economic statistics for categories of countries. URL: https://www.imf.org/external/pubs/ft/weo/2017/01/weodata/weoselgr.aspx (Accessed 19. 02.2019).

Jalles, J.T. (2017). Forecasting performance of private sector's unemployment forecasts in advanced economies. International Review of Applied Economics, 31(6), pp. 707–733.

Jia, S., Qin, C., Ye, X. (2018). The evolution of regional multi-pole growth. Annals of Regional Science, 61(1), pp. 189–207.

Kupina, Q., Salko, D. (2015). Banking system performance on actual stage of economic development of (A comparison analysis of banking systems of Albania and Kosovo). Mediterranean Journal of Social Sciences, 6(2), pp. 345–353.

Meza-Bolaños, D., Compañ Rosique, P., Satorre Cuerda, R. (2019). Analysis of Relevant Factors to Measure the Impact of Investment in e-learning Ecosystems in Public Universities. Advances in Intelligent Systems and Computing, 918, pp. 781–790.

Mitrouli, M., Roupa, P. (2018). Estimates for the generalized cross-validation function via an extrapolation and statistical approach. Calcolo, 55(3),24.

Mohammadi, A., Ahmadi, M.H., Bidi, M., Ghazvini, M., Ming, T. (2018). Exergy and economic analyses of replacing feedwater heaters in a Rankine cycle with parabolic trough collectors. Energy Reports, 4, pp. 243–251.

Peter, T., Bröckling, U. (2016). Equality and excellence. Hegemonic discourses of economisation within the German education system. International Studies in Sociology of Education, 26(3), pp. 231–247.
Pirker, S., Lichtenegger, T. (2018). Efficient time-extrapolation of single- and multiphase simulations by transport based recurrence CFD (rCFD). Chemical Engineering Science, 188, pp. 65–83.
Popkova, E.G., Bogoviz, A.V., Lobova, S.V., Alekseev, A.N. (2018a). "Underdevelopment of whirlpools" as manifestation of disproportions of economic growth in modern Russia. Studies in Systems, Decision and Control, 135, pp. 155–162
Popkova, E.G., Bogoviz, A.V., Lobova, S.V., Romanova, T.F. (2018b). The essence of the processes of economic growth of socio-economic systems. Studies in Systems, Decision and Control, 135, pp. 123–130
Raźniak, P., Dorocki, S., Winiarczyk-Raźniak, A. (2018). Eastern European cities as command and control centers in a time of economic crisis | [Vzhodnoevropska mesta kot središča Vodenja in upravljanja med gospodarsko krizo]. Acta Geographica Slovenica, 58(2), pp. 101–110.
Shahbaz, M., Shahzad, S.J.H., Mahalik, M.K., Sadorsky, P. (2018). How strong is the causal relationship between globalization and energy consumption in developed economies? A country-specific time-series and panel analysis. Applied Economics, 50(13), pp. 1479–1494.
Stafford, M.B.R., Reilly, T., Grove, S.J., (. . .), Bhandari, R., Copeland, J. (2011). The evolution of services advertising in a services-driven national economy: An analysis of progress and missed opportunities. Journal of Advertising Research, 51 (SUPPL.1), pp. 136–152.
The Best Schools (2019). The 100 Richest Universities: Their Generosity and Commitment to Research 2018. URL: https://thebestschools.org/features/richest-universities-endowments-generosity-research/ (Accessed 19.02.2019).
Zou, H., Liu, W., Zou, D. (2017). The optimal investment strategies for university endowment funds based on principle component analysis. Proceedings of the 29th Chinese Control and Decision Conference, CCDC 2017, 7978981, pp. 2755–2760.

Marina L. Al'pidovskaya, Pavel S. Seleznev

18 Purely Public Benefits: The Issue of Inequal Consumption

Introduction

Justice is one of the most complicated and obvious issues of human thought. Many misunderstandings, contradictions, and dissent arise out of inexplicitness, blurriness, and sometimes impreciseness of this concept.

Aristotle explored the virtues in the context of the public life of ancient society and defined the fair thing as the middle between the two kinds of fairness – breach of the law and discrimination towards equal. Modern democrats consider the inequality of people obvious, declaring about dissimilarity (inequality?) od people. From their point of view, this is the definition of fairness. To prove their views, they cite as an example *the principle of differences and individuation* by Gottfried Wilhelm Leibnitz, the completer of the 17th century philosophy and the predecessor of the German classical philosophy: "there are not two absolutely identical things . . ." (The general principles of the philosophy by Leibniz). Therewith, at first, they mistakenly even *equality and similarity*; at second, having approved *the principle of differences and individuation (the law of differentiation)*, Leibniz, in contrast, states *the principle of identity of indistinguishable things* and interpret it as *a law of contradiction*, more precisely, a law of consistency or prohibition of contradictions.

Essentially, a man and a woman as well as an adult and a child, or representatives of different human races are unsimilar and not identical, but . . . they may have equal rights. As equality is not of anthropological nature in this situation, but of a social one, equality of rights to life, freedom, and labor is the pursuit of happiness.

About the unnatural inequality was written by J.-J. Rousseau. Another democrat of the past, one of the representatives of German classical philosophy I.G. Fichte discussing the nature and law as prime causes of equality-inequality noted: "Let nature be responsible for physical inequality that has arisen accidentally; social inequality seems moral one; in respect hereof arises a completely natural question: by what right do different classes exist?" (Fichte, 1993).

Marina L. Al'pidovskaya, Pavel S. Seleznev, Federal State-Funded Educational Institution of Higher Education "Financial University under the Government of the Russian Federation", Moscow, Russia

https://doi.org/10.1515/9783110636147-018

Methodology

However, it was the end of the 13th century. Today, in the 21st century, the age of information and high technologies, the logic of rights and the laws of modern redistribution stipulate the opposite philosophy contradicting the human essence and human society as such. The principle of the right naturalness towards the gradual acquisition of public benefits is being lost and regularly manifested. For this problem to be resolved we suggested a political and economic analysis of socio-economic relations emerging in the course of production, distribution, exchange, and consumption of purely public benefits and services, concepts of fairness and virtue in the context of public life and human activities. Also, we studied the importance of a public (purely public) benefit not limited to the area of private economic interests, which cannot be invalidated or rejected by the socio-economic system.

Results

The role of the welfare state is not an ordinary understanding of the essence of redistribution function, i.e. the transfer of wealth from the rich to the poor. "It consists in funding public services and substituting income that is equal for all people to a greater or lesser extent, foremost in education, health care, and pension support . . ." (Picketti, 2015). We would like to mention that pursuant to the Constitution (Article 7), the Russian Federation is a social welfare state. The main objective hereof is to achieve social progress, which is based on the legally enshrined principles of social equality, universal solidarity and mutual responsibility. The welfare state is aimed at helping to the weak, influence on the distribution of economic benefits proceeding from the principle of fairness to provide a dignified human existence (Kozlova and Kutafin, 2001).

As for education and health care, we are talking about true equality of access for everyone regardless of the income of a person and his parents, at least from a theoretical point of view. "The modern redistribution is based on the logic of rights and the principle of equal access to a certain number of benefits, which are considered fundamental" (Picketti, 2015). And, arguing in this vein, we cannot limit the list of fundamental benefits solely to health care, education and pension support. They should include purely public benefits, and not only referred to them by definition.

The most economic benefits are certainly private (purely private). They are acquired by and consumed by private parties. Nevertheless, the significance of a public (purely public) benefit, which is not limited to the area of private economic interests, cannot be invalidated or rejected by the socio-economic system. State defense, communications, keeping public law and order, science, national libraries, and so forth having all three properties of the public benefit simultaneously (non-competitiveness, non-excludability, indivisibility) should not be classified as private (purely private) benefits from the point of fairness.

The step-by-step transformation of purely public benefits to purely private in modern Russia often becomes an unsolvable problem not only for the individual consuming these benefits but also for the socio-economic system in general. Society faces a choice: either it must upgrade the social welfare state in a way that deductions in favor of the state should eventually fund almost all needs, or remove it.

The model of a commercial enterprise is by far not the only one form of economic activity and finally poses severe problems, primarily in the system of economic interests that is quite conflict-ridden in essence. The idea that there is only one admissible form of capital ownership and, respectively, the arrangement of production does not meet the real facts of modern socio-economic life.

World experience shows that the commercialization of public (purely public) benefits leads to the growth of their prices and nothing else. A considerable part of the population of the Russian Federation completely excludes public benefits as such from their consumption little by little (Alpidovskaya, 2016). Paid mayor parking, federal highways, and the notorious system "Platon" with the subsequent increase in prices for all foodstuffs,[1] uncontrolled growth of housing and utility tariffs, including energy, wastewater disposal and water supply that are out of concern of the economic bloc of the Russian Government, commercialization of education, healthcare, science, and culture is a distinctive approach of liberal-minded reformers of Gaidarist orientation who mastered in turning the problems into an instrument of personal enrichment. This approach is banally reduced to the privatization of profits under the nationalization of costs and losses respectively (Delyagin, 2015).

The General Agreement on Trade in Services (GATS) included in the legal framework of the WTO and signed in July 2012 will lead to similar inextricable (from the point of adverse effects) consequences for the population of our country (Al'pidovskaya, 2013). The WTO in this agreement challenges both the social welfare state and the modern understanding of public benefits bringing them exclusively under the category of "commodity". The international trade union of public sector employees uniting 600 trade unions from 150 countries of the world officially stated in relation to Russia's accession to the WTO: "Our member organizations have been suffered for a long time from negative consequences of the WTO in public services' sector, including privatization, job cuts, deterioration of infrastructure as well as a depreciation of employees' qualifications, limited access to the services for people who are not able to pay them" (Zhdanovskaya, 2012).

1 It is stated that this system will lead to an increase in foodstuff prices up to 30–50 percent.

We would like to note that the UN Commission on Human Rights recognized GATS contravention of the universal and inalienable human rights: the rights to education, medical care, water supply, and financial stability should be accessible to everyone. That is, they should be natural rights available to everyone just by birth (Alpidovskaya, 2016).

Undoubtedly, modern capitalism has turned a particular majority of home country into wealthy people, while having not eliminated both the ever-increasing gap in the financial status of various groups of the population and having not addressed the problem of true privation and poverty. Absolute impoverishment at one pole is accompanied by an absolute enrichment at another (Semenov, 2013). By the beginning of the 1990s, the proportion of wealthy people in the United States belonging to the upper one percent of the population doubled and amounted to over 40 percent in comparison with the mid-1970s (Semenov, 2013). The process of absolute impoverishment of most employees and a sharp rise in wealth inequality emerged in the United States covers all other countries. Today the proportion of total wealth belonging to one percent of the wealthiest people in the country is 70 percent of all Russian funds.

The trend of reduction of social costs is typical not only for modern Russia. In the West, talks of the scientific community about the removal of the social welfare state come to fruition. "After the reforms of the social democratic heritage follows a history-scale counter-reform; a movement into the future is backward one" (Martin, H. Schumann, 2001). Continuous cuts of social costs are being ideologically justified. The views of J. Townsend, T. Malthus, G. Spencer re-emerge. The works of the proponents of the free capitalist market F.A. von Hayek, L. von Mises, and M. Friedman imposed today by educational programs in the "global high school" are still relevant.

The ongoing cuts in the wages of the most working population and, as a consequence, the contraction of the taxable base entailed a reduction in state budget revenues. As a result, the cost reduction was not long in coming. At the same time, corporatocracy put forward requirements for the transfer of all economic sectors previously controlled by the state into their hands as the essential condition for investments in the country's economy. Now privatization of communications, housing and utility sector, aircraft traffic, railways, and highways, etc. are passing.

In the new conditions, the once-powerful state loses its monopoly on violence in addition to financial and tax control. " . . . Organized crime is now the most growing sector of the global economy that gains a profit of 500 billion dollars annually" (Martin, H. Schumann, 2001). Being entangled in the rigid web of earlier-developed financial pyramids and having lost huge profits, representatives of the financial services industry were trying by any means to find new sources of enrichment and profit generation that have not been discovered before. These sources turned out to be the sector of public services.

After the publication of the work “Beyond the Growth” by E. Pestel, in 1991 the Club of Rome first presented own report reflecting the common position of its members. Editing hereof was entrusted to Alexander King and Bertrand Schneider.

The authors of the report have conducted great research and have suggested a program of action based hereon to tackle the world problem. On the pages of this report, it was noted: “The world has never been captured by the money-dictated laws. Capitalism impudently expresses confidence in its . . . superiority. He rewards winning and punishes the defeated. But the success of capitalism itself encourages its failure . . . The dream of an infinite, unlimited choice can lead to a horrible situation when there will be no choice at all. The world of abundance can be wrapped into the age of general poverty” (King and Schneider, 1991).

Conclusions

The global system crisis is a true-to-life circumstance of today. At the same time, the crisis promotes the conceptual search but does not deny the scientific classics. By virtue hereof, currently there is an urgent need for the economic experience of past generations and the corresponding scientific, expert and research thought. Since tomorrow everything can change drastically, the crisis situation will advance it.

References

A. King, B. Schneider. The first global revolution. Report of the Rome Club. M.: Progress-Pangeya, 1991.

A. Zhdanovskaya Capturing of services//Tomorrow. 2012 No. 26 (970). p. 4.

E.I. Kozlova, O.E. Kutafin. The constitutional law of Russia. Textbook. Edition 2, revised and enlarged. Recommended by the Ministry for General and Professional Education of the Russian Federation as a textbook for university students majoring in Jurisprudence. MOSCOW. JURIST, 2001. // (Internet resource) // URL: http://www.bibliotekar.ru/konstitucionnoe-pravo-4/27.htm

G.-P. Martin, H. Schumann. The trap of globalization: attack on prosperity and democracy. M.: Al’pina, 2001.

I. G. Fichte. Essays in two volumes. V. II. / Content and notes by Vladimir Volzhskii. SPb.: Mithril, 1993.

Lester C. Thurow The Future of Capitalism: How Economic Forces of Today Form the World of Tomorrow / Lester C. Thurow; Translated from English by A.I. Fedorov. Novosibirsk: Siberian Chronograph, 1999.

M.G. Delyagin. Crimean power bridge. The brilliance and poverty of Russian liberalism in the mirror of the new federal district challenges. //Zavtra. 2015, No. 49 (1150). p. 4.

M.L. Al’pidovskaya. Accession to the WTO, or the “new economic chimera” of the present postmodern society. The Age of Globalization, 2013, No.1. pp. 132.

M.L. Al'pidovskaya. The issue of reproduction of purely public benefits in modern Russia// The Agrarian Issue in Political Economy: Theoretical and Practical Points: A Collection of Articles Based on the Proceedings of a Scientific Conference Dedicated to the 150th Anniversary of the Political Economy Department of the Russian State Agrarian University. Moscow Agricultural Academy named after K.A. Timiryazev/Under general editorship by R.S. Gaisin. M.: Publishing house of Russian State Agrarian University-Moscow Agricultural Academy, 2016. pp. 34–39.
The general principles of the philosophy by Leibniz//Digital Library of Philosophy. [Internet resource] // URL: http://filosof.historic.ru/books/item/f00/s00/z0000005/st062.shtml
Thomas Picketti. Capital in the 21st century. Moscow: Ad Marginem Press, 2015.
Yu.I. Semenov. Philosophy of history. The general theory of the historical process. M.: Academic Project; Tricksta, 2013.

Tair M. Makhamatov, Timur T. Makhamatov,
Saida T. Makhamatova

19 Principles of Democracy as the Foundation of the Market Economy

Introduction

This article aims to identify the relationship and interdependence of the basic universal principles of modern democracy with the principles of the market economic system. It also reveals the negative impact of the limited freedom of entrepreneurship and the political and financial weakness of the state power on the economic growth of the country. The article substantiates the position of non-identity of political and legal inequality with natural inequality of citizens on the basis of the thesis of socio-political and biosocial essence of man.

To solve this problem, we use methods of comparative logical and historical analysis, unity of the historical and the logical, of conceptual modeling, idealization, systematic and structural approach and other methods and principles of the modern research of social phenomena and institutions.

Methodology

Contradictions of the Principle of Equality

Modern concepts of democracy recognize equality as a basic principle of democracy. Modern social and political practice shows that the real democracy takes place only where the equality of citizens before the public laws of society and equality in participation in the management of public life dominate and where the social, economic and political rights and interests of each member of the community are protected. K. Mannheim wrote that democracy "is convinced of the essential equality of all men, and rejects all vertical division of society into higher and lower orders. This belief in the essential equality of all human beings is the first fundamental principle of democracy" (Mannheim, 2000).

Tair M. Makhamatov, Timur T. Makhamatov, Saida T. Makhamatova, Federal State-Funded Educational Institution of Higher Education "Financial University under the Government of the Russian Federation" (Financial University), Moscow, Russia

https://doi.org/10.1515/9783110636147-019

However, equality as a social phenomenon is inextricably linked to inequality. "The sad irony of world history is, writes N. Bolz – that the ideal of equality perpetuates the hatred generated by the reality of inequality" (Bolz, 2014). Therefore, he believes that "egalitarianism is nothing but a guide to misfortune" (Bolz, 2014), for "it is impossible to change the "unjust advantages", i.e. the ability and talent of people by nature, without endangering the freedom of society. Based on the fact that all people are different, the material inequality of their living situation follows from their observance of the principle of equality" (Bolz, 2014). However, if society does not create the necessary legal, social, financial and economic conditions to contain the strengthening of social and economic inequality, then there is a fall in the rate of economic growth, according to J. Stiglitz, E. Atkinson, Ha-Joon Chang, and other researchers (Stiglitz, 2017; Atkinson, 2018; Chang, 2019).

Even Hegel noted that any social organism for its development needs to create certain conditions for the realization of each citizen's differences and creative abilities (Hegel, 1990). A prominent researcher of management problems R. Waterman writes that "when an organization suppresses an individual, it jeopardizes its ability to change. When the organization stimulates the self-expression of personality, it's hard *not to be* renovated. Individuals are the only source of renewal in the company" (Waterman, 1988; Gratton, 2005).

Each person will be *fully equal* to the other person only when he/she can show his/ her creative difference from the other. A high-performance and creative team is formed from such complementary and unique personalities.

K. Marx on the Economic Foundations of Equality

K. Marx, overcoming Hegel's abstract understanding of equality, *reveals its economic ontology* and proves that the principle of equality, as *the legal equality of citizens before the law*, is an objective requirement of the market economy. According to K. Marx, in the capitalist mode of production, all forms of social relations are directly or indirectly subject to the objective law of the market. Equality is determined by *the personal legal independence of a person in society, which creates a legal space* of capitalist production. "Civil rights", Thomas H. Marshall wrote, "were necessary for a competitive market economy" (Marshall, 2011).

Therefore, *legal equality is a form of realization of the objective requirement of, first of all, the market economy*, i.e. an exchange of goods, including labor, in the commodity market at cost. In the commodity market, a worker sells his labor as a commodity *at the market value*. Here, an equal exchange is implemented between the buyer capitalist and the seller worker, *based on the equality of exchange values.* In this process, the labor owner receives, as K. Marx wrote, "the exact equivalent, since the price he received allows him to remain the owner of the same exchange value that he had had before. The amount of materialized labor, which was contained in his life activity, was paid to him with capital" (Marx, 1968).

Equality, which is exercised and manifested with regard to exchange, allows abstracting from natural, class, national, religious and other differences and constitutes *an economic ontology* of *equality* of people as citizens.

Due to legal equality, it is more clearly manifested that each person is an abstract unit of the social organism. Here, objectively and necessarily, the principle of *"everyone is replaceable" is applied,* which is a necessary basis for preserving the integrity of the social organism and the rule of law in it. In modern society, *due to its "abstractness", as Hegel put it, legal equality* allows establishing a single criterion for all members of society, to equalize people of different abilities and health.

However, the exchange of goods is also implemented due to the difference in use values, which is the result of specific work, specific abilities, professions, as a reflection of the diversity and qualitative dissimilarity of people.

The difference in the needs of exchanging subjects, the difference in the goods produced by them "is the occasion for exchange and for their being socially equated in it. Hence this natural difference is the precondition of their social equality in the act of exchange . . . " (Marx, 1968). This statement of K. Marx shows objective dialectical unity, complementarity of legal equality, allowing normal market relations, and natural diversity of needs, abilities of individuals.

Reasoning of Hegel, K. Marx and other authors on equality allow us to say that legal equality as a social attitude and the basis of the unity of society, has as its ontological condition the natural difference of individuals and their abilities, that is, *specific equality as one of the sources of development of society*. It is also the objective basis of the principle of *"everyone is indispensable"*. Consequently, equality as a social attitude of a democratic society is realized as an organic unity of *the abstract, i.e. legal equality* and *concrete equality*, which includes an individual, natural particularity, *uniqueness*, and in this context the *irreplaceability* of each person. "The principle of the inherent equality of all human beings, – K. Mannheim writes, – "in itself, does not presuppose a mechanical equalization, as hasty critics of democracy are recklessly inclined to think. The point is not that all people are equal in their qualities, merits and talents, – he continues, – but that they all embody *the same ontological principle of humanity*. The democratic principle does not deny that in conditions of fair competition, some individuals will stand out and surpass others; it only requires that competition be fair, i.e. that one is not granted a higher initial status than hereditary privileges" (Mannheim, 2000)

Revealing the dual nature of work, K. Marx showed the objective interdependence of the democratic principle of equality with the market economy. "Freedom and equality are not only respected, – he wrote, – in exchange based on exchange values, but, also, the exchange of exchange values is the productive, real basis of all *equality* and *freedom*" (Marx, 1968).

Results

The Institution of the State, Democracy and the Economy

The positive relationship between legal equality and natural inequality in the economic sphere is achieved by the action of the market, as the relationship between the seller and the consumer. In the society, abstract equality manifests itself as the principle of *"everyone is replaceable"* and acts as an ontological basis for the centralizing functions of the state, achieving stability of public life. Specific equality as an individual identity of citizens is implemented in the principle of *"everyone is indispensable"*, which acts as the ontological basis of the objective necessity of democratization of the society as the creation of foundations for the sustainable economic development (Chang, 2019), the aspirations of citizens to realize their natural abilities, talents, expanding the boundaries of social groups of their freedom, autonomy and relative independence from state supervision. These trends must also be ensured, regulated and protected through legislation and relevant state institutions.

The full implementation of both trends in democracy by the state is necessary not only for the sustainable development of society but also for the "dynamic efficiency" of entrepreneurial activity. In his book "Socio-economic theory of dynamic efficiency", a prominent representative of the Austrian school of Economics Jesus Huerta de Soto considers entrepreneurial activity, creativity of the entrepreneur, creation and transfer of information in the business space, competition, coordination and business ethics as the main factors of dynamic efficiency (Huerta de Soto, 2011). The state, which, as noted by C. Lindblom, creates the legal framework, the entrepreneurial space (Lindblom, 2010), J. U. de Soto is not considered as a necessary factor of dynamic efficiency.

However, he further writes that society, in order to encourage "most vigorously" "the entrepreneurial creativity of all its members . . . should a priori guarantee each person that he will be able to appropriate the results of his entrepreneurial creativity and no one will take them from him either completely or partially (and certainly the authorities will not do it)" (Huerta de Soto, 2011). Even John Dewey, criticizing such social and political philosophy and referring to the authority of state power, wrote that "the essence of the issue is not to distinguish between special "spheres" for authority and freedom, stability and change, but to stimulate their interpenetration. We need an authority that, unlike the old forms of its embodiment, is able to direct and use change, and needs a different type of personal freedom than the one that gave rise to and justified unlimited economic emancipation, namely – we need a universal and all acceptable type of personal freedom, where a socially organized reasonable control would serve as the background and a guiding principle" (Dewey, 2003).

If you look at the concept of J. Huerta de Soto through the prism of the statements of J. Dewey, it raises a number of issues related to the relationship of the entrepreneur as a citizen with the institute of the state. Firstly. To perform its functions, the state collects taxes, i.e. "partially" will take away "the result of entrepreneurial creativity". Secondly. The entrepreneur must pay the wages to his employees within the minimum established by the state. Thirdly. He is subject to all laws and regulations of state institutions regulating the life of its citizens in all spheres of society, including the competitive relations of entrepreneurs. As Charles Lindblom notes, "the ability to influence governmental adoption of programs in which the population is interested requires not a weaker government, but a stronger one, which is able to cope with taxation and management" (Lindblom, 2010). It also concerns the efficiency of entrepreneurship.

Thus, entrepreneurial activity, on the one hand, is based on the freedom of the labor force, free competition and full appropriation of the results of entrepreneurship. But it, on the other hand, requires a guarantee of protection of the domestic market, its economic interests from foreign companies, stability in the activities of the Central Bank, tax regulations, etc. Modern democratic society should combine these objective contradictious needs of the economic sphere and the whole society in the activities of its state institutions. The dialectical unity of the above-mentioned obligations of the state of democratic societies forms the principle of democratic centralism.

Centralization of the State and Democracy

Centralization is an ontologically necessary activity of the institute of the state, aimed at the maximum concentration at its disposal of the main functions of military-political, financial-economic and other decisions and control over the main financial and economic resources of society, it is a policy aimed at strengthening the integrity of society, stability and security of its life. F. Fukuyama writes that "there is a long-term attraction to the inevitability of higher degrees of decentralization and horizontal distribution of power in the organizational structure in society. However, this trend is questionable, since decentralized organizations have their own shortcomings, the problem of elimination of which has no technical solution. Decentralization of an organization often generates high internal organizational costs, and such organizations may be slower and less decisive than centralized ones" (Fukuyama, 2006).

The weakness of the centralizing activity of the state can lead to the emergence of decentralizing trends in society and as a result – to the weakening of the integrity of the social organism, which prevents further stable and sustainable socio-economic growth of the country. In any society there are ontological bases of decentralizing tendencies what causes the objective need for the centralizing policy in the management of public processes. Ludwig von Mises writes that "the state and the government are not a goal but a tool. . . . Recognized authorities resort to deterrence and coercion to ensure the smooth functioning of a certain system of social organization" (Mises, 2012). However, centralization, with the weakness of civil society and legislative mechanisms to limit power, can turn the state power into a dictatorship.

Consequently, in order to ensure the harmonious development of society from the transformation of the institution of the state into a dictatorship, it is necessary to create a political and legal basis for ensuring and protecting the democratization of society.

Democratization in the Activities of the State

Democratization is actions of public authorities of society aimed at creating political and legal foundations for the development of the autonomy of local authorities, expansion of the independence of social groups, civil society institutions, business and other forms of activity of citizens.

Society needs not only to preserve itself, its integrity and stability, but also political and legal conditions to ensure its immanent change and development. This is possible only through the expansion of independent economic, social and spiritual activity of every citizen and public institutions in all spheres of society. The historical experience of the world's leading economies shows that the basis for the development of the market economy of society, first of all, is the democratization of society (Lindblom, 2010; Chang, 2019).

The ontological basis of democratization in the activities of state power is the need to implement the principle "*everyone is indispensable*", which also meets the objective needs of the market-competitive economy. A person is creatively active when he is independent and free, has the right to self-realization and self-determination, but at the same time is protected by a strong legal state. Hegel wrote: "The principle of the modern state has prodigious strength and depth because it allows the principle of subjectivity to progress to its culmination in the extreme of self-subsistent particularity and yet at the same time brings it back to the substantive unity and so maintains this unity in the principle of subjectivity itself" (Hegel, 1990). Here you can add the words of L. von Mises who said that "as individuals have different abilities, it requires the authorities to study their personalities" (Mises, 2012). Such a task is carried out by the democratic education policy.

The process of democratization of society cannot be developed only on the basis of the relevant political and legal activities of the institute of the state. Deepening and expansion of democratization of society need to increase the activity of civil society institutions. The state can only create a legal framework. The actual development and the deepening of democracy mean the transformation of it, as

John Dewey dreamed and wrote, in the way of life of the people. The success of non-profit non-governmental organizations of citizens in the field of social and political life of the social organism, the process of digitalization of the information space of society can turn the dream of the great thinker into reality in the future (Stuhr, 1993; Keane, 2013).

A democratic society needs a combination of centralizing policies with democratic principles for the formation and exercise of power in the activities of the state. John Dewey wrote: "I simply cannot imagine a person who would not consider it an urgent need to initiate and establish some organic unity of freedom and authority" (Dewey, 2003). This "organic unity" is *the principle of democratic centralism*. The application of this principle dialectically connects the centralizing activity of the state power with its democratizing policy aimed at expanding the rights of citizens, civil society institutions and the media. In this principle, with its undistorted application, all positive, consisting both in the centralizing and democratizing policy of the state, should be synthesized.

Thanks to the gradual, to some extent spontaneous transition of democratic states in their activities to the principle of democratic centralism and the simultaneous increase in the activity of civil society institutions and "monitor democracy" (Keane, 2013), democracy today goes beyond its political form, acquires a cultural and civilizational meaning and gradually turns into a way of life of the people (Dewey, 2002; Dewey, 2003). As Taiwan's President Chen Shuibian rightly wrote, "democracy cannot be considered mature if it is manifested only in the form of a political system" (Larin, 2004).

As the practice of political struggle in modern democracies shows, despite the constant ideological and political struggle between the various institutions and movements of civil society (Kapustin, 2011) thanks to the activity of civil society, a culture of democracy is being formed and developed, the entrepreneurial space is being democratized and the organic link between the fullness of the principles of democracy and the sustainable economic development of society is becoming increasingly clear.

Conclusion

Our study showed that one of the basic principles of democracy, equality, means, first of all, universal legal equality. This principle creates a legal space of equal starting conditions, which contributes to the formation and development of the market economy. However, its implementation necessarily increases the socio-economic inequality of citizens, to mitigate which conditions are created for the identification and realization of citizens of their natural, individual abilities, talents and the corresponding social and educational policy of the state in the democratic society. Such a policy of the state and the public life contribute to the implementation of the principle *"everyone is indispensable"*.

The analysis of ontological bases of modern democratic society demonstrates that democracy with objective necessity is based on the centralizing policy of the state power. The centralizing policy of the state ensures security, sovereignty of the country, creates political and legal conditions for stability and sustainable development of its socio-political and economic spheres.

The following conclusion was made based on a comparative analysis of studies on democracy and the evolution of civil society institutions. The principle of democratic centralism, as it is understood by D. Dewey, L. von Mises, F. Fukuyama, is one of the effective guarantees for the further development of market economy, deepening democracy in modern developed democracies, despite their internal contradictions, and also the revitalization of civil society institutions.

References

Atkinson, Entoni B. (2018). Neravenstvo: kak s nim byt'? [Inequality: how to deal with it?] / Per. s angol. – M.: Izd. dom "Delo" RANKHiGS. – 536 p (in Russian).

Bol'c, N. (2014). Razmyshleniya o neravenstve. Anti-Russo [Reflections on inequality. Anti Russo] / per. s nem; Nac. issled. un-t "Vysshaya shkola ek-ki". – M.: Izd.dom Vysshej shkoly ek-ki (in Russian).

CHang, Ha-Dzhun [2019]. Kak ustroena ekonomika. [How the economy works.]/Per. s angl. – 6-izd., dop. – M.: Mann, Ivanov i Ferberg. – 320 p (in Russian).

D'yui D. (2003). Rekonstrukciya v filosofii. Problema cheloveka [Reconstruction in philosophy. Human problem] / Per. s angl. – M.: Respublika. – 494 p – (Mysliteli HKH veka) (in Russian).

D'yui, Dzhon. (2002). Obshchestvo i ego problemy. [Society and its problems.] / Per. s angl. – M.: Ideya-Press. – 160 p (in Russian).

Fukuyama F. [2006]. Sil'noe gosudarstvo: Upravlenie i mirovoj poryadok v XXI veke [A Strong State: Governance and World Order in the 21st Century]/ per s angl. M.: AST. – 220 p (in Russian).

Gegel' G. V. F. (1990). Filosofiya prava. [Legal philosophy] M.: Mysl'. – 524 p (in Russian).

Gretton Linda (2005). Demokraticheskoe predpriyatie. Raskreposhchenie biznesa blagodarya svobode, gibkosti i priverzhennosti. [Democratic enterprise. Free business through freedom, flexibility and commitment] – SPb., Stokgol'mskaya shkola ekonomiki (in Russian).

Kapustin B.G. (2011) Grazhdanstvo i grazhdanskoe obshchestvo. [Citizenship and civil society.] – Vysshaya shkola ekonomiki; pril. T.H. Marshall / per. s angl. – M.: Izd. dom gos. un-ta. – 224 p (in Russian).

Keane, John (2013). Democracy and Media Decadence/ Cambridge Univ. Press, NY.

Larin A. [2004]. Prezident ili demokratiya s tajvan'skoj specifikoj. [President or democracy with Taiwanese specifics.] M.: Muravej. – 136 p (in Russian).

Lindblom CH. [2010] Rynochnaya sistema: chto eto takoe, kak ona rabotaet i chto s nej delat'. [Market system: what it is, how it works and what to do with it] / Per. s angl. – M.: Izd. dom gos. un-ta – Vysshaya shkola ekonomiki. – 320 p (in Russian).

Manhejm K. [2000] Esse o sociologii kul'tury. [Essay on the sociology of culture] //Izbrannoe: Sociologiya kul'tury. M.–SPb (in Russian).

Marks K., Engel's F. (1968). Sochineniya: v 50 t. 2-e izd. M.: Politizdat. T. 46, ch. 1. – pp. 188, 190 (in Russian).
Marshall T.H. Grazhdanstvo i social'nyj klass. Prilozhenie [Citizenship and social class. Application]/ per. s angl. – / Kapustin B.G. (2011) Grazhdanstvo i grazhdanskoe obshchestvo. – M.: Izd. dom gos. un-ta. – Vysshaya shkola ekonomiki. – pp. 145–223 (in Russian).
Mizes, fon Lyudvig (2012). CHelovecheskaya deyatel'nost': traktat po ekonomicheskoj teorii. [Human activities: a treatise on economic theory.]/Per. s angl. – CHelyabinsk: Socium. – 878 p (in Russian).
Stiglits, Dzhozef. (2017). TSena neravenstva. CHem rassloyeniye obshchestva grozit nashemu budushchemu. [The price of inequality. Than the stratification of society threatens our future.]/Per. s angl. – M.: Izd-vo "E". – 512 p (in Russian).
Stuhr John J. [1993] Democracy as a Way of Life /Philosophy and the Reconstuction of Culture: Pragmatic Essays after Dewey. Edit by John J. Stuhr. – New York: State Univ. of NY. pp. 37–58
Uerta de Soto H. (2011). Social'no-ekonomicheskaya teoriya dinamicheskoj effektivnosti [Socio-economic theory of dynamic efficiency]/ Per. s angl. – CHelyabinsk: Socium. – 409 p (in Russian).
Uoterman R. (1988). Faktor obnovleniya. [Update factor.]/ Per. s angl. – M.: Bantam, 368 p (in Russian).

Karina V. Khaustova, Nelli V. Tskhadadze,
Mariya A. Ekaterinovskaya

20 Socio-Economic Differentiation of the Population of Russia in the Conditions of Scientific and Technical Progress

Introduction

The accumulation and expansion of knowledge, advanced scientific discoveries and inventions, which a few years ago seemed fantastic, incessant and rapid improvement of technology, the digital world and means of communication, which allow people from different ends of the planet to be so close and at the same time so distant from each other – All of these are the reality of the scientific and technological progress of the modern world.

The importance and benefits of scientific and technological progress cannot be underestimated, but there are also many obvious shortcomings and its disastrous consequences, which include: exhaustion of resources, global environmental problems that can lead to a global catastrophe and are posed above the problems of nuclear war, rapid obsolescence of professional skills and abilities, the socio-economic stratification of society that increase each passing day. This article will address the last of these problems, as the differentiation of incomes of the population increases, and, as a result, inequality and poverty rise (Ekaterinovskaya, 2016; Ekaterinovskaya, 2017; Khaustova, 2017; Lyubimov, 2016; McConnell and Brue, 1993; Novikova, 2005; Tskhadadze and Alpidovskaya, 2017).

Both economists and statisticians, sociologists, politicians and philosophers consider the problem of unevenness in the distribution of monetary incomes and public goods for a long time. Assessment and analysis of socio-economic differentiation and the level of well-being of the population become particularly relevant in the conditions of scientific and technological progress, because rising inequality and polarization of society can lead to significant social, economic, and political upheavals in modern Russia. Constant analysis of statistics characterizing inequality and poverty allows state authorities to take the necessary measures of social support for the population, including preventive ones, and to monitor the implementation of national goals and strategic objectives of the development of the Russian Federation.

Karina V. Khaustova, Nelli V. Tskhadadze, Mariya A. Ekaterinovskaya, Financial University under the Government of the Russian Federation, Moscow, Russia

https://doi.org/10.1515/9783110636147-020

The relevance of this work is also determined by the compliance of the chosen subject with a number of strategic goals and objectives, which are formulated in the Message of the President of the Russian Federation to the Federal Assembly on March 1, 2018 and in Presidential Decree No. 204 of May 7, 2018 "On the national goals and strategic objectives of the Russian Federation on period until 2024" and should be achieved and resolved already at the turn of 2024–2025. These include providing the growth rate of the Russian economy higher than the world ones, increasing the gross domestic product per capita by one and a half times and halving the number of the poor.

Methodology

The works of the classics of economic theory, the works of foreign and domestic scientists on the problems of economic growth and development, distribution relations and socio-economic differentiation were used as the methodological basis of this work.

The legal basis were the legislative and regulatory acts of the Russian Federation, the data of the Federal State Statistics Service (Rosstat), including the microdata base of the Comprehensive Survey of the Living Standards of the Population, as well as statistical data and special survey data contained in foreign and domestic literature.

The authors also used such theoretical methods of scientific knowledge as the method of ascent from the abstract to the concrete, the method of idealization, the method of formalization and others. Methods of comparison, modeling and statistical analysis were used as experimental ones.

Results

Macroeconomic indicators characterizing inequality in the distribution of monetary incomes and the level of welfare of the population (distribution of monetary incomes by percentage of the population, the ratio of funds, the Gini index, the distribution of the population by the size of the ratio of monetary incomes and the subsistence minimum, as well as other indicators) being regularly published by the State Statistics Service of the Russian Federation (Rosstat) remain the main method for quantifying inequality and poverty. The distribution of total monetary incomes and the characteristics of the differentiation of monetary incomes of the population of the Russian Federation are presented in Table 20.1 in retrospect from 1995 to 2017.

Statistics show that the Russian Federation clearly refers to countries with a high degree of inequality – almost half of all incomes of the population (divided into 20 percent groups) over the past decades belongs to the fifth group with the highest incomes, the poorest (the first group with the lowest income) owns about 5 percent of

Table 20.1: Distribution of total money incomes and characteristics of the differentiation of money incomes of the population of the Russian Federation.

		including by 20% population groups, in %:						
	Total cash income	1st (with the lowest income)	2-nd	3-rd	4-th	5th (with the highest income)	Decile coefficient of funds, in times	Gini coefficient
1995	100	6.1	10.8	15.2	21.6	46.3	13.5	0.387
2000	100	5.9	10.4	15.1	21.9	46.7	13.9	0.395
2005	100	5.4	10.1	15.1	22.7	46.7	15.2	0.409
2010	100	5.2	9.8	14.8	22.5	47.7	16.6	0.421
2011	100	5.2	9.9	14.9	22.6	47.4	16.2	0.417
2012	100	5.2	9.8	14.9	22.5	47.6	16.4	0.420
2013	100	5.2	9.8	14.9	22.5	47.6	16.3	0.419
2014	100	5.2	9.9	14.9	22.6	47.4	16.0	0.416
2015	100	5.3	10.0	15.0	22.6	47.1	15.7	0.413
2016	100	5.3	10.1	15.0	22.6	47.0	15.5	0.412
2017	100	5.4	10.1	15.1	22.6	46.8	15.3	0.410

Source: Population. Inequality and poverty // Federal State Statistics Service.

total revenues. It is worth noting that the trend of increasing the concentration of incomes among the richest has continued since 1995 and only refracted in the last few years – from 47.6% of all incomes of the population in 2013, the share fell to 46.8% in 2017, but still remains unacceptably large.

The decile ratio of funds is a component of the group of income differentiation coefficients of the population. It describes how many times the average cash income level of 10% of the population with the highest incomes exceeds the average money income of 10% of the population with the lowest incomes. In 1995, the level of money incomes of 10% of the richest population exceeded the level of incomes of 10% of the poorest population by 13.5 times, in 2017 it was already 15.3 times (URL: http://www.gks.ru/wps/wcm/connect/rosstat_main/rosstat/ru/statistics/population/poverty/#, Population. Inequality and poverty, Federal State Statistics Service, 2019).

According to Rosstat, the Gini coefficient has not undergone fundamental changes since 1995 and even gradually decreased, reaching 0.41 in 2017, which is even slightly higher than the estimates of a number of international organizations in Russia. Official statistics attribute Russia to countries with a moderate degree of inequality, while according to other international analytical centers, Russia is the most unequal economy in the world, in which almost all wealth is owned by literally 1% of the population.

The study of socio-economic differentiation cannot do without the naturally emerging problem of poverty as a consequence of the uneven distribution of income and public goods among the population. The main indicator and the official "poverty line" is the subsistence minimum, and the poor are those whose monthly income is below the established subsistence minimum.

However, the traditional statistical toolkit assesses the financial situation of the population, but does not fully characterize the real level of poverty and socio-economic differentiation, since it does not allow to assess the social aspects of the population: housing conditions and intentions to improve them; working conditions; health status and access to quality health care; education; the presence of children; opinion on the living conditions in the village; transport service and communication; recreation.

This information on socio-demographic problems is collected by Rosstat as part of federal statistical observations. Thus, the Comprehensive Monitoring of the Living Conditions of the Population is organized in all the constituent entities of the Russian Federation and covers about 60 thousand households. The purpose of this observation is to obtain official statistical information that will reflect the real living conditions of Russian households (families).

Comprehensive observation of the living conditions of the population (hereinafter referred to as CMLC) is carried out on the basis of a personal survey of members of households (respondents) at their place of residence, thus the household itself gives a subjective assessment of its welfare. The CMLC microdata base consists of approximately 60 thousand observations (interviewed households) and about 300 variables (questions asked to respondent households).

Table 20.2 presents the information on the CMLC for 2016 and 2018. Data analysis allows us to conclude that the situation has improved by the majority of criteria characterizing the differentiation of households by financial situation.

So, taking into account the incomes of all household members, in 2016 compared to 2018, 88.5% of the total number of respondents had the opportunity to pay for vital (most important) medicines (while in 2016 this share was 86.4%), could cope with unexpected expenses (expenses for urgent repair of housing or replacement of durable goods, urgent medical services, and so on) – 45.7% (55.3% in 2016), replace the most simple furniture that has become unusable – 45.9% (37.6% in 2016) buy new clothes for family members as far as it wears out – 88.5% (85.5%), buying each family member two pairs of comfortable and seasonally suitable shoes (one for each season) – 63.8% (50.3%), eating meat, poultry or fish (or equivalent vegetarian food) every 2 days – 89.6% (91.5%), eating fruit at any time of the year – 78.4% (74.5%), inviting guests to a family celebration (birthday, New Year and other holidays) – 74.2% (70.5%), spending one week per year on vacation outside the house (including spending time in second dwelling, with relatives, friends) – 49.1% of respondents compared to 54.5% in 2016.

Thereafter, in 2018, 11% of the total number of respondents did not have the ability to pay for vital (most important) medicines, could not cope with unexpected expenses (expenses for urgent housing repairs or replacement of durable items, urgent

Table 20.2: The financial situation of households by type of settlement.

	All households		**urban areas – total**		**rural areas – total**	
	2016	**2018**	**2016**	**2018**	**2016**	**2018**
All households	100.0	100.0	100.0	100.0	100.0	100.0
taking into account the incomes of all household members						
having the opportunity to						
pay for essential medicines	86.4	88.5	87.0	88.9	84.6	87.3
cope with unexpected expenses (the cost of urgent repairs to housing or the replacement of durable use, urgent medical services and so on)	53.3	45.7	55.3	47.2	47.1	41.0
replace the most basic furniture that has become unusable	37.6	45.9	39.5	47.2	31.7	41.5
buy new clothes for family members as it wears out	85.5	88.5	85.9	88.8	84.5	87.5
buy each family member two pairs of comfortable and seasonally-appropriate shoes (one for each season)	50.3	63.8	52.8	65.3	42.2	58.9
allow eating meat, poultry or fish (or equivalent vegetarian food) every 2 days	91.5	89.6	92.1	90.3	89.8	87.1
eat fruit any time at any time of the year	74.5	78.4	77.3	80.3	65.4	72.3
invite guests to a family celebration (birthday, New Year, etc.)	70.5	74.2	72.1	75.5	65.3	69.9
spend one week of vacation per year outside the home (including time spent in a second dwelling, with relatives or friends)	43.2	50.1	48.0	54.7	27.9	35.1
unable to						
pay for essential medicines	12.1	11.0	11.3	10.5	14.6	12.3
cope with unexpected expenses (the cost of urgent repairs to housing or the replacement of durable use, urgent medical services and so on)	44.2	52.9	41.9	51.2	51.3	58.4
replace the most basic furniture that has become unusable	59.6	53.1	57.4	51.5	66.8	58.0
buy new clothes for family members as it wears out	13.6	11.2	13.2	10.9	14.7	12.4

Table 20.2 (continued)

	All households		urban areas – total		rural areas – total	
	2016	2018	2016	2018	2016	2018
buy each family member two pairs of comfortable and seasonally-appropriate shoes (one for each season)	48.0	35.4	45.3	33.8	56.6	40.8
allow eating meat, poultry or fish (or equivalent vegetarian food) every 2 days	7.9	10.1	7.3	9.3	9.9	12.8
eat fruit any time at any time of the year	24.4	21.1	21.4	19.2	33.9	27.5
invite guests to a family celebration (birthday, New Year, etc.)	28.0	25.3	26.2	23.9	33.7	29.8
spend one week of vacation per year outside the home (including time spent in a second dwelling, with relatives or friends)	54.5	49.1	49.4	44.3	70.6	64.6
unable to do any of the above	1.7	1.8	1.5	1.8	2.4	2.0

Source: Comprehensive observation of the living conditions of the population // Federal State Statistics Service.

medical services, etc.) – 52, 9%, could not replace the most basic furniture that has become unusable – 53.1%, could not buy family members new clothes as it wears out – 11.2%, could not buy each family member two pairs of comfortable and seasonally suitable shoes (one for each season) – 35.4%, could not allow eating meat, poultry or fish (or equivalent vegetarian food) every 2 days – 10.1%, could not eat fruit at any time of the year – 21.1%, could not invite guests to a family celebration (birthday, New Year and other holidays) – 25.3%, could not spent a holiday week per year outside the house (including spending time in the second dwelling, with relatives, with friends) – 49.1% of households. 1.8% of the respondents were unable to carry out any of the above (URL: http://www.gks.ru/free_doc/new_site/KOUZ16/index.html, Comprehensive observation of the living conditions of the population, Federal State Statistics Service, 2019).

Consideration of the differentiation by financial situation in terms of types of settlements suggests that in rural settlements the number of households that can meet all the needs in Table 20.2 is obviously less than in urban areas.

As was already said in the introduction, the life and development of modern society in the conditions of scientific and technological progress have become unthinkable without a wide range of communications and television. Today, telecommunication technologies and the Internet allow us not only to erase the boundaries between states and people, but also to solve many problems in such areas as education, medicine, management and commerce.

Table 20.3 presents the information on the status of households' provision with communications and television by demographic and social groups in the Russian Federation in 2016. It is not surprising that 99% of households surveyed have a color TV, while 97.6% have a mobile phone. In the second decade of the 21st century, the absence of these objects seems unreal. At the same time, the presence of a landline phone is observed only in 47.3% of households surveyed, as there is a tendency to gradually stop using this type of communication, as it is replaced by cellular communication and the Internet. It is important to note that only 67.9% of households surveyed have a home stationary computer and/or a laptop. This figure does not seem to be enough, because the access to the Internet offers unlimited opportunities for education and development. It can be assumed that the remaining 32.1% of surveyed households that do not have a computer compensate the absence by using the mobile Internet.

Table 20.3: Provision of households with telecommunications and television by demographic and social groups.

	All households	Young families	Large families	Single-parent families	Consisting only of pensioners	Consisting of the disabled only
	1	2	4	5	6	7
All households	100.0	100.0	100.0	100.0	100.0	100.0
That have						
color TV	99.0	97.7	98.5	99.3	99.1	98.3
satellite antenna	27.6	23.4	42.8	23.8	22.2	16.3
cable TV	47.3	52.2	36.7	50.5	40.6	35.6
landline phone	42.2	24.3	26.0	35.5	51.0	53.9
cell phone	97.6	99.8	99.4	99.6	93.0	86.9
PC and/or a laptop	67.9	88.1	77.2	83.8	29.9	17.2
That do not have						
color tv	1.0	2.3	1.5	0.7	0.9	1.7

Table 20.3 (continued)

	All households	Young families	Large families	Single-parent families	Consisting only of pensioners	Consisting of the disabled only
satellite antenna	72.4	76.6	57.2	76.2	77.8	83.7
cable TV	52.7	47.8	63.3	49.5	59.4	64.4
landline phone	57.8	75.7	74.0	64.5	49.0	46.1
cell phone	2.4	0.2	0.6	0.4	7.0	13.1
PC and/or a laptop	32.1	11.9	22.8	16.2	70.1	82.8

Source: Comprehensive observation of the living conditions of the population // Federal State Statistics Service.

Considering the household structure in terms of demographic and social groups gives the following results: 11.9% of young families surveyed, 22.8% of large families, 16.2% of single-parent families, 70, 1% of families consisting only of pensioners, 82.8% of families consisting only of persons with disabilities do not have a home PC and/or a laptop. Thus, supporting the most vulnerable groups of the population such as retirees, disabled people, and large or incomplete families is an important task of the state and society.

Conclusion

In this paper, we analyzed the trends in the distribution of monetary income among various groups of the population of Russia, which characterize the standard of living. Also, on the basis of the Comprehensive Survey of the Standard of Living of the Population, the distribution of benefits and goods was considered including the financial situation of households and the provision of households with communications and television, which characterizes the quality of life of the population of modern Russia in the context of scientific and technological progress. Due to the fact that in any really existing economic system, the distribution of monetary incomes and benefits cannot be completely even, the emphasis was placed on the study of socio-economic differentiation by population groups, which should not be excessive, but leading to increased inequality and poverty.

In view of the foregoing, the search for a new concept of the socio-economic development of the Russian Federation is becoming increasingly important, which will ensure not only sustainable growth, but also the quality of economic growth, including a focus on a more even distribution of the benefits of economic growth among various population groups.

References

Comprehensive observation of the living conditions of the population, Federal State Statistics Service. [Electronic resource] URL: http://www.gks.ru/free_doc/new_site/KOUZ16/index.html

Ekaterinovskaya M.A. *K voprosu ob otsenke effektivnosti mezhgosudarstvennykh tselevykh program*. [The issue of evaluating the effectiveness of interstate targeted programs]. Economy and Entrepreneurship, 2016, No. 10, p. 3 (in Russian).

Ekaterinovskaya M.A. *Otsenka effektivnosti makroekonomicheskoy sistemy v koordinatakh strategicheskogo planirovaniya*. [Evaluation of the effectiveness of the macroeconomic system in the coordinates of strategic planning]. Economy and Entrepreneurship, 2017, No. 3 p. 2 (in Russian).

Khaustova K.V. *Analiz sotsial'no-ekonomicheskoy differentsiatsii i urovnya blagosostoyaniya naseleniya Rossii*. [Analysis of the socio-economic differentiation and the level of well-being of the population of Russia]. Innovations and investments No. 1, 2019, pp. 269–277 (in Russian).

Khaustova, K.V. *Inklyuzivnost' ekonomicheskogo rosta v sovremennoy Rossii*. [The inclusiveness of economic growth in modern Russia]. Global economy in the XXI century: the dialectic of confrontation and solidarity. Collection of scientific papers / Ed. dr. econ Sciences, Professor D. Sorokin, edited by Dr. of econ. Sciences, associate professor Alpidovskoy M.L., Krasnodar, Science. 2017, p. 494 (in Russian).

Lyubimov I.L. *Neravenstvo i ekonomicheskiy rost: vyzovy dlya rossiyskoy ekonomiki*. [Inequality and economic growth: challenges for the Russian economy]. Russian Entrepreneurship, 2016, Vol. 17, No. 1, pp. 11–22 (in Russian).

McConnell K., Brue S. Economics: principles, problems, politics. Trans. from English Moscow: Respublika Publishing House, 1993, pp. 399–400.

Novikova V. *Vozmozhno li spravedlivoye raspredeleniye dokhodov?* [Is a fair distribution of income possible?]. The Economist, 2005, No. 4, pp. 63–67 (in Russian).

Population. Inequality and poverty, Federal State Statistics Service. [Electronic resource] URL: ",1,0,0>http://www.gks.ru/wps/wcm/connect/rosstat_main/rosstat/ru/statistics/population/poverty/#>

Population. Standard of living, Federal State Statistics Service. [Electronic resource] URL: http://www.gks.ru/wps/wcm/connect/rosstat_main/rosstat/ru/statistics/population/poverty/#.

The social situation and the standard of living of the population of Russia. 2017: Stat.sb., Rosstat, M., p. 332.

Tskhadadze N.V. *Vosproizvodstvo Rossii v XXI veke: dialektika reguliruyemogo razvitiya: Kollektivnaya monografiya. Tom 1*. [Reproduction of Russia in the 21st Century: Dialectics of Regulated Development: A Collective Monograph. Vol.1]. Ed. M.L. Alpidovskaya, Moscow, Science. 2017, p. 256 (in Russian).

Tskhadadze N.V. *Vosproizvodstvo Rossii v XXI veke: dialektika reguliruyemogo razvitiya: Kollektivnaya monografiya. Tom 2.* [Reproduction of Russia in the 21st Century: Dialectics of Regulated Development: A Collective Monograph. Vol.2]. Ed. M.L. Alpidovskaya, Moscow, 2017, p. 286 (in Russian).

Julia A. Berger, Zarema M. Khasheva, Ekaterina A. Chumakova

21 The Availability of Education as a Foundation for Innovative Development of the Country

Introduction

Progressive capabilities of the state are usually formed from the complex of human, information, social, material, technical and other reserves that determine its innovative development. The increase in such resources provides greater opportunities for the development of the competitiveness of the regions and the whole country. Human capital has been and remains a basis of such resources, which performs not just a providing function but acts as the main creative force.

There is no doubt about the value of human capital which is the basis and driving force of innovative development of territorial entities in the current state of financial relations.

The human capital of the subject of the Russian Federation, and not the concentration of material and financial resources within it, is considered the main condition for the growth of competitiveness, which is beneficial to the economy and to the social sphere of a particular region.

The predominance of information and communication technologies as a tool for the dissemination of knowledge contributes to far-reaching structural changes that ensure the stable development of the region's economy, the formation of society and the material well-being of its people.

The aim of the study is to determine the impact of the availability of education at different levels on the innovative development of the country.

In connection with this goal, it is necessary to solve the following interrelated *tasks:*

- to justify the correlation of notions: "access to education" – "human capital" – "innovative development"
- to assess the availability of education through the prism of the education index
- to identify the impact of the level of education on the innovative development of the country

Julia A. Berger, Volgograd State University, Volgograd, Russia
Zarema M. Khasheva, Southern Institute of Management, Krasnodar, Russia
Ekaterina A. Chumakova, Volgograd Institute of Management – Branch of the Russian Academy of National Economy and Public Administration, Volgograd, Russia

https://doi.org/10.1515/9783110636147-021

Methodology

In the conditions of the innovative economy high-tech spheres take on a center stage, and the prevailing condition for development and competitiveness is human capital that raise the economy to a much high level of efficiency and competitiveness. Speaking of human capital, modern economic science refers to a set of knowledge and skills used to meet different needs of the man and the society as a whole.

Main means of production (potential) are high professionalism, exceptional features, the art of adapting them to the ever-changing conditions of functioning. Investments in intellectual human resources are transformed into the most effective method of capital allocation. The human factor is incomparable not only at the micro level of specific industries, but also on a national scale. The competitiveness of each state is highly dependent on the work of an individual.

In the Economic Encyclopedia, human capital is defined as a special type of investment, a set of costs for the development of human reproductive potential, improvement of the quality and functioning of the labor force. The composition of the objects of human capital usually include knowledge of general and special character, skills, experience (Abalkin, 1999; Anikina et al., 2016; Bowles and Gintis, 2002; Ciring, 2012; Konstantinovskij et al., 2008; Morgan; Vejher et al., 2004).

One of the main issues of any country is the creation of criteria for assessing human capabilities. In international statistics, the human development index (HDI) has been widely used since the early 1990s. HDI is a coefficient that determines the social formation of the state in terms of health, education and actual income of citizens.

The HDI is based on the following indices: life expectancy index (average life expectancy at birth), education index (average life expectancy) and gross national income index.

The substance of the index is the national search for the projected social development not only from an economic point of view, but also taking into account the achievements of the state in the field of health and education.

In other words, the formation of human development is based on the satisfaction of the desire to spend a long and full life, to obtain the required knowledge and have the means to achieve the goal of a decent standard of living (Klyucharev, 2014).

The individual is transformed into the initial and final point of social formation, there is a change of direction to the domination of human capital over the material one. The theory of human development is directed towards the formation of human capabilities through education.

Thus, according to this concept, education is considered to be the main component of social development responsible for the quality and development of human capital. For this reason, HDI and its elements are taken into account with an emphasis on educational indicators.

In the Concept of long-term social and economic development of the Russian Federation for the period up to 2020, approved by the order of the Government of the Russian Federation of 17.11.2008 No. 1662-p, it is noted that the strategic goal of the state policy in the field of education is to increase the availability of quality education that meets the requirements of innovative development of the economy, the modern needs of society and every citizen.[1] Its solution involves the formation of appropriate educational policies, organizational measures, as well as mechanisms for their implementation. However, their development and implementation is complicated not only by the economic situation in the education sector, but also by the lack of theoretical and practical education of psychological and pedagogical aspects of the problem, the lack of criteria for assessing the achievement of goals.

Speaking of the availability of education, in total, we refer to the possibility of access of different social categories of the population to quality educational services (Shklyar, 2012). Perfectly accessible educational services can be defined as the absence of any barriers to access. Education should remain a public good, that is, it should be acceptable to all without restrictions and discrimination of different users. Increased accessibility contributes to the formation of new democratic models of education, and has an impact on public mobility (Ponomareva, 2018).

According to article 10 of the Federal law "On education", in Russia education is divided into general education, vocational education, additional education and vocational training, providing the opportunity to fulfil the right to education throughout life (continuing education).[2]

In its turn, general and vocational education has an even more detailed gradation.

This paper discusses the availability of pre-school education, school education, secondary and higher professional education.

While characterizing the coverage of children with preschool education, statistics of recent years has a positive trend. Namely, about 30% of children aged one to six years are not able to attend kindergartens. In other words, the number of places in kindergartens still lags behind the total number of children in need. The lack of places leads to a violation of the state-guaranteed right of the child to be fully developed earlier.

This fact is confirmed by the statistics of social and economic indicators for the regions of Russia (Table 21.1).

The system of pre-school education in Russia includes about 50 thousand institutions, which cover 56% of children aged 1 to 6 years inclusively. In recent years,

---

1 Order of the Government of the Russian Federation of 17.11.2008 N 1662-p (edition of 28.09.2018) "About the Concept of long-term social and economic development of the Russian Federation for the period till 2020" – URL: http://www.consultant.ru/document/cons_doc_LAW_82134/ (accessed 19.02.2009).

2 Federal law "On education in the Russian Federation" of 29.12.2012 N 273-Federal Law (latest version). URL: http://www.consultant.ru/document/cons_doc_LAW_140174/ (accessed 02.04.2009)

Table 21.1: The coverage of children by preschool education.

Federal district/ subject of the Russian Federation (min and max coverage)	The coverage of children by preschool education, %			The provision of children of preschool age with places in kindergartens, places for 1000 children		
	2015	2016	2017	2015	2016	2017
Central federal district	66.0	66.6	66.5	648	651	649
Kursk region	52.5	55.6	55.4	447	475	492
Vladimirskaya oblast	80.8	82.7	81.9	810	822	828
Northwestern Federal District	76.3	76.6	76.2	753	757	750
Kaliningrad region	66.2	69.2	70.6	655	706	703
Novgorod region	85.4	85.5	85.7	867	866	875
Southern Federal District	60.1	62.2	62.3	534	558	582
Krasnodar region	63.4	67.1	65.3	504	549	593
North Caucasus Federal District	39.8	42.9	45.1	341	373	392
The Republic of Ingushetia	14.0	17.4	21.3	109	153	197
Stavropol Territory	59.9	62.2	63.2	583	602	604
Volga Federal District	69.3	70.8	70.8	657	667	668
Saratov region	60.3	62.9	63.7	626	649	669
Chuvash region	78.0	79.0	77.7	790	789	778
Ural Federal District	72.3	73.8	74.1	677	692	707
Kurgan area	63.9	63.7	66.4	653	655	704
Chelyabinsk region	79.7	80.6	80.3	706	711	751
Siberian Federal District	60.9	63.5	64.2	570	595	611
The Republic of Tuva	42.5	46.6	48.1	365	400	399
The Republic Of Khakassia	68.8	70,	69.8	665	712	719
The Far Eastern Federal District	67.8	68.4	68.2	655	660	679
Primorsky Krai	65.1	65.7	64.7	636	640	649
Chukotka Autonomous Okrug	92.6	91.9	92.0	1059	1066	1048

after the decline of the mid-1990s, the number of children in pre-school education has gradually increased, although it has not reached the level of 1985 – 68.3% of children of the appropriate age.

In addition, the lack of places in kindergartens has an impact on the country's labor potential, as mothers of children do not have the opportunity to go to work in a timely manner and they lose professional skills and experience.

At this time, social inequality in pre-school education takes a variety of forms, one of which are discriminating conditions of access to educational services. An alternative solution to the availability of pre-school education is seen in the introduction of changes in urban planning legislation related to the procedure for granting construction permits with the obligation of the developer to build social facilities in the construction of microdistricts. (Ivanova, 2016).

One of the most important criteria for a decent life is the availability of quality school education, which is the foundation for the development of human capital. Human capital, as a socio-economic category, includes the level of intellectual development, health, nature of work, quality and level of knowledge. Due to the fact that knowledge is a fact of innovative development, the issues of access to education in all regions of the country have become relevant in recent years.

The legislation of the Russian Federation guarantees accessibility and free basic general education. The level of enrolment of children of school age is in line with that of the developed countries. In 2000s, due to demographic trends, the number of students decreased, which led to an excessive supply of places in schools. According to the statistical studies of the Research University of Higher school of Economics, presented in the collection "Indicators of education", the coverage of children with primary general, basic general, secondary general education in 2016 amounted to 100.1%, compared with 2000–91.2%.

To date, the popularity of secondary vocational education is growing steadily. There are about 2,6 thousand educational organizations implementing this level of education in more than 300 specialties. 2.3 million people are enrolled in secondary vocational education programs.

Currently, the system of secondary vocational education is undergoing major changes associated with the introduction of new standards in the top 50 most popular specialties in the labor market, the introduction of a demonstration exam on the standards of World Skills and others.

Accessibility of higher education consists not only of the opportunities to enter a higher education institution, but also to obtain a diploma. And as practice shows, the main reason for the non-completion of higher education programs is not the material component, but the lack of the ability to adapt to changing conditions, increased educational demands, of the ability to organize themselves.

In pedagogical science, the acceptability of higher education is defined as a combination of opportunities associated with admission and successful completion of higher education, implemented on the basis of the activation of the internal potential of self-development and self-realization of the individual with the help of pedagogical support in this process (Apevalova, 2017).

The need to analyze the placement of young people in the market and the cost guidelines in terms of the choice of professional activity is caused by two factors. First of all, young people constitute a significant share of the working population of the country and occupy a central place in the labor market, and at the same time remain the most vulnerable segment in the personnel market.

In this regard, the relationship between the country's development prospects, its economic and social success and the starting conditions for the professional activity and activities of young people, and the degree of its integration into all spheres of social and economic life of the society is undeniable.

Results

The multidimensional and mediated impact of education on financial and economic activities and development requires, on the one hand, the assessment of the contribution of education to the achievement of economic results, and, on the other hand, the development of a kind of system of indicators that allow such an assessment to be implemented.

This task is implemented in the framework of the statistical approach by calculating various indices. First of all, the education index and the human development index should be mentioned.

Every year, in the Human Development Reports, United Nations specialists regularly focus on the correlation between human development and economic growth.

This relationship includes the possibility of an upward spiral development: the high level of human development contributes to the acceleration of economic growth, which, in turn, stimulates the further development of human potential.

The composition of the indices demonstrates the contribution of education to this movement, concretizing its importance in the new knowledge economy. Since the HDI elements can be considered as human development resources, therefore, the high values of the index components provide more opportunities for the realization of human potential (Klyucharev, 2014).

The identified directions become the foundation of the state policy in the field of education, which are reflected in various federal and regional regulations that guide the development of the Russian education system.

The Ministry of education has developed a national doctrine of education in Russia to better coordinate the actions aimed at further development of education. This state document is closely linked to the strategic plans and goals of education with the further development of the country and society and includes:

- the formation of basic principles for stable socio-economic development of the country, ensuring high quality of life of the people and national security
- the promotion of democratic rule of law and development of civil society
- the provision of personnel to the actively developing economy, globalizing into the world economy, having high competitiveness and increasing investment activity

The Concept of long-term socio-economic development of the Russian Federation for the period up to 2020[3] fixes the increasing importance of human capital as a basic element of socio-economic development, namely, "the level of competitiveness of the modern innovative economy is largely determined by the quality of professional staff, the level of their socialization and cooperation. Russia cannot maintain a competitive position in the world economy at the expense of cheap labor and savings on the development of education".

Conclusion

Thus, the high level of professional education acquired by the residents of the country makes it possible to improve the quality of life of the population through improving their health and longevity, increasing the level of education and culture, that is the relationship between the human development index and education.

In addition, the human development index and education of citizens, according to UN experts, significantly affect the state of economic and social progress of the country.

In the state programs implemented in the subjects of the Russian Federation it is supposed to widely apply educational programs of magistracy and postgraduate study. Also, new standards and technologies for the general and pre-school education, as well as additional education systems, should be introduced.

In addition, it is planned to introduce the most successful all-Russian independent assessment of the quality of education, created on the principles of participation of employers who are professionals and public organizations.

Thus, the main factor in the innovative development of the modern economy and the improvement the quality of life of the population is human capital, and the main component of human capital is an individual with a high level of education and development. Today, the human capital itself determines the bulk of the national wealth of countries, regions, municipalities and organizations.

3 The concept of long-term social and economic development of the Russian Federation up to 2020 (approved by the order of the government of the Russian Federation from 17.11.2008 № 1662). – URL: http://www.consultant.ru/document/cons_doc__LAW82134/ (accessed 02.04.2009)

References

Abalkin L. I. EHkonomicheskaya ehnciklopediya [Economic encyclopedia] / Ed. count: E. I. Alexandrov, A. V. Anikin, R. S. Asatryan, etc.; GL. ed. by L. I. Abalkin. M.: Economics; Institute of Economics of the Russian Academy of Sciences, 1999. -1055 p (in Russian).

Anikina E.A., Ivankina L.I., Silifonova E.V. Problemy i perspektivy dostupnosti vysshego obrazovaniya v usloviyah sovremennyh preobrazovanij v Rossii [Problems and prospects of higher education accessibility in conditions of modern transformation in Russia] / edited nauch. the editorship of doctor. Econ. Sciences G. A. Barysheva. – Tomsk: STT, 2016. – 162 p (in Russian).

Apevalova Z.V., Bulkina K.I., Semenova A.A. Znachenie tekhnologij vosproizvodstva chelovecheskogo kapitala v kontekste zadach obespecheniya dostupnosti vysshego obrazovaniya v RF [The Importance of human capital reproduction technologies in the context of problems of accessibility of higher education in the Russian Federation]//Modern science: actual problems of theory and practice. Series: Economics and law. 2017. No. 4. pp. 4–8 (in Russian).

Bowles S., Gintis H. Schooling in capitalist America. Revisited // Sociology of education. 2002. Vol. 75. N 1. pp. 1–18.

Ciring R.A. Teoreticheskie podhody k izucheniyu problemy dostupnosti vysshego obrazovaniya v sovremennom obshchestve [Theoretical approaches to the study of the problem of accessibility of higher education in modern society] Vestnik of Kostroma state University. N. Ah. Nekrasov. 2012. No. 1 (18) (in Russian).

Ivanova E.YU. Dostupnost' doshkol'nogo obrazovanie v Rossii: praktiki vyravnivaniya sprosa i predlozheniya v sbornike: Social'nye dvizheniya, kollektivnye dejstviya v usloviyah social'nogo neravenstva [The Accessibility of preschool education in Russia: practices of alignment of supply and demand in the book: Social movements, collective action in conditions of social inequality] // the Collection of materials of the Round table. MGGER. Moscow, 2016. pp. 23–44 (in Russian).

Klyucharev G.A., Didenko D.V., Latov YU.V., Latova N.V. Nepreryvnoe obrazovanie stimul chelovecheskogo razvitiya i faktor social'no-ehkonomicheskih neravenstv [Continuous education the stimulus of human development and the factor of socio-economic inequalities] / Under the General ed. M.: CSEM, 2014. / Pod obshch. red. YU.V. Latova. M.: CSPiM, 2014 (in Russian).

Konstantinovskij D.L., Vahshtajn V.S., Kurakin D.YU. Kachestvennoe obrazovanie: dostupnost' i social'naya politika V knige: Social'naya politika v sovremennoj Rossii: reformy i povsednevnost' [Quality education: accessibility and social policy In the book: Social policy in modern Russia]: reforms and everyday life Burawoy M., Vakhshtein S. V., Zdravomyslova E. A., Zubarevich N. In. Konstantinovsky D. L., Lezhnina Yu. P., Pilkington, H., Richter, D., P. V. Romanov, E. R. Yarskaya, Atoyants M. S., Yarskaya V. N., Chagin, K., Kurakin D. Yu., Kuznetsova-Morenko, I. B. Center for social policy and gender studies. Moscow, Science. 2008. pp. 52–79 (in Russian).

Morgan R. In debate over welfare reform, work trumps education // http://Chronicle.com/weekly/v48/i41/41a02401.htm19.06.02.

Ponomareva M.N. Dostupnost' professional'nogo obrazovaniya v usloviyah cifrovoj obrazovatel'noj sredy [Availability of vocational education in the digital educational environment] //Innovative development of vocational education. 2018. Vol. 19. No. 3. pp. 63–69 (in Russian).

SHklyar A. H. Dostupnost' professional'nogo obrazovaniya [The Accessibility of professional education]: monograph / A. H. Shkliar, Y. I. Krichevsky. – Minsk: RIPO, 2012. 87 p (in Russian).

Vejher A.A., Kremenickaya I.V. Izmenenie stepeni dostupnosti vysshego obrazovaniya v rossijskih usloviyah: prevrashchenie chasti vysshego obrazovaniya iz professional'nogo v obshchee [Change the degree of accessibility of higher education in the Russian context: the transformation of a part of higher education of the professional in General] // Accessibility of higher education in Russia. OTV. editor S. V. Shishkin. Independent Institute of social policy. – M., 2004 (in Russian).

Vladlen G. Budashevsky, Konstantin V. Krinichansky,
Olga N. Pastukhova

22 The Development of Disciplines with a Flexible Subject Area in the Digital Age: Logical and Heuristic Methods and Models

Introduction

University disciplines which affect such areas of modern finance as financial markets, banking, credit, money and monetary systems are currently experiencing a real crisis. It is caused by significant transformations in the above-mentioned areas. Thus, financial services markets are deeply transformed under the influence of the development of remote access technologies, digital transaction processing, the use of big data to develop various solutions, the use of blockchain technologies for transactions, contracts (smart contracts) and fixing the rights of the parties to contracts. The structure of financial systems changes significantly during the introduction of these innovations into the markets. New segments are emerging, the role of traditional players, in particular, commercial banks, is changing in the markets, their business models are being modified. Opportunities are opening up for new players to enter certain niches.

These processes determine the need to re-formulate the subject area of disciplines studying this area of finance, to revise tools and methods of their teaching, even tasks and goals to some extent, bearing in mind that the modern market requires a specialist to have a different set of competencies and skills than it was in the period preceding the digital era of the 21st century.

The present study aims to identify the basic contradictions, the beginning of which lies in the area of the technology revolution affecting the subject area disciplines, the contradictions that professors and universities have to face today. In addition, it is recommended to apply methods, the use of which will contribute to more effective work of the teacher with disciplines which have a flexible subject area.

Vladlen G. Budashevsky, Olga N. Pastukhova, South Ural State University (National Research University), Branch in Miass, Miass, Russia
Konstantin V. Krinichansky, Financial University under the Government of the Russian Federation, Moscow, Russia

https://doi.org/10.1515/9783110636147-022

Methodology

The issue raised in this study affects an extremely wide range of scientific fields, including epistemology, logic, ontology, other areas of philosophy, pedagogy, finally, economics as the subject area. Returning to the above-mentioned goal of our study, we note the following. According to the authors, there are two fundamental contradictions that determine the above complexity of teaching disciplines with a flexible subject area. A number of financial disciplines could be used as an example of these contradictions, namely:

(A) the contradiction between disciplinary approach and discreteness as a generally accepted way of organizing knowledge, on the one hand, and the uniqueness and the unity of the object under study, on the other hand;

(B) the contradiction between the understanding of the object in the time continuum, determining the flexibility and the inevitable variability of the studied subject, on the one hand, and, the need to use various subjects in the study of the discipline, thus, there are a problem of the formulation of the constant methodological apparatus, primarily conceptual one, on the other hand.

Today, in practice, we can often see that these contradictions determine significant difficulties with the postulation of the goals of academic disciplines, the definition of the boundaries of their subject area and, in fact, the formulation of didactic units to be mastered by university students, etc. Both teachers and students suffer from the rapid obsolescence of the textbook material. Against this background, the value of the teacher's ability to form the student's competence to work not so much with the subject as with the tool significantly increases. The task is to teach students to master and apply methods, to understand the methodology, to create their own algorithms and analytical approaches. All this, of course, should be combined with the development of skills in the use of modern technical means and software.

In order to show the topicality of this study, we turned to the problems of disciplines which study financial markets and the work of financial intermediaries. Indeed, today we can see that such an object of study as the banking market is completely changing its appearance under the influence of digital technologies. Providers of such services today are not only banks, but also FinTech companies, large companies in the ICT sector, social networks, major retailers. A number of studies show significant advantages of these companies in comparison with traditional financial intermediaries in providing consumers with financial services. For instance, Dallerup et al. (2018) and Dietz et al. (2017) indicate that banks are losing to FinTech companies in terms of the cost of providing financial services. Banks' costs are about 1.8–1.9 times higher than those of their competitors who have recently entered the financial services market. FinTech players, if we compare them with banks, have 65–75% lower costs of opening and maintaining an account,

40–60% lower costs of providing cash withdrawals and depositing, 90–95% lower costs of supporting cash payments and money transfers.

As a result, the market partially changes its structure in favor of new players, in addition, traditional players begin to adapt to the situation, for example, changing their own business models and structure, implementing takeover strategies, creating their own platform solutions and marketplaces.

The presence of these processes indicates the increasing complexity of the development and teaching, for example, such a discipline as Banking, the expansion of its subject area, the need to improve the methodological apparatus, making significant adjustments to it.[1] Drawing the attention to the second of the abovementioned contradictions, we note that the advent of the digital age has led to the effect that, as shown by the example of Banking, a number of financial disciplines today are increasingly becoming, as they say, disciplines in dynamics. This leads to an increase in the demand for the use of pedagogical techniques that focus on the subject-problem field, aimed at finding an answer regarding the future states of the object under study, the search for opportunities, and not the analysis of the current state of this object. Thus, the subject of the discipline becomes a kind of vector in its future.

The analysis showed that in order to develop methods of teaching disciplines with a flexible subject area, in fact, knowledge in philosophy, pedagogy, system analysis and other areas, which has already been accumulated, can be used. This will help to overcome the crisis of these disciplines. Among the most well-known works, which the developers of academic disciplines should pay attention to, are works on the theory of organizational learning, systems and project thinking (Senge, 1990; Dim et al., 2005), the theory of knowledge management (Toffler, 1980; Bukowitz and Williams, 1999), research in the field of decision-making under conditions of uncertainty (Kahneman, 2011), the theory of system dynamics (Forrester, 1968; Sterman, 1994), ways of learning (Polya, 1957, Bandler, 1985, Korczak, 1990, Robbins, 2002), the theory of system constraints (Goldratt, 2000; Goldratt & Cox, 2014). Let us also pay attention to the current trends of research in the field of human resources management (Liu, Tangirala, Lee, and Parker, 2019, Parker and Collins, 2010, Mensmann and French, 2019, Chamberlin, Newton, and Lepine, 2017). One of them is the analysis and management of proactive behavior of people, bringing benefits to both individuals and teams or organizations.

The first thing we will pay attention to from the point of view of the content side of the learning process is the need to teach the vision of systematic interaction of the

1 This may include, for example, the need to reflect the emergence of alternative financing options built on a loan contract, but without the bank as a financial intermediary in the traditional sense. We are talking about so-called crowd model – crowdfunding and crowdlending. Another case that does not fit into the known schemes is a financial contract built on the model of a smart contract that has the features of a share.

key activities of the organization (see Figure 22.1). This requirement is well known, but it is rarely a goal in the training practice. At the same time, an employer often points out that such a vision is a key condition for the ability of a university graduate to develop an innovative high-performance solution, especially in conditions of uncertainty of the socio-economic environment (Townsend, Hunt, McMullen, Sarasvathy, 2018) and problems arising from so-called diseases of the transition period.

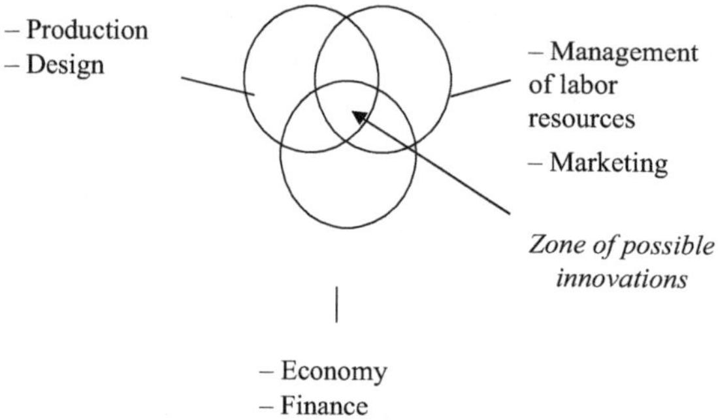

Figure 22.1: The interaction of the key activities.

The second thing to focus on is the need to develop the graduate's problem thinking. In this regard, it is advisable to understand what is the problem? It can be noted that the concept of problem in the literature and in scientific and applied research is not usually formulated in the sense that it is not given a definition. In this sense, the word problem is widely used, so that its meaning remains quite unclear. In practice, it complicates the process of analysis, forecasting and decision-making greatly. We will try to correct this shortcoming by giving the following definition. The problem is characterized by a gap between the initial and desired (given) states of the system (object, process), which is caused by the insufficiency or incompatibility of available resources (information, financial, labor, material and other) or methods to overcome this gap (Budashevsky, 2014). The desired state of the system is determined by the condition of achieving the goal. We illustrate this concept with the following model (see Figure 22.2).

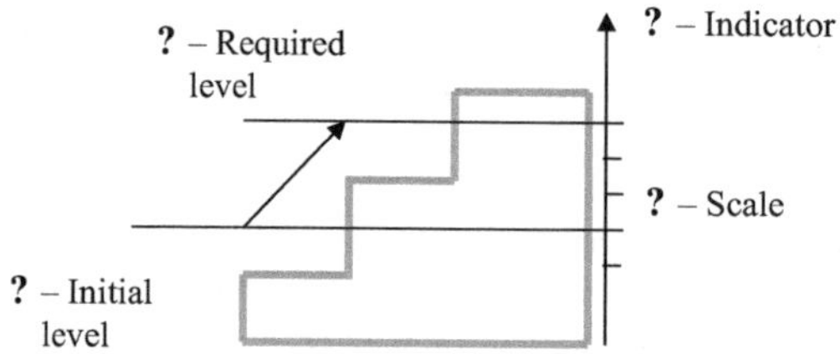

Figure 22.2: Schematic representation of the concept of problem.

As can be seen, the concept of problem implies an attempt to give comments, explanations on four issues for the person using it in his analysis. These issues are:
- What is the key metric used to fix the problem as well as to set a goal?
- What is the scale of its measurement?
- What is its initial level?
- What is the required level?

Let us pay attention to some nuance, which is expressed in the need to distinguish between the problem and the problem situation. The problem, as discussed above, must be expressed quantitatively, be specific and objective. On the contrary, the problem situation is considered as the situation expressing the conflict between possession by the subject of some potential (resources), on the one hand, and the purposes, tasks of this subject, on the other. Thus, there is a need to find a solution to bridge the gap between limited capacity and the need to achieve some objective.

Since the organization or some socio-economic system at the same time face a whole set of problems, the important task is to prioritize them. Simplifying, we will talk about the need to find a key problem among a number of problems. To do this, it is advisable to apply the method of pre-project analysis and ranking of problem, that is the MARP method (Budashevsky, 2012, 2016). The method is based on a preliminary search and analysis of the proposed links between the selected initial problems, their expert ranking (in several successive stages), quantitative assessment of the statistical significance of the results. At the output, the analyst must present a generalized ranking chart. Then the cause-and-effect relations between the selected most significant problems are identified and analyzed, the connections that are fundamentally important from the point of view of management decisions are highlighted.

The measurement required to adequately analyze and solve any problem can be carried out with varying degrees of objectivity, using different indicators and scales. Scales can be both strictly quantitative and qualitative. It is also possible to use qualitative and quantitative comparative analysis, which is achieved, for example, through the use of logical and heuristic methods.

The third thing that we emphasize is the orientation of the teaching methods used on the harmonious combination of development from the outside and self-development. This is the key to modern human resource management (Senge, 1990). Besides, it is important to find a balance between the requirements for in-depth specialization in a particular area and the possession of general cultural competencies, including the development of erudition. To do this, we propose to use an expanded version of the T-model (see Figure 22.3). It allows visualizing specific requirements for a specialist, assessing the initial level of the performance of each of them, optimizing the program of balanced self-development (Budashevsky, 2014). This model is aimed at the formation of the required skills, improving the competitiveness of the specialist, his willingness to innovate, to actively diversify in various areas of work and career development.

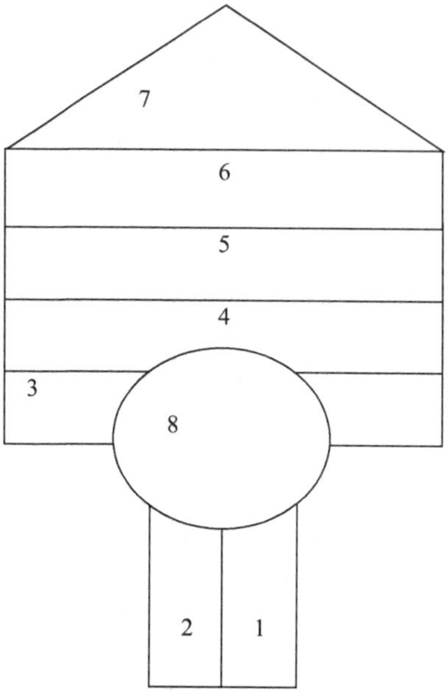

Figure 22.3: Specialist T-model.
Notes: 1 – necessary professional skills, their use
2 – mastering the critical mass of professional knowledge
3 – common sense, clear thinking
4 – comprehension of experience (the positive and negative one; the own and foreign one)
5 – the culture of thinking (development of three levels of thinking, critical thinking and error resistance, logic, argumentativeness)
6 – formulation and analysis of problems, rational problem solving
7 – continuous self-development
8 – regulation of synergetic interaction of model elements on the basis of formation of key competences, development of innovativeness, productive creativity.

The explanation of this model to students opens the possibility of purposeful management of development (and self-development) of key skills of a specialist, his adaptability in the modern rapidly changing world.

The formation and development of the necessary skills of a new level of specialist should be carried out individually, taking into account its mental characteristics. The interaction of cognitive activities of people with their professional (business) life is studied by D. Kahneman (Kahneman, 2011). The author discovered *the systemic irrationality* of human attitude to risk in decision-making and in the management of their behavior. The confrontation to irrationality is possible in the case of the interaction of two systems of thinking, logical-mathematical and mental-heuristic ones, the use of which varies depending on the degree of complexity of the problem.

Human thinking can be represented as a model (Budashevsky, 2014), which reflects the degree of complexity of a problem in relation to the level of preparedness of a decision-maker. Here we conditionally distinguish three levels of thinking. The first, the basic level, assumes that the available information containing the thought, which is already known, is transmitted without distortion. Control over the development of the material is carried out by checking the ability of the student to build illustrative examples and anti-examples. The achievement of this level reflects the ability of a specialist to work competently according to the instructions.

The next level will be called a standard one. Its achievement corresponds to the ability of a specialist to solve typical problems in the professional field, independently and consciously choosing the most rational methods of the known. Thus, there must be an effective application of available knowledge.

The problem of mastering disciplines with a flexible subject area requires achieving a creative level of reflection. This third level of productive creative thinking is achieved when a given (or chosen) problem is solved in an extraordinary way, with elements of original techniques and, ultimately, more effectively than using standard solutions.

An important component of the effective training is the ability of a person to self-development and self-management. At the same time, it is necessary to take into account the relationship between the level of training of a specialist and the level of his needs (Budashevsky, 2009). The matrix presented in Figure 22.4 can significantly help teachers and students to build individual trajectories of self-study.

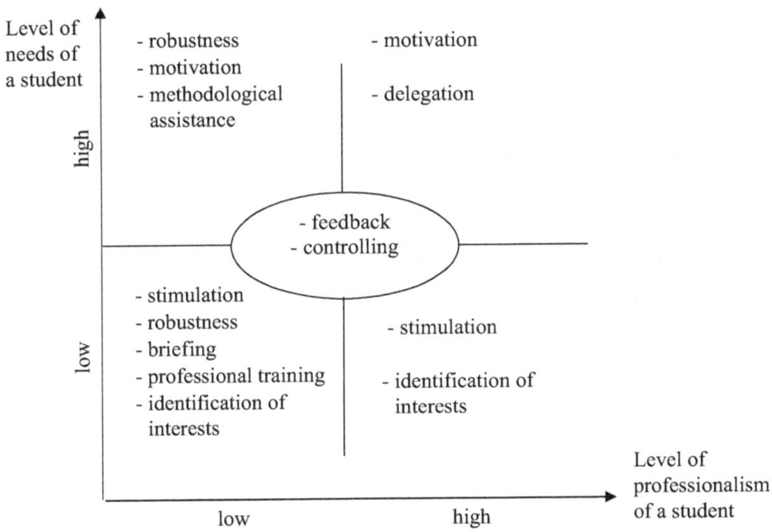

Figure 22.4: Effective coaching model.

The improved coaching model should be applied at all stages of training, taking into account the subjective characteristics of each student and each coach.

Finally, the fourth point of our analysis is devoted to the use of elements of systems analysis and synergy in the teaching of disciplines with a flexible subject area. Being limited by the scope of this publication, we will drastically narrow the set of these elements by proposing only one of them, namely, the program-target approach (PTA).

The essence of the PTA can be represented compactly but succinctly in the form of ten key components, which are at the same time, the conditions for the effectiveness of solutions: Goals – Measures – Consequences – Criteria – Resources –

Models – Compatibility – Program – Mechanism – Controlling – Risks (Budashevsky, 2016). PTA as a universal tool is applicable both to the analysis of already established and stable functioning systems, and to dynamic systems, which are designated as a flexible subject area in this paper.

Results

As can be seen from the previous material, the considered methodological tools are developed and used by the authors of this work in their research and teaching activities. Assessing the subjectively achieved result as positive, the authors recommend the use of the considered methods, that is a systematic approach, logical-heuristic methods of problem thinking, self-development techniques, etc., in the practice of training specialists in higher education programs. First of all, we insist that these methodological tools will be useful for teachers of those disciplines, which are characterized by contradictions, indicated at the beginning of this work. These are disciplines with a flexible subject area. Besides, it is possible to notice that universality of the methods, opened in this work, allows hoping that they can be productively used in other fields of activity, apart from the educational one, in research, in the solution of business problems and so forth. Thus, the result of their use can affect several levels from the personal one to the level of the firm or the organization as a whole.

Conclusion

The development of digital technologies, their penetration into the markets of financial services and products have led to a significant transformation of financial systems, in view of their structure, membership, sets of tools, interaction technologies, etc. A number of concepts and methodological techniques, which previously set clear boundaries of the study of financial disciplines, cease to work today. It radically complicates the task of teaching a number of disciplines, named in this work, that are disciplines with a flexible subject area.

In this paper, first of all, an explanation of the nature of this problem is given. It is based on two fundamental contradictions. The first one is between discipline and discreteness as a common way of organizing knowledge and uniqueness and the unity of the object under study. The second is the contradiction between the inevitable variability of the subject and the conservatism of the methodological apparatus used.

In addition, the paper presents methods and recommendations for the development of methods of teaching disciplines with a flexible subject area, relying on such methodological principles as system analysis, problem thinking, approaches to self-stimulation and self-development, etc. Due to the increasing demand for the problem, creative, innovative, inventive solutions in the financial industry (although not in it alone) requires specific, difficult algorithmizable heuristic methods and techniques. The authors recommend to develop methods of teaching these approaches and techniques in universities, believing that the ongoing digitalization in its most diverse manifestations will only lead to increasing complexity in economic systems and further collapse of the existing methodological apparatus.

References

Bandler, R. (1985), Using Your Brain for a Change, Real People Press, Moab, Utah.

Budashevsky V. G. *Tekhnologiya razrabotki innovatsionnykh resheniy i upravleniya chelovecheskimi resursami s primeneniyem usovershenstvovannoy matritsy kouchinga* [Technology of development of innovative decisions and human resources management with the use of advanced coaching matrix]. Socio-economic, institutional, legal, cultural and historical components of the development of municipalities. Proceedings of the VI scientific and practical conference, Russia, 2009, Geotur Publishing, 2009, Miass, pp. 14–16 (in Russian).

Budashevsky V. G. *Tekhnologiya predproyektnogo ranzhirovaniya problem, na osnove vyyavleniya i logiko-evristicheskogo analiza svyazey mezhdu nimi* [Technology pre-ranking of the problems based on the detection of logical and heuristic connections between them]. Socio-economic, institutional, legal, cultural and historical components of the development of municipalities. Proceedings of the VIII scientific and practical conference, Russia, 2012, Geotur Publishing, 2012, Miass, pp. 10–12 (in Russian).

Budashevsky V. G. *Prinyatiye upravlencheskikh resheniy: logika i tekhnologiya vybora i prakticheskogo primeneniya metodov razrabotki, obosnovaniya i prinyatiya upravlencheskikh resheniy: uchebnoye posobiye* [Managerial Decision Making: Logic and Technology Choice and Implementation of Methods for the Development, Justification and Management Decisions], SUSU Publishing Center, Chelyabinsk, 2016, 187 p (in Russian).

Budashevsky V. G. *Prakticheskaya logika (Osnovy tekhnologii produktivnogo myshleniya): uchebnoye posobiye* [Logic: Foundations of Productive Thinking], SUSU Publishing Center, Chelyabinsk, 2014, 191 p (in Russian).

Bukowitz, W. and Williams, R. (1999), The Knowledge Management Fieldbook, Prentice Hall, Financial Times.

Chamberlin, M., Newton, D. W., and Lepine, J. A. (2017), "A meta-analysis of voice and its promotive and prohibitive forms: Identification of key associations, distinctions, and future research directions", Personnel Psychology, Vol. 70, pp. 11–71.

Dallerup, K., Jayantilal, S., Konov G., Legradi A., Pereira N., Stockmeier H.-M. (2018), "A bank branch for the digital age", McKinsey.

Dietz, M., Lemerle, M., Mehta, A., Sengupta, J., and Zhou. N. (2017), "Remaking the bank for an ecosystem world", McKinsey Global Institute Report, October.

Dym, C. L. et al. (2005), "Engineering design thinking, teaching, and learning", Journal of Engineering Education, Vol. 94(1), pp. 103–119.

Forrester, J. W. (1968), Principles of Systems, Pegasus Communications, Waltham (MA).

Goldratt, E. (2000), Necessary but not Sufficient, North River Press, Great Barrington, MA.

Goldratt, E. and Cox, D. (2007), Objective. Continuous improvement process, Publishing house Medley.
Kahneman, D. (2011). Thinking, Fast and Slow, Farrar, Straus and Giroux, New York, NY, US.
Korczak, J. (1990), How to love a child, a book about education, Politizdat, Moscow.
Liu, W. Tangirala, S., Lee, C., and Parker, S. (2019), "New directions for exploring the consequences of proactive behaviors: Introduction to the special issue", Journal of Organizational Behavior. Vol. 40 Is. 1, pp. 1–4.
Manyika, J., Lund, S., and Singer, M. (2016), "Digital Finance for All: Powering Inclusive Growth in Emerging Economies", McKinsey Global Institute Report, September.
Mensmann, M. and French, M. (2019), "Who stays proactive after entrepreneurship training? Need for cognition, personal initiative maintenance, and well-being", Journal of Organizational Behavior, Vol. 40, pp. 20–37.
Parker, S. K. and Collins, C. G. (2010), "Taking stock: Integrating and differentiating multiple proactive behaviors", Journal of Management, Vol. 36, pp. 633–662.
Polya, G. (1957). How to Solve It (2nd Ed.). Princeton. NJ: Princeton University Press.
Robbins, E. (2002), Unlimited Power: The New Science of Personal Achievement. Meganewton, Potpourri.
Senge, P. M. (1990), The Fifth Discipline: The Art & Practice of the Learning Organization, Doubleday/Currency, New York.
Sterman, J. D. (1994), "Learning in and about complex systems", System Dynamics Review. Vol. 10 No. 2–3, pp. 291–330.
Toffler, A. (1980), The Third Wave, Bantam Books, New York.
Townsend, D. M., Hunt, R. A., McMullen, J. S., and Sarasvathy, S. D. (2018), "Uncertainty, knowledge problems, and entrepreneurial action", Academy of Management Annals, Vol. 12 No. 2, pp. 659–687.

Nadezhda Golubeva, Olesya Digtyar

23 The Role of Emotional Intelligence in Forming Critical Thinking on ESP Employments (English for Special Purposes)

Introduction

The doctrine of vocational education of the Russian Federation and the standards being developed provide a gradual transition to a more professionally oriented content of the learning process. Moreover, the content should be formed taking into account the needs of the national economy and not to be a dogma, because the needs of the national economy are changing. Therefore, all changes should be reflected in educational programs, and this requires feedback, i.e. scientists, authors of educational standards and programs should be constantly aware of the changes that are occurring in the national economy (Golubeva, 2015a).

This study aims to show that the vocational education can be characterized as peer-to-peer pedagogy and is based on subject-subject relations. Since the study is devoted to finding ways to optimize the formation of professional skills of non-philological students, we just need to consider this problem from the point of view of the second subject, i.e. the learner, especially since in the process of vocational education the learner plays one of the main roles in shaping the content of vocational education, and therefore it is impossible to optimize the process of forming skills without the participation of the learner (a student, in our case).

The purpose of this work is to determine the role of emotional intelligence in the development of critical thinking, as a key professional skill, in the process of teaching professionally oriented foreign language in universities. According to D. Halpern, critical thinking is the use of cognitive techniques or strategies that increase the likelihood of obtaining the desired end result. This definition characterizes thinking (intelligence) as something different in controllability, validity, and purposefulness – the type of thinking that is used to effectively achieve the goal (Fedotovskaya 2002).

In the development of cognitive science in a certain period of time, too much attention was paid to informational, "computer-based" models of intelligence, and the affective component of thinking, at least in Western psychology, faded into the background. The concept of social intelligence is precisely the link that binds together the

Nadezhda Golubeva, Financial University under the Government of the Russian Federation, Moscow, Russia
Olesya Digtyar, Financial University under the Government of the Russian Federation, Suzdal, Russia

https://doi.org/10.1515/9783110636147-023

affective and cognitive aspects of the process of cognition. In the field of social intelligence, an approach was developed that understands human cognition not as a computational activity, but as a cognitive-emotional process (Melnichuk, Nenyuk and Alisevich, 2014).

When preparing a specialist with knowledge of the language in the field of professional activity, it is necessary to take into account the profile specificity. There is no doubt that a university graduate must quickly adapt to changing circumstances, to independently acquire knowledge, to be able to competently work with information, i.e. to find the necessary sources to solve the task, analyze it, summarize, compare, make reasoned conclusions and make decisions based on them (Golubeva, 2015b).

The next section will describe the methods of studying the influence of emotional intelligence in the development of critical thinking, which is one of the key professional skills in the process of teaching a professionally oriented foreign language in universities, the third section will present the results of the study, and in the last section, respectively, the conclusions.

Data and Methods

Theoretical Analysis of Pedagogical, Psychological and Methodical Literature

The theoretical analysis of the pedagogical, psychological and methodical literature on the research topic allows noting the following. The authors of the technology of critical thinking are C. Temple, D. Steele and K. Meredith. In the 1980s in the United States, and later in the 1990s in Europe, the development of critical thinking became one of the main goals of education. One of the most common is the definition of D. Kluster: "Critical thinking is a special kind of thinking activity, the characteristic features of which are: the development of strategies for making the right decisions when solving any tasks based on receiving, analyzing, and processing information; the implementation of reflexive actions (analytical, testing, controlling, evaluative) performed in relation to any object or phenomenon, including its own thinking process; a balanced analysis of various opinions and views, the manifestation of one's own position, an objective assessment of the process and the result of both one's own and other activities" (Goleman, Boyacis and McKee, 2005).

All formulations of critical thinking are fairly close in content, and critical thinking is such intellectual activity of people, which can be characterized by the presence of a high level of perception, understanding and objectivity of the approach to the surrounding information field.

The process of developing critical thinking is of particular relevance in the era of global development of the information space. It allows us to confidently work with an ever-increasing and renewing stream of knowledge, to systematize them, to express our thoughts on the basis of understanding existing judgments and experience correctly, to solve problems and also to promote independent learning. Of particular importance is the development of critical thinking of students as an important factor for perception, evaluation and analysis of information, as well as the ability to respond adequately and implement foreign language communication. Technology development of critical thinking is aimed at the formation of a diverse personality, able to treat any information critically, but at the same time open to new ideas and methods (Digtyar, 2018).

Synthesis

Today, various methods of forming critical thinking in teaching foreign languages to students of economic specialties are offered, for example, problem assignments, training in discursive analysis skills, implementation of the project method as enhancing students' ability to independently perceive and evaluate information in a foreign language context, a method of analyzing specific situations or case method.

The method of projects, as the teaching technology of critical thinking, involves a combination of research and search methods for the purpose of their creative implementation. The method involves active independent work on the formulation of the problem, the search for its solutions, as well as the formulation, detailed analysis and evaluation of a specific solution (Digtyar, 2017).

The project method thus helps to unleash the creative potential of students, develops practical skills of applying the obtained theoretical knowledge of future economists in a foreign language, taking into account all modern 21st century skills in the audience, particularly creativity and critical thinking, communication and collaboration as well as digital literacy (Melnichuk, Osipova and Kondrakhina, 2017).

A distinctive feature of this method is the formulation of a specific problem and the proposal of solutions. Through this method, students are offered a number of problems or even one that bring them to an independent decision based on previously acquired knowledge. In the process of resolving the problem, students are faced with a lack of certain knowledge, which they fill in through self-study. The results of using this training method are the development of critical thinking, the ability to learn independently, a high interest in the educational process, etc.

The case study method or case method was based on the principle of a "precedent" or "case study". The essence of the method lies in the analysis of real problem situations in organizations using the brainstorming method and the formulation of solutions and their subsequent implementation.

The results of this training method are interest in studying the subject, activity in learning and improving skills in collecting, processing and analyzing information in various situations, finding non-trivial solutions, as well as practical teamwork skills.

The use of these technologies and techniques in the educational process involves using the approach of "pedagogy of peers", that is, the active involvement of students in the didactic process, which contributes to the development of personal, intellectual and professional activity, as well as the formation of the necessary competencies that the future specialist should possess.

When implementing the technology of critical thinking in teaching foreign language the students of economic specialties, the role of the teacher is not to assign "ready" knowledge, but to help students in constructing their own, which is born in the learning process. The teacher uses the communicative-active principle in teaching, conducts an interactive mode of study, a joint search in solving problems and building partnerships with students. Teachers need to pay maximum attention to the very meaning of critical thinking. It is necessary to show that the essence is not in the search for flaws, but in an objective assessment of the positive and negative aspects in the object under study. Thus, when learning a foreign language, in particular, learning is not limited to just a set of theoretical knowledge and practical skills. It forms the personality of the student with a complex of specific skills.

Innovative technology development of critical thinking is the practical implementation of a student-centered approach to learning. Within the framework of this approach, the student himself constructs the learning process, defining specific goals, tracking the directions of his development and evaluating the final result. In addition to this, the use of this technology enhances the development of skills of thoughtful work with information. The most effective form of teaching critical thinking to students is the implementation of group work, which allows them to develop the qualities of independence, curiosity, the ability to make an independent assessment, to argue their opinions, to prove or refute their decision. Each group develops integrative teamwork skills, which represent the professional competence of future professionals.

Results

Discussion

The formation of critical thinking in the process of teaching a foreign language for special purposes (ESP) of students is based on a critical analysis of incoming information from employers who highlight this skill as the main workplace. These technologies, aimed at developing critical thinking, effectively combine all types of speech activity by creating the necessary linguistic professional environment. Thus, the use of case and project tasks during the study of a foreign language is dictated by the need for successful employment and career ambitions of students.

Critical thinking helps to analyze information, formulate sound conclusions and assessments, correctly apply the results to situations and problems (Golubeva, 2015a). However, the open nature of the studied problems contributes to the construction of a logically thought-out and reasoned decision. The collective nature of work in class helps the manifestation of the strengths of each participant in the discussion in shaping the final decision, which leads to the active inclusion of each student in the group, regardless of their level of knowledge and language base. The modern didactic process is characterized by the need for collaboration, with the result that each of the participants can show their most pronounced abilities and talents: for example, one student is talented in information technology, another has the necessary charisma for a convincing presentation, the third is capable of quick analysis and synthesis information, etc. Jointly solving a common task, united by a single goal, students have the opportunity to demonstrate individual competences, and also have a chance for self-expression, which contributes to the growth of motivation of the group members, and ultimately – a successful result.

The overall goal in solving a case or project task not only leads to the formation of critical thinking, but also helps to systematize existing theoretical knowledge. Consequently, critical thinking is a way of forming a systematic approach to the analysis of information, which turns out to be the most important tool in the process of applied knowledge utilization. Systematic thinking in the professional sphere is a logical and rational approach not only to collecting and analyzing information, but also to making a decision, assessing the possible consequences of a given choice.

Systematic thinking, on the other hand, implies knowledge and skills in various fields of science and practice, which means that critical thinking has an interdisciplinary character. The interdisciplinary is an integration approach, without which it is impossible to develop any academic discipline in modern higher educational institutions. Indeed, all breakthrough modern discoveries in the professional sphere are interdisciplinary. By itself, the nature of a foreign language for special purposes, as a subject, combines the possession of foreign language competences and competencies in the professional field of knowledge (financial, tax, legal, etc.). Therefore, in our opinion, it is appropriate to note that innovative pedagogical technologies in the field of teaching a foreign language, and not only, relate to interdisciplinary or intersectoral communication.

Among the most important skills allocated by employers in assessing the qualifications of graduates of economic universities is the ability to manage projects. Design tasks, as an innovative technology of teaching ESP, thus, becomes especially relevant. Project management is characterized by time constraints, therefore, to be effective, each team member must demonstrate not only professional competence and creativity, but also some other qualities, without which the success of an undertaking is not possible. Thus, along with rational and pragmatic critical thinking, graduates should possess some emotional competences (charisma, adaptability, tolerance, communication skills, etc.) that would contribute to the development of critical thinking and professional success, in general.

Therefore, in parallel with the practice-oriented approaches to the teaching didactics, teachers and psychologists began to pay more and more attention to emotional intelligence. The idea of a successful personality combining cognitive and affective natural qualities belongs to A. Maslow. In the middle of the last century, he conducted research in the field of psychology, which led to the conclusion that professional realization is not possible without an affective component.

Since the nineties of the last century, the theme of combining emotionality and rationalism has become increasingly popular in the publications of psychologists on the topic of professional success. The term "emotional intelligence" becomes especially widely used after the appearance of the article of the same name (Caruso and Salovey 2004). In particular, P. Salovey wrote that the attitude towards human emotions has changed in the professional environment. Pure rationalism does not necessarily lead to career growth, which is appropriate to combine emotionality with cognitiveness. Further, the authors noted that emotions are of practical importance especially when it comes to the psychological determination of the type of personality. They emphasized that meaningful affectiveness is justified and useful in a professional environment, that it helps to better understand and manipulate colleagues. They defined emotional intelligence as a substance that includes the following components: the ability to express one's own and perceive other people's emotions; the ability to control their own and manipulate other people's feelings.

Developing the idea of the benefits of feelings in the profession, D. Caruso emphasized that there is no contradiction between the rational and the emotional, that the realization of ambitions is possible only in a combination of both components. The authors successfully implemented the experience gained in the process of research, having founded the society "Six Seconds", the purpose of which was to conduct practice-oriented seminars on emotional intelligence. Psychologists of society conduct classes to improve the emotional climate in families, companies and government organizations. They offer their understanding of this phenomenon, based on the practical conclusion that the ability to get the best result in relationships with oneself and other people is possible with the appropriate emotional state.

The relevance of these seminars is especially important in the conditions of VUCA (VUCA: volatility, uncertainty, complexity, ambiguity) of the world; this is some context in which the business community and the people working inside it consider their present existence. Volatility involves the variability of conditions, which requires the ability to adaptability, tolerance, and patience for success. Uncertainty – is an uncertainty that negates the efforts of groups of people, suggests that they lose hope for the best, do not see the point in exerting effort, lose their motivation and endurance. In such a situation, the leader is required to be able to resist the general mood, not to lose faith, inspiration so that, despite the general mood, to keep his presence of mind, to calm, instill confidence in his strength, lead. Complexity (complexity) – about the difficulties that organizations face in a difficult political and economic world. The real leader is a talented communicator, able to explain the difficult in simple words, to encourage, to interest, to see the appeal of the call, to positively evaluate the work done – all this will help to cope with an increasingly aggressive professional environment. Ambiguity means uncertainty. There are no right and wrong decisions. Be always ready to take a punch, remember the possible consequences, understand the essence of change and understand the relationship of variables. The leader requires high moral and ethical qualities of the individual, particularly: high self-control in chaos, responsibility for making their own decisions and decisions of subordinates, professional intuition, ability to predict the potential result and its consequences for business and team members, the ability to take responsibility for potential negative result. All the above-mentioned qualities of a leader relate mainly to personal qualities, that is, to the competences of emotional intelligence, which in the conditions of the World Science Academy of the world becomes a guarantee of not only success, but also survival.

The concept of emotional leadership became especially popular due to D. Goulman, an employee of a well-known American publishing house, whose book aroused interest among professionals in the field of professional growth in the US (Goleman, 2005). What can explain such high popularity? For almost the entire 20th century, scientists emphasized the importance of rational, pragmatic intelligence, which was determined by numerous tests on IQ (intelligence quotient). It was on the basis of mental and technical abilities that professional and career prospects were assessed. However, practical observations and conclusions disproved the correctness of the popular theory that a high IQ test result guarantees professional success. The author presented research data, according to which IQ in different versions affects the success of a leader with an average probability of up to 15%. The researcher explains this by the fact that in order to become a leader, you must gain a certain number of points on testing for IQ. However, to move up the career ladder, you need something else. When in numerous studies they compared what the leaders – super successful managers of companies – are different from the average statistical managers, the research showed that completely different competencies, particularly affective ones, are needed.

D. Goleman, referring to neurophysiology, proves that the emotional center of the brain affects the activity of the cerebral cortex, which is responsible for rational thinking. The theory of emotional intelligence initially led to active rejection among representatives of the professional community, refuting one of the main ideas of success in the 20th century that emotions have no place at work. The author shows with examples that successful leaders are emotional, charismatic people who use the affective component to benefit themselves and others. They are creative extroverts, talented communicators, effective motivators, which contribute to rapid career growth.

In modern didactic literature, great attention is paid to the element of cooperation between the teacher and students in the learning process; we have already mentioned the collaboration above. Other scientists in this field refer to the term peer-to-peer pedagogy. What is the role of a teacher – a teacher in ESP classes, in the conditions of the VUCA University? In many theoretical papers, the term "ecological thinking" is becoming increasingly popular, and is understood in the broad sense of adaptability and tolerance to today's rapidly changing world. We understand this term as treating respect for all participants in the pedagogical process, as pedagogy of non-violence. In a professional environment, this is the idea of creating a comfortable environment that provides opportunities for the realization of creativity for all, an emotionally comfortable climate that contributes to full-fledged teamwork, growth of trust and respect for each other. In this sense, the teacher of a higher educational institution is an eco-preacher, which means that he is not just a carrier of knowledge, a seller of educational services, he is a person, a teacher, a communicator of moral values. The teacher is a respected person, by virtue of the proposed conditions, having the right to exercise control, reprimand and management. We want to emphasize that eco-thinking is the creation of comfortable conditions for all participants in the pedagogical process, including, above all, the teacher.

Assuming proper communication, success of which is based on the competencies of emotional intelligence (intuition, empathy, ability to motivate and inspire, evaluate work, encourage, etc.), a successful professional result of the pedagogical process is guaranteed. Critical thinking implies the ability to apply basic intellectual competences (knowledge, skills, abilities) to analyze, synthesize and understand the information critically, as well as to solve complex and ambiguous problems. This may include skills for working with a complex audience, when the teacher needs to properly assess the scientific potential of each student and group, in general, to relate it to the personal characteristics of each, to select the desired trajectory of movement in accordance with the program of the discipline. In this sense, the competence of the teacher's critical thinking makes him the developer of the educational trajectories (mind-fitness trainer) in the eyes of students. On the other hand, the product of critical thinking is the result of cognitive activity. Mental activity is expressed in speech. However, it is emotionally colored! The important concept of charisma is inseparable from such qualities of a teacher-leader as the ability to communicate, motivate, convince, lead, be (or seem to be) successful. Charisma and interpersonal skills are closely related.

Practice-Oriented Recommendations

Teachers of a foreign language for special purposes pay attention to the development of personality traits of students in teaching various types of speech activity (telephony, negotiation, presentation, etc.). When reading and listening to authentic text, we ask students to evaluate information not only from the point of view of their professional value, thereby developing critical thinking skills, but also to characterize the text from the point of view of intercultural characteristics, thus forming the basis of tolerance and empathy. In the process of work, trainees should perceive and evaluate the author's thoughts and position, comparing with their professional guidelines and experience. Taking into account the lack of professional and life experience of students, teachers become moral and professional values carriers, due to communication conditions, become the main source for the formation of correct assessment criteria and, therefore, emotional competence of students.

Above, we have already discussed very popular technologies of teaching a foreign language for specific purposes, such as the project method and case studies. These technologies combine all innovative teaching methods: collaboration – collaboration approach (the teacher and the students together develop solutions to the problem); peer-to-peer pedagogy (in a professionally-oriented environment, students act on an equal footing with a teacher, as they are better oriented in their field of knowledge than a foreign language teacher), shifting the focus of the goal (a foreign language for special purposes helps students in professional competencies, not language skills). These technologies undoubtedly develop the competence of critical thinking, since they require not only the ability to analyze and evaluate someone else's arguments, but also the ability to interpret information in different styles of communication (presentation, essay, business letter, scientific article, etc.). However, the perception of information is based on our life experience, which is emotionally colored. We choose the way of presentation and argumentation, relying on the intuition and positive (negative) emotions of the listeners, on their cultural and historical features. The existing system of knowledge is not possible to transfer without taking into account the specified features, without – belonging to a certain area of knowledge, traditions, etc.

E. Fedotovskaya, exploring the topic of critical thinking in the application to speech activity, noted in particular that communicative competence is a complex phenomenon, including linguistic, sociolinguistic and pragmatic components (Fedotovskaya, 2002).

The author emphasized that these components cannot be formed without socialization, that is, without acquiring knowledge and certain skills of socialization in a certain area of communication. Examining in detail the linguistic component, the researcher noted not only the need to master the new terminology of the professional sphere, but also the mastery of realities, phraseological expressions and behavioral norms. The scientist believed that the sociolinguistic component is formed in accordance with the speech task. With the use of case and project tasks in ESP classes, an example of a speech problem is, for example, writing a theoretical basis for a project that requires the selection and analysis of literature on a professional topic. Or a speech task may be the preparation of a presentation using information technologies, etc. Depending on the speech (professional task) set, students are offered to master various means of communication. Discussion, disputes, brainstorming, finding a compromise, negotiating (at different management levels and in different business situations), writing business correspondence and much more, require the formation of sociolinguistic competence. Paying tribute to speech skills, we should note that the presence of social knowledge about the features of communication is much closer to emotional intelligence than to rational, since speech is emotionally colored. It is interesting, from our point of view, how the author allocates a pragmatic component. It emphasizes the effectiveness, the successful outcome of the negotiations, the persuasiveness of the argument, as the main characteristics of this component. However, along with pragmatism (rational choice of arguments), the effectiveness of the result also depends on the emotional fullness of the polylog.

As a recommendation for developing critical thinking in ESP classes, we would like to highlight the benefits of case assignments. D. Goulman, among others, attributed the striving of leaders to self-improvement to emotional competencies. High school teachers have to work with representatives of the Z generation, that is, they are, as a rule, introverts, self-righteous, interested in the opinions of others, poorly influenced by outside conditions and are individualists. However, such qualities hinder productive teamwork, create a false sense of self-righteousness, and do not lead to the correct formation of reflection. D. Goleman believes that these leaders are distinguished by a high level of emotional self-consciousness, which does not prevent them from being constructive in their criticism. Cases assignments teach students to work in a team, in the proposed conditions, they must learn to listen and hear each other. Assessing the options proposed solutions, students develop the skills of adaptability and acceptance of their own kind.

By learning how to criticize correctly, students learn tolerance and empathy. A case study helps students to open up, to discover the potential of a hidden leader in themselves, especially in the case of recognition in a team. Emotional pleasure from recognition of victory, success encourages and motivates to great creative discoveries, both in oneself and in the surrounding world. Adaptability leads to flexibility of thinking, develops interest in related professional and scientific areas. Gradually, under the influence of the teacher, students begin to more positively relate to the professional manifestations of others, see the benefits of teamwork, learn to communicate correctly. Leaders are gradually formed with the right emotional attitudes that are able to see and evaluate potential occupational risks.

An incarnation of a manager who is able to manage his feelings is an employee who remains calm and prudent in the face of severe stress or during a crisis – he remains calm even when faced with a problem situation. This competence, among creativity, critical thinking, ability to work in a team, was named by representatives of employers, as the main one when recruiting graduates, at an economic forum in Valdai in 2018. In other words, emotional intelligence is the result of sociolinguistic and pragmatic competences, which E.I. Fedotovskaya mentioned in her work, and which successfully develop in the classroom of a foreign language for specific purposes in the conditions of use of innovative educational technology design and case studies.

Conclusion

Modern pedagogical process in universities of economic profile must meet the requirements of employers that exist in the VUCA world. In order for our graduates to meet the requirements of employers to have certain competencies, particularly, critical thinking, emotional competence, creativity, etc., we tried to define the pedagogical environment in which our colleagues have to work and determine the pedagogical technologies that contribute to solving our tasks.

The study helped us to conclude that modern didactic methods (project method, case assignments) facilitate the formation of foreign language competencies, since they shift the focus of the goal from learning a foreign language to studying professionally oriented topics. They are based on a communicative-active approach and contribute to the formation of critical thinking through tasks that require emotional involvement. As a result, these technologies help to form not only the skills of correct assessment, but also respect for one's own, other people's thoughts and experience; sharpen curiosity and initiative; develop active listening, empathy; increase student self-esteem; form a critical attitude to stereotypes; promote adaptability through the development of sensitivity and tolerance. That is, they create the prerequisites for our graduates to become true leaders in the broad sense of the word.

We believe that it's time, paying tribute to digital technologies, to pay attention to the fact that for the full formation of a specialist in the field of economics – a leader, we need a teacher – a teacher – a personality. Teachers – pedagogues should develop and use didactic approaches, in which human knowledge is considered not as a "computational operation", but as a cognitive-emotional process, the effectiveness and success of which is directly related to the personal characteristics of all participants in educational activities.

References

Golubeva N.B. *Kriterii otsenki sformirovannosti inoyazychnoy professional'noy kommunikativnoy kompetentsii na primere prepodavaniya inostrannogo yazyka v neyazykovom VUZ-e* [Criteria for assessing the formation of a foreign language professional communicative competence on the example of teaching a foreign language in a non-linguistic university] // Modern science, topical issues of theory and practice. – M. Scientific technologies, 2015. No. 5–6 – pp. 41–44 (in Russian).

Golubeva N.B. *Razvitiye kriticheskogo myshleniya kak vazhnyy element formirovaniya professional'no-oriyentirovannoy inoyazychnoy kompetentsii.* [The development of critical thinking as an important element in the formation of professional-oriented foreign language competence] // University Bulletin (SUM). – M.: Publishing House of the GUU, 2015. No. 3 – pp. 257–262 (in Russian).

Goleman D., Boyacis R., Mackey E. *Emotsional'noye liderstvo. Iskusstvo upravleniya lyud'mi na osnove emotsional'nogo intellekta.* [Emotional leadership. The art of managing people based on emotional intelligence]. – M, Alpina Business Books, – 2005 (in Russian).

David R. Caruso, Peter Salovey. The Emotionally Intelligent Manager: How to Develop and Use the Four Key Emotional Skills of Leadership. Josses-Bass, – San Francisco. – 2004.

Digtyar O. Yu. *Ispol'zovaniye metoda "CASE-STUDY" v obuchenii angliyskomu yazyku studentov neyazykovykh vuzov. English Language Teaching Upgrade: Practices And Innovations.* [The use of the CASE-STUDY method in teaching English to students of non-linguistic universities. English Language Teaching Upgrade: Practices and Innovations]. // Collection of scientific papers. M.: Scientific technologies, 2017. p. 21 (in Russian).

Digtyar O. Yu. *Formirovaniye kreativnogo obraza sistemnogo myshleniya studentov neyazykovykh vuzov pri obuchenii angliyskomu yazyku. – Mir nauki, kul'tury, obrazovaniya.* [Formation of a creative way of system thinking of students of non-linguistic universities in teaching English. – The world of science, culture, education]. // International scientific journal. April 30, 2018. Number 2 (69). 2018. pp. 492–494 (in Russian).

Fedotovskaya E.I. *K probleme razvitiya navykov kriticheskogo myshleniya pri rabote s inoyazychnymi tekstami.* [To the problem of developing critical thinking skills when working with foreign language texts. // "Text. Perception, information, interpretation. Sat reports of the I International Scientific Conference of the Russian New University]. – Moscow, 2002. – pp. 279–283 (in Russian).

Melnichuk M.V., Nenyuk E.A., Alisevich M.V. *Psikholingvisticheskiye aspekty kak osnova prakticheskogo izucheniya inostrannogo yazyka.* [Psycholinguistic aspects as a basis for practical learning of a foreign language] // Austrian Journal of Humanities and Social Sciences. -2014.- No. 9–10, – pp. 100–104 (in Russian).

Melnichuk M.V., Osipova V.M., Kondrakhina N.G. Market-oriented LSP training in higher education: towards higher communicative skills // Eurasia Journal of Mathematics, Science and Technology Education. 2017. V.13. No. 8. pp. 5073–5084.

Nelli V. Tskhadadze, Aza D. Ioseliani

24 Informal Labor Relations: The Evolution of Concepts

Introduction

Informal labor relations are extremely common at present. Evaluation of this phenomenon in the scientific field is ambiguous. To understand the current situation better, it seems reasonable to make clear the origins of the formation of this phenomenon and highlight the main theoretical approaches to its conceptualization.

Initially, informal economic activity was investigated in relation to developing countries. This was done in the context of studying the informal sector, which was an organized group of people who created their own employment system, subordinate to the system of survival. These included a variety of types of employment, based on informal, personalized relationships with consumers, employees, and creditors. Naturally, workers involved in such activities dropped out of the officially organized labor market.

Additional interest in the problem of informal employment in developed countries appears in connection with the rapid spread of various new forms of employment that do not fit into the current concept of formal, standard employment. Such forms of employment were developed due to the emergence of new information technologies, which in turn determined a new, specific organizational environment for economic activity.

Methodology

The methodological basis of the work was the works of the classics of economic theory, foreign and domestic scientists on the problems of informal labor relations.

Initially, several different terms were used to refer to the informal sector. So, J. Beeke in the early 1950s noted the phenomenon of "dual economy" (Boeke, 1953). A little later, K.Geertz proposed a division into "bazaar" and "firm-oriented device" economies ("bazaar-economy" and "firm-centered economy") (Geertz, 1963). The first was characterized as labor-intensive, low-productivity, small-scale and low-income, while the second is vice versa – more efficient, capital-intensive, with a higher labor

Nelli V. Tskhadadze, Aza D. Ioseliani, Financial University under the Government of the Russian Federation, Moscow, Russia

https://doi.org/10.1515/9783110636147-024

productivity. Thus, the problem of "informality" gradually matured in the scientific community, acquiring more and more distinct contours.

Evolution of Informal Employment Concepts

The study of the informal sector has shifted to a higher quality level thanks to research carried out under the guidance of the World Bank and the International Labor Organization. The work of the English sociologist Keith Hart (Hart himself considered his predecessor in the study of the informal economic activities of an English publicist of the mid-19th century, G. Mayhew, a researcher for the "culture of poverty" in London), who is considered a pioneer in the study of "informality", gained the greatest fame. During field studies of the late 1960s of the 20th century, in the urban slums of Accra, the capital of Ghana, one of the backward countries of Africa, the scientist noted that the local population for the most part has nothing to do with the official economy. "The urban economy of backward countries was a huge accumulation of small and tiny workshops, shops and other "microfirms" supplying city residents with simple everyday goods (food, clothing, transport services, etc.), without any official registration, ignoring tax and other government requirements for business". (Hart, 1973).

The researcher interpreted the economic system of developing countries in the framework of the dual concept, opposing the formal sector to the informal one. For each sector, the opposite characteristics were distinguished. According to Hart, the key criterion in distinguishing between formal and informal is the degree of rationalization of labor, its constancy and regularity, as well as the presence or absence of fixed earnings. Based on these criteria, K. Hart identified three main income groups of citizens:

- Formal income: salaries in the public and private sectors, transfer payments
- Legal informal income: employment in the primary (agriculture), secondary (artisans, shoemakers, beer producers, etc. working independently or under contract), tertiary (construction, trade, transport) sectors, the provision of services (medical and funeral services, musicians, hairdressers, etc.), private transfers (gifts, loans, begging)
- Illegal informal incomes: services (labor of illegal usurers, drug business, smuggling, etc.) and transfers (theft, gambling, etc.) (Hart, 1973)

Hart categorically objected to the neglect of unorganized workers and stressed their important role in the provision of goods and services to ordinary citizens. He combined such workers with the notion of "informal sector".

Hart's innovation was met with great interest and very soon many scientists began to pay close attention to the problems of informal employment. A number of similar studies have been conducted in other third world countries. In 1972, the ILO published a study on employment in Kenya, where the concept of informal economic activity was already used as the main scientific paradigm. In this study, the differences between the formal and informal sectors were explained as follows.

Informal activities characteristics:
- ease of entry (into production)
- reliance on own resources
- family ownership of enterprises
- small scale activities
- labor-intensive and flexible technologies
- skills acquired outside the formal school system
- unregulated and competitive markets

The activities of the informal sector are usually ignored by the government, rarely supported, often regulated and sometimes actively suppressed.

The characteristics of activity in the formal sector are opposites:
- the entry into it is difficult
- constant reliance on external resources
- corporate property
- large scale operation
- capital-intensive, often imported technologies
- formally acquired skills
- the markets are under protectionist regulation (with the help of tariffs, quotas, trade licenses) (Hart, 1973)

Gradually, the term "informal sector" received scientific recognition and became generally accepted in English literature. Researchers from developing countries in Latin America and Asia quickly joined researchers in African countries. In addition to the "geographical" expansion, a disciplinary expansion gradually took place – in addition to economists, sociologists, anthropologists, and political scientists actively joined the study of this phenomenon.

English expert on the problems of the "third world" Ray Bromley pointed out that the terminology offered by Hart and the concept connected with it were in the right place at the right time. The concept of the informal sector quickly gained international popularity, primarily because it offered such recommendations, which in the 1970s turned out to be very convenient for international organizations and for non-extreme governments. Supporting the informal sector implies the possibility of helping the poor without threatening the rich, that is, redistributing part of the income and wealth to the "poor", but to such an extent as to leave the "elite" feeling calm in an atmosphere of stability and well-being.

Expansion of the circle of researchers led to some discrepancies in the understanding of the object of research, which is also associated with the country characteristics of the phenomenon. Thus, researchers from African countries highlighted such features of the informal economy as the small size of economic entities and their poor technical equipment. Scientists exploring the countries of Latin America, focused mainly on its illegality.

In this aspect, the collaboration of Donald Mead and Christian Morrisson (Mead and Morrisson, 1996), revealing the difficulties in determining the key features of the informal sector, is of interest. In 1990, American and French economists conducted research on small entrepreneurs in the third world countries. The sample includes 2,200 enterprises from seven countries: two Latin American countries (Ecuador, Jamaica), four African countries (Algeria, Tunisia, Nigeria, Swaziland), and one Asian country (Thailand). Mead and Morrisson consistently analyzed three main criteria of informality:

- Legality:
- registration of the enterprise
- payment of taxes
- regulation of working conditions (payment of the minimum wage, pension and insurance payments, safety, etc.)
- legislative measures restricting the activities of subjects of the informal sector
- The size of the enterprise (usually the informal sector includes enterprises with no more than 5–10 employees)
- The level of capital intensity of production

In practice, these characteristics are closely interrelated, so it does not matter which of them is decisive.

As a result of the study, Mead and Morrisson come to the following conclusions:

- There is no clear relationship between the "small size" criterion of the enterprise and the degree of its registration.
- Registration of the enterprise is neither a mandatory nor a sufficient condition for the payment of taxes.
- There is no explicit relationship between registration and regulation of labor relations.
- There is also no unambiguous consistency between the level of capital intensity and the size of the enterprise.

It soon became apparent that informal economic activity was not spread only in underdeveloped countries. In 1977, almost simultaneously in the United States, two conceptual articles were published on the forms and scales of shadow economic activity in the Soviet economy: American Sovietologist Gregory Grossman (Grossman, 1977) and the former Soviet economist who emigrated to America, Aron Katsenelinboigen (Katsenelinboigen, 1997). They laid the foundation for the study of independent economic activity in the USSR and the countries of Eastern Europe.

In the 1980s, sovietologists concluded, that despite centralized planning and total accounting, informal economic activity took place. Moreover, the general over-regulation actually hides a mixed-type economic system, where informal, uncontrolled production sometimes plays the same role with official production. However, the elimination of a command economy led to the collapse of research in this socio-economic system.

It is believed that the study of the informal economy in the developed countries of the West began in the second half of the 1970s. Thus, P. Gutmann became a "pioneer" in 1977. The American economist published an article in which he argued that unrecognized activities in developed capitalist countries had grown so much that it was simply unacceptable to neglect it (Gutmann, 1977). An article by another American economist, E. Feige, published in 1979, received an impressive response (Feige, 1979). The scientist made a calculation according to which the irregular economy of the United States covers about a third of GNP, that is, comparable in level with the countries of the Third World.

Over the years of research, several conceptual approaches to the analysis of the informal economy and employment have been developed. Let us consider the main ones.

Conceptual Approaches to the Analysis of the inFormal Economy and Employment

The Structuralist Approach of the International Labor Organization (ILO)

This approach is presented in the publications of the organization itself, as well as in the works of such Latin American scholars as Tokman, Mezzera, Marquez and Cartaya. Supporters of this approach see the fundamental reason for the growth of the informal sector in combination of oversupply of labor with low demand for it. They explain the oversupply of labor by switching from labor-intensive technologies to capital-intensive technologies; the peculiarity of local labor resources, expressed in insufficient education and low labor skills; the presence of internal migration (from village to city), contributing to the rapid growth of urban labor, which is much faster than the growth of provided jobs in the formal sector of the economy. In accordance with the structuralist approach of the International Labor Organization, the informal sector is characterized by small business units (mainly self-employment or family-owned firms), technology primitiveness, ease of market access. Proponents of this approach recognize the heterogeneity of informal employment, that is, its internal heterogeneity. In this case, there are three types of participants in informal activities:

1 The poor with low human capital or content with marginal work due to their objective characteristics.
2 "Conjunctively unemployed", losing legal income due to structural changes in the official economy.
3 Informal entrepreneurs, owners of micro enterprises. It is believed that macroeconomic policies are needed for economic growth and poverty eradication, aimed primarily at supporting the formal, not the informal sector. However, ones support other measures leading to an increase in employment, productivity and income.

Marxist Approach

(Other names – Structuralist approach of the "left", the approach from the standpoint of the concept of "black market", the approach from the standpoint of the concept of "underground economy", Alejandro Portes approach).

The most famous representatives are Portes and Castells. The roots of this approach go back to the ideas of neo-Marxism, so the focus is on analyzing production relations (in particular, the subordination of labor), commodity turnover (the relationship between informal activities and large legal firms), class contradictions and reorganization of production under the influence of changing economic, institutional, social legal conditions. Thus, Castells and Portes, as a result of a number of studies, proposed a functional classification of informal activities (which are a priori carried out outside the framework of state regulation), depending on their goals (Table 24.1 and Table 24.3).

All these types of economies are not mutually exclusive and differ not only in the motivation of participants, but also in the increasing level of social organization necessary for each listed type of economy.

This classification implies an important conclusion that not only formal, but also informal activities can contribute to the function of accumulating capital, since firms operating within the formal sector are able to go underground and do it quite consciously.

The main thing in which the ILO's structuralist approach and the Marxist approach differ is the definition of the informal sector.

The main similarities and differences of these approaches are presented in the table.

Table 24.1: Classification of informal activities depending on the goals.

Subject	Purpose	Type of informal activities	Economy type
Individual or household	Survival	Natural economy or sale of goods, works or services on the market	Economics of survival
Firms belonging to the formal sector (i.e. relatively large firms)	Increased managerial flexibility, reduced labor law compliance costs	Shadow employment or use of subcontracting relationships with informal entrepreneurs	Economics of dependent exploitation
Small firms	Capital accumulation, network mobilization, increased flexibility, cost reduction	Shadow employment or use of subcontracting relationships with informal entrepreneurs	Economics of growth

Source: compiled by author according to Portes and Sassen-Koob (1987).

Table 24.2: The main similarities and differences of the ILO structuralist approach and the Marxist approach.

ILO Structuralist Approach		Marxist approach
The fundamental reason for the growth of the informal sector is the combination of an oversupply of labor with low demand for it.		
Recognizing the heterogeneity of the informal economy		
Recognizing the relationship between informality and the impoverishment of workers.		
Formal activity	⇦ ⇨ Capital accumulation function	Both formal and informal activities
A special segment of labor market	⇦ ⇨ Informal sector is. . .	A special segment of the economy as a whole
– The size of the business entity – Access to the market – The level of technology	⇦ ⇨ Informal sector definition	– Labor Status – Working conditions – Form of firm management – The nature of labor

Source: compiled by the author according to (Tskhadadze, 2015a; Tskhadadze, 2015b).

Table 24.3: The main differences between the structuralist approaches (ILO and Marxist) and the legalist approach.

Structuralist approaches	Legalistic approach
government intervention in the economy is *necessary*	government intervention in the economy is *categorically undesirable*
the fundamental reason for the growth of the informal sector is in *the combination of excess labor supply with low demand for it*	the fundamental reason for the growth of the informal sector is *in the legal and bureaucratic activities of the state itself*
members of informal activities are *passive object of help*	participants of informal activities are *the basis of the development of the national economy*

Source: compiled by the author according to Tskhadadze (2015b).

The Legalist Approach of the Institute for Freedom and Democracy (Desoticism)

This approach is proposed by the Peruvian Hernando de Soto.

In 1989, the Peruvian economist Hernando de Soto published the book "The Other Way. The invisible revolution in the third world", which revolutionized the researchers' views on the causes, role and significance of the shadow economy in the modern market economy and impugned the negative characteristics of the informal sector. (De Soto, 1995).

The cornerstone of the de Soto concept is the thesis that the main reason for the growth of the urban informal sector is the excessive bureaucratic organization of the legal sector of the economy, which impedes the free development of competitive relations. The scientist criticizes the understanding of the informal economy as the inability of a part of the population to find its place in the formal economy. According to supporters of this approach, those employed in the informal sphere are not a burden to society, but rather constitute the basis for the development of the national economy, as they are entrepreneurs who make their way under difficult conditions of bureaucratic regulation.

According to supporters of this approach, the division of the economy is not connected with structural reasons, but with the legal and bureaucratic activities of the state itself, which uses its power in the interests of the authorities. Thus, the development of informality is presented as the answer of the poor strata of the population to the state's conscious defense of the status quo, when the creation of privileges by one is associated with the violation of the rights of others. In fact, the proposed new segmentation of the economy of the type is not "formal – informal", but "a privileged entrepreneur – an unprivileged entrepreneur".

The legalist approach is based on legal determinism related to the direction of neoinstitutionalism, which focuses on the development of legal institutions in the development of society. Such well-known economists as R. Coase, D. North, R. Posner, H. Demsetz also belong to this direction.

The main differences between the structuralist approaches (the International Labor Organization and the Marxist) and the De Soto approach are shown in the table.

Myrdalism

Myrdalism is a cultural approach, founded by the Swedish economist G. Myrdal, one of the first economists who noted the illegitimacy of using Western stereotypes to analyze Eastern societies.

The main emphasis is made not on formal legal norms, but on traditions, values, routines that determine the behavior of large social communities (classes, ethnic groups, denominations) and form a certain economic culture. Thus, in order to contain the shadow economy, it is necessary to develop such forms of entrepreneurship that are approved by the traditional economic culture and to promote the values that stimulate entrepreneurship.

Conclusions

Summing up, it can be noted that with the development and expansion of research in the informal economy (both geographically and substantively), the concept of formal-informal dualism gives way to considering the problem of the informal economy as the nature of economic relations in different degrees and different forms presented in all forms of management. The informal economy as an equal model of management, along with the formal one, has excellent mechanisms for coordinating the interests of participants and levers of influence on their behavior. Such consideration of the informal economy became possible due to the transition to a post-industrial society, when the number of small firms increased significantly. Now, in terms of the total volume of goods, works, services provided and income received, they can be compared with large industrial enterprises.

The informal economy is interpreted not as a separate segment, but as the withdrawal of economic entities from various forms of government regulation and statistical accounting. Thus, there is a significant expansion of the object of study of the informal economy due to the inclusion in these relations of subjects, both having and not having official status.

References

Barsukova Neformalnaya ekonomika. Ponyatiye. istoriya izucheniya, issledovatelskiye podkhody [Informal economy. Concept, study history, research approaches]. // Sotsiologicheskiye issledovaniya. 2012. No. 2. – S. 31–39 (in Russian).

Boeke J.N. Economics and economic policy of dual societies. New York: IRelations, 1953.

British Social Attitudes / R. Jowell, S. Witherpoon (eds.). Gower: Aldershot, 1985. Bromley R. Introduction – the Urban Informal Sector: Why Is It Worth Discussing?//World Development. 1978. N 6., pp. 1034–1035.

Feige E. L. How big is the irregular economy? // Challenge. 1979. – Vol. 6. – No. 22. – pp. 47–58.

Geertz C. Peddlers and princes: Social change and economic modernization in two Indonesian towns. Chicago: University of Chicago Press, 1963.

Grossman G. The "Second Economy" of the USSR // Problems of Communism. 1977. Sept. – Oct. – Vol. 2. No. 1.

Gutmann P. The Subterranean Economy // Financial Analysis Journal. – 1977. – Vol.33. – pp. 28–24.

Hart K. Informal-Income Opportunities and Urban Employment in Ghana // The Journal: of Modern African Studies. – 1973; – Vol. 11, – No. 1. – pp. 60–74.

ILO. Employment, incomes and equality: a strategy for increasing productive employment in Kenya. – Geneva: ILO, 1972, 189 p.

Katsenelinboigen A. Coloured Markets in the Soviet Union // Soviet Studies. – 1997. – Vol. 29. – No. 1.– pp. 57–68.

Mead D., Morrisson C. The informal sector elephant // World development. 1996. Vol.24. No. 10.– pp. 25–36.

Partes A., Sassen-Koob S. Making It Underground: Comparative Material on the Informal Sector in Western Market Economies // American Journal of Sociology. 1987. Vol.93. No.l. – pp. 79–85.

Rakowski C.A. Convergence and Divergence in the Informal Sector Debate: A Focus on Latin America, 1984–1992 // World Development. 1994. Vol. 22. No. 4. pp. 501–516.

Soto E. de. Inoy put. Nevidimaya revolyutsiya v tretyem mire [The other way. Invisible Revolution in the Third World]. M.: Catallaxy. 1995.- 267 p (in Russian).

Tskhadadze N.V. Neformalnaya ekonomicheskaya deyatelnost v Rossii: otritsatelnyye i polozhitelnyye posledstviya [Informal economic activity in Russia: negative and positive consequences]. // Innovatsii i investitsii". No. 7. 2015a. – pp. 50–55.i upravleniye". No. 4. 2015. – S.102–112. (in Russian).

Tskhadadze N.V. Sotsialno-ekonomicheskiye posledstviya razvitiya neformalnoy zanyatosti v Rossii [Socio-economic consequences of the development of informal employment in Russia]. //Vestnik Tverskogo gosudarstvennogo universiteta. Seriya "Ekonomika i upravleniye". No. 4. 2015b. – pp. 102–112. (in Russian).

Nelli V. Tskhadadze, Karina A. Skriabina

25 Regional Migration Processes in Modern Russia

Introduction

The most important achievement of modern Russia in population migration is the granting of freedom of movement and place of residence within the country and freedom of traveling abroad to Russian citizens. The Russian migration policy has specific strategic goals arising from the characteristics of modern demographic, economic and political development of Russia, such as: replenishing the natural decline of the Russian population by stimulating the influx of migrants from abroad and stabilizing the number of its permanent population. There is also an important issue to meet the needs of the Russian labor market for additional labor in the face of declining national labor resources by attracting temporary international labor migrants. The "regional migration differentiation" observed in the country stimulates interest in the issue under study and determines the need for a comprehensive review to identify regions that are in the "migration stagnation" stage.

The lack of state interests concerning internal migration represents a separate problematic issue. Spontaneous trends emerging in internal migration in Russia over the past 25 years are the following: low internal mobility of the population and a steady exodus of population from the eastern and northeastern regions of Siberia to the European part of Russia, which creates the prerequisites for extremely adverse economic, demographic and political consequences. This spontaneous internal migration is becoming a factor which contributes to an even more uneven, asymmetrical distribution of the population throughout Russia. This unevenness has objective historical and climatic reasons. However, it is aggravated by unfavorable migration vectors from the point of view of the country's strategic development. Instead of engaging vast territories of the Asian part of the country and developing the economy of regions that are strategically important for Russia, the population migrates to European regions and concentrates in the metropolitan region, which contributes to the formation of migration enclaves (Ivakhnyuk, 2017). The development of a set of state measures aimed at stabilizing the production potential and preventing negative migration consequences, particularly, implies the

Nelli V. Tskhadadze, Financial University under the Government of the Russian Federation, Moscow, Russia
Karina A. Skriabina, Financial University under the Government of the Russian Federation, Russia

https://doi.org/10.1515/9783110636147-025

existence of a comprehensive analysis of regional features of migration processes observed in the constituent entities of the Russian Federation.

Methodology

The authors have chosen federal districts as research units. This review is based on statistical data, which includes: migration rate, regional percentage of incoming migration flows, employment and unemployment rates, average regional wage rate, category of migration groups, dates of migration, educational level of migration groups. In 2018, about 5 million people were involved in migration processes, of which 2.2 million in intraregional migration, 2.3 million accounted for interregional migration, and about 500,000 are foreign labor migrants (Bulletin "Number and Migration of the Population of the Russian Federation, 2018). The authors suggest considering the overview table for the federal districts, which takes into account all the above indicators (Table 25.1).

Results

Based on the presented data, it is possible to determine a number of regions that are most attractive for the realization of internal and international migration.

It obvious that the Central and North West Federal Districts, which annually attract migratory flows, are the outstanding leaders in this review. These regions are represented by high rates of employment and profitability. In most cases, labor migrants, people from other regions and countries migrate to these regions. As a rule, internal migrants migrate for a period of 1 to 3 years, and foreign migrants from 1 to 2 years. The educational structure of arriving groups is mainly represented by persons with higher education. It should be noted that in the studied districts, the maximum concentration of migrants with a scientific degree has been established. This indicates a significant demand for intellectual and scientific capital. It is noted that the predominantly incoming migration (in relation to the citizens of the country) is temporary, 18–19% of the total number of arriving migrants is registered for a long period (from 5 years). This can be explained by the following facts:

1. Not all migrants have the material resources to purchase their own housing. In most cases, migrant arrivals live in rented accommodation. Taking into account the requirements of the current legislation, it is very difficult to find individuals (landlords) who agree to register a migrant on a long-term or permanent basis, since this may lead to certain risks primarily for the landlord.

Table 25.1: Analysis of migration processes in the context of a regional review.

Federal districts	Migration rate1	% of arriving migrants 2	Employment rate	Unemployment rate	Wage level3	Main group of migrants4	Migration period 5	% arrival for a period of 5 years and more 6	Educational level of migration
Central Federal District	+5.1	30%	69.2	3.1	65683	Labor, mostly international	1–3 years	19%	Predominantly higher education
North West Federal District	+5.5	18%	68	4	57674	Labor, mostly international	1–3 years	18%	Predominantly higher education
South Federal District	+2.7	14%	63	5.8	36123	Labor, mostly international	1–2 years	18%	Predominantly higher education
North Caucasian Federal District	−2.6	4%	58.3	10.8	31412	Labor, mostly international	9 months to 1 year	9%	Predominantly higher education
Volga Federal District	−1,2	13%	65	4.6	37162	Labor, mostly international	1 year	7%	Predominantly college education
Ural Federal District	0	10%	65.8	5.2	55129	Labor: international and internal	1 year	19%	Predominantly college education
Siberian Federal District	−1.6	7%	62.7	6	42989	Labor, mostly international	1 year	29%	Predominantly college education
Far East Federal District	−2.8	4%	66.3	5.7	64821	Labor, mostly international	9 months to 1 year	18%	Predominantly higher education

Source: compiled by the authors (Statistical Bulletin Number and Migration of the Russian Federation, 2018).

2. Migrants who have a family, as a rule, move alone and for a period of not more than 1 year. This is characterized by significant current costs for relocation and socio-economic adaptation of all family members. Consequently, these regions can be classified as *migration-attractive*.

The second place is occupied by the South and Ural Federal Districts, which are represented by positive and neutral migration growth. These districts are characterized by a fairly high level of employment, but a very significant difference in the level of labor remuneration (the South District is inferior in this indicator to the Ural District). As the analysis shows, citizens of the country mainly migrate to these regions for no more than a two-year period, with higher and college education. Incoming migration (in relation to citizens of the country) is mainly temporary, thus, 18–19% of the total number of arrived migrants is recorded for a long period (from 5 years). Given the dynamics of the increase in migration characteristic of the South District and the absence of negative migration in the Ural District, these regions can be classified as: *migration-positive*. Next, the authors consider less attractive regions for migration, such as the Volga and Siberian Federal Districts, which are marked by negative migration and natural growth. The educational structure of incoming groups is represented by persons with college education, which indicates that they have a relatively low level of demand for intellectual and scientific work. It should be noted that the regions are characterized by an average level of labor remuneration and migration flows mainly consist of international labor. As the analysis shows, incoming migration is of a short-term nature, for a period of up to 1 year. An important distinguishing feature for the Siberian District is the presence of a high rate of incoming migrants who are registered at the place of residence for a long period of time (from 5 years and above). This figure is 29%, while in the *attractive regions*, it is between 18 and 19%.

This phenomenon is explained by the possibility of getting district coefficients for pensions and social benefits. Thus, the possession of a "northern residence permit" increases the pension content, which encourages people to register in the northern regions. But as practice shows, the number of persons registered in the studied region does not actually live there. Therefore, the effect of "dead souls". After overviewing the dynamics of migration processes occurring in the analyzed districts and the presence of negative migration indicators, these regions can be classified as: *migration-negative*.

Now we will define the category of *"migration outsiders"*, which include the North Caucasus and Far East Federal Districts, which are characterized by a negative migration increase. However, it is fair to note that the migration losses for the North Caucasus region are fully compensated by the natural increase (record for the country as a whole).

The educational structure of the incoming groups is represented by persons with higher education. In these regions, the differentiated level of wages, the Far East, is far ahead of the North Caucasus, which is characterized by the highest unemployment rate in the country. The structure of migration flows consists of international labor. Citizens of the country migrate to these regions for a period of 9 months, up to 1 year. The lack of migration attractiveness of the North Caucasus is a consequence of ethnic conflicts. The small attractiveness of the Far Eastern District is a consequence of the remoteness of the area and the unfavorable climatic conditions.

The study of the dynamics of migration processes occurring in these districts allows us to classify these regions as: *migration-depressive*. As part of this study, an analysis was conducted that allows us to determine the proportion of citizens of the country (an indicator of regional migration) and foreign citizens involved in the migration processes observed in Russia (Figure 25.1).

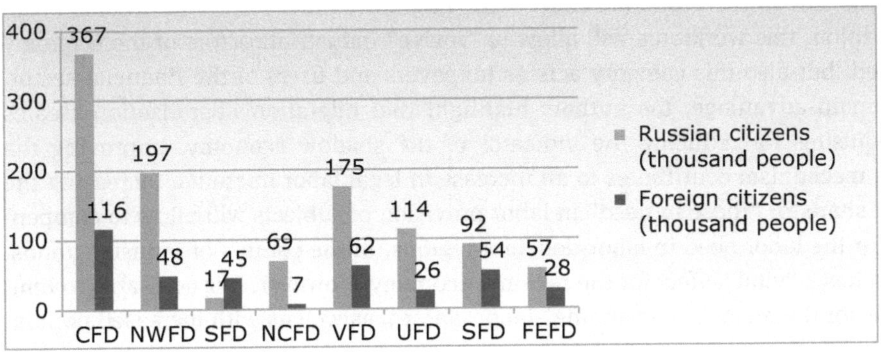

Figure 25.1: Comparative analysis of interregional and foreign migration in the context of the district review.
Source: compiled by the authors (Statistical Bulletin "Number and Migration of the Population of the Russian Federation", 2018).

The analysis revealed that the rate of interregional migration exceeds the rate of international migration, but in some cases it may be reversed.

Consequently, international migration is of a labor nature and can affect the structure of regional labor markets. The indicator of the impact of international labor resources on labor markets should be regulated by the state, depending on the qualifying needs of regional labor markets.

In some cases, a dense accumulation of internal and external labor migrants can lead to increased competitiveness in labor markets, taking into account the current trends of job losses observed in the whole country (excess of liquidation over job creation).

In order to maximize income, by minimizing costs, the employer is forced to reduce the cost of labor, which lowers the attractiveness of employment for the internal migrant, and as a result, an international migrant takes the workplace.

The description of this scenario has a similarity with the U.A. Lewis's model of "economic development with unlimited labor supply", the authors can consider the concept of "unlimited supply of foreign labor" (Lewis, 1954) only as unlimited labor supply. Consequently, both international and internal labor migration, requires institutional quantitative and qualitative analysis, determining the optimal tools for regulating, encouraging and deterring migration flows of interregional, as well as international types. Professional liberalization of foreign migration policies can have a beneficial economic impact by amending existing legislation. Professional liberalization of foreign migration policy implies a selective approach to choosing foreign labor, based on the level of professional (qualified) training of a foreign migrant and on the needs of regional labor markets (Zayonchkovskaya, 2019).

The introduction of professional liberalization will contribute to the transparency of the migration environment, not only for the supervising bodies, but also from the side of the economic effect – the migratory labor force will become legal. In addition, this workforce will allow to "revive" industrial sectors of the economy in need, but also this category acts as taxpayers and users of the financial sector. As a main advantage, the authors highlight that migration liberalization creates prerequisites for reducing the indicator of the shadow economy. Improving the quota mechanism contributes to an increase in legal labor migrants. Increasing the quota share for "those in need" in labor provision of subjects will allow to compensate for the labor need in labor-deficient regions, in the context of industry trends, which has a "vital" effect for the regional economy. However, it is advisable to limit quotas for the regions "consuming" labor masses, as well as with increased population indices.

It is the definition of targeted production "needy" areas that leads to economic benefits and losses for various market actors. For example, in the Russian Federation, foreign labor migrants are prohibited from doing a retail trade, as well as selling alcohol and pharmaceutical products.

As a result, it should be noted that the national labor market is formed at the expense of regional markets, the structure of which is determined by the following: indicators of employment and unemployment of the population, sectoral professional shifts, movement of workplaces (by the creation and elimination of jobs and enterprises), intersectoral differentiations, the presence of differences and the order of formation of nominal wages, labor law institutes, the nature of enforcement, indicators of regional clustering, and so on. All of the above is part of the market formation structures and are catalysts for migration supply and demand (push and pull) (The State of Food and Agriculture, "Migration, agriculture and rural development", The state of the world series of the food and Agriculture Organization of the United Nations, 2018).

Active migration processes are dual in nature, which means that migration is able to smooth out the uneven distribution of productive forces, acting as a "reserve labor army". In the absence of a clear definition of migration strategy, taking into account the socio-economic analysis, the opposite effect takes place, when migration "flows" into economic centers and agglomerations, leaving the "donor" regions, aggravating the economic state of the latter. This leads to very serious socio-economic and demographic consequences. An example of such a phenomenon is the "western drift" that began in the 1990s, during which the population of Russia as a result of domestic migration is redistributed from the country's eastern regions to central and western districts (Tskhadadze and Bogatskaia, 2016).

Recommendations

The authors proposed a number of measures aimed at stabilizing the "migration crisis", which creates a socio-economic imbalance, which can contribute to the slowing down and gradual cessation of the migration outflow, the attraction of capital-intensive migrants and the creation of a healthy adaptation migration environment.

The main socio-economic problems in regions with negative migration and depressive dynamics are as follows:

- countering the growth of real unemployment and the improving employment mechanisms
- developing social infrastructure in order to attract and retain specialists
- developing and implementing a system of measures within the framework of the State Program to assist voluntary resettlement to the Russian Federation of compatriots living abroad, taking into account the needs of the district and implementing a system of measures that stimulate labor productivity (Decree of the Government of the Russian Federation "On Amendments to "Promotion of Employment", 2019)
- modernization of industries with low labor productivity
- increasing quality and competitiveness of the workforce based on the implementation of the principle of continuous professional development, which includes the development of a training system within the organization, further training and retraining, as well as vocational training and retraining of unemployed citizens
- promoting professional and labor mobility of the population
- expanding job search opportunities by improving the quality and availability of public services in promoting employment
- developing a long-term forecast of the balance of labor resources for the districts with a view to the subsequent development of long-term plans for the further training and retraining of specialists
- optimizing the size of quotas for issuing temporary residence permits and invitations to enter the Russian Federation to foreign citizens in order to carry out labor activities, taking into account the demographic situation and opportunities for foreign citizens to settle in migration-negative, migration-depressive districts

- creating administrative and regulatory legal conditions for ensuring inter-regional labor mobility and attracting it from other subjects of the Russian Federation
- harmonizing the structure of migration flows with the needs of sustainable socio-economic development of the district and individual regions, including the suppression of illegal migration, the development and implementation of programs for the effective migration of retired labor resources from the economy, social adaptation and integration of foreign citizens, strengthening tolerance, harmony, and also socially political stability in the region ("Migration as a tool to promote trade and sustainable development", Information and analytical publication of the International Center for Trade and Sustainable Development, 2018)
- creating abroad a network of information and analytical centers aimed at attracting qualified foreign specialists for training and internships in migration-negative, migration-depressive districts with the possible granting of advantages in obtaining Russian citizenship after graduation, as well as encouraging the return to the macroregion of emigrants
- attracting qualified foreign specialists, including graduates of Russian higher educational institutions, for permanent residence
- developing and implementing socio-economic measures to increase migration attractiveness in migration-negative, migration-depressive districts
- forming and implementing special regional and macro-regional programs aimed at creating favorable conditions for the adaptation of immigrants to new conditions and their integration into Russian society on the basis of respect for culture, religion, customs, traditions and lifestyles of people in migration-negative, migration-depressive districts, as well as for the development of tolerance in relations between the local population and representatives of other countries in order to prevent social conflicts
- creating a favorable cultural environment for qualified foreign specialists recruited into the macroregional economy, including assistance in publishing specialized mass media and communications, joining clubs, representation in community and youth organizations of the district, as well as creating civilized conditions for the work and life of migrants and protecting their civil rights (Kapralova, 2015)

The adoption of comprehensive measures to resolve the socio-economic problems of the region helps to ensure the rise of the level and quality of life of the population and attract investments for the implementation of priority investment projects. The practical application of the described toolkit will contribute to the stabilization of migratory regional exodus, maintenance and increase of the working population (Barkenkhoyeva, 2017).

References

Decree of the Government of the Russian Federation of 28.03.2019 No. 348 "On Amendments to the State Program of the Russian Federation "Promotion of Employment".URL:https://rulaws.ru/goverment/Postanovlenie-Pravitelstva-RF-ot 28.03.2019-N-348 (Accessed 12.03.2019).

Barkenkhoyeva R. (2017) Improving the Level and Quality of Life of the Population as the Dominant of Regional Development. The quarterly peer-reviewed scientific journal "Vestnik ASU-Regional Economics" Issue No. 1, ISSN 2410-3683– vol. 2, – pp. 13–22.

Kapralova E. (2015) The Impact of the Media on Human Consciousness. Annual state newspaper of the civil service, issue No. 3, pp. 87–93.

Tskhadadze N. Bogatskaya K. Migration of Labor and Its Impact on Reproduction Processes. Collection of theses of reports / ed. R.M. Nureev, M.L. Alpidovskaya – M .: Financial University, 2016, – pp. 277–283.

Bulletin "Mosty" (2018) Migration as a Tool to Promote Trade and Sustainable Development. Information and analytical publication of the International Center for Trade and Sustainable Development URL: https://www.ictsd.org/sites/default/files/review/mosty_february_issue_-_2018.pdf (Accessed 10.09.2019)

Zayonchkovskaya Z.A. Proposals for the Migration Strategy of Russia until 2035. Center for Strategic Research. URL:https://www.csr.ru/wp-content/uploads/2017/11/Report-Demography-web.pdf (Accessed 05.09.2019)

Statistical Bulletin. Number and Migration of the Population of the Russian Federation. Federal Service of State Statistics. URL: http://www.gks.ru/bgd/regl/b18_107/Main.htm (Accessed 05.09.2019).

Lewis W. A. (1954) Economic Development with Unlimited Supplies of Labor. Available at: https://la.utexas.edu/users/hcleaver/368/368lewistable.pdf (Accessed 07.05.2019)

FAO. 2018. The State of Agricultural Commodity Markets 2018. Agricultural trade, climate change and food security. Available at: http://www.fao.org/3/I9542EN/i9542en.pdf (Accessed 07.05. 2019).

List of Figures

https://doi.org/10.1515/9783110636147-026

List of Tables

https://doi.org/10.1515/9783110636147-027

Index

https://doi.org/10.1515/9783110636147-028